The Globetrotting Shopaholic

The Globetrotting Shopaholic: Consumer Spaces, Products, and their Cultural Places

Edited by

Tanfer Emin Tunc and Annessa Ann Babic

Cambridge Scholars Publishing

The Globetrotting Shopaholic: Consumer Spaces, Products, and their Cultural Places,
Edited by Tanfer Emin Tunc and Annessa Ann Babic

This book first published 2008

Cambridge Scholars Publishing

12 Back Chapman Street, Newcastle upon Tyne, NE6 2XX, UK

British Library Cataloguing in Publication Data
A catalogue record for this book is available from the British Library

ISBN (10): 1-4438-0027-9, ISBN (13): 978-1-4438-0027-3

As always: for those we have lost and loved along the way

TABLE OF CONTENTS

LIST OF FIGURES

PREFACE

Tanfer and Annessa have known each for eight years now, and in that course of time have spent numerous hours discussing their work, lives, heartbreaks, and the things they love. Annessa comes from a working-class background; Tanfer does not. Tanfer helped educate Annessa on the beauty of a Coach handbag (now they both own *cough cough* a few), and Annessa told Tanfer stories about stretching a penny so far you could see straight through it. Many of our best conversations have come from window shopping, long lazy ambles through Port Jefferson, NY, and enjoyable explorations of Ankara, Turkey. Some of our best questions concerning sources and theory emerged during our shopping excursions. Annessa's favorite shopping memory is when Tanfer stepped in fish at a market in Ankara. She tried to hide her disgust, while Annessa cackled uncontrollably at her friend's unfortunate mishap.

What happened recently, however, supercedes the horror of the aforementioned "day of fish decay." In July 2008, Tanfer came to New York, and we did what we always do. We talked about life, Annessa's recent breakup, and our work. We had not seen each other in eight months, so we had a lot of catching up to do. We headed to Huntington Village. Downtown Huntington used to be a happening place, with sidewalk vendors, folks on afternoon strolls, and assorted characters singing and laughing in the street. What we found instead was a sad and decrepit ghost town. So we bailed on the Huntington Depression, and headed to Walt Whitman Mall. While there, we went into Macy's. As luck would have it, a delightful shoe clearance was going on. Annessa bought a pair of gold jacquard slip-on sandals with a shiny gold Coach buckle. She promptly put them on, shedding her just as fashionable Anne Klein high-healed sandals. For the rest of the afternoon she skipped through the mall chanting "Look at my pretty new shoes!" Even though the mall created some special memories for both of them that day, it was clear that the same culprit was responsible for the decay of their beloved Huntington.

The idea for this anthology emerged in January 2007, while wandering through Ankara's AnkaMall in an effort to escape the snowy winter weather. As we thought of what we could present at the American Studies Association of Turkey's annual conference, the mall atmosphere spoke to

The above story came from a friend who willingly gave up the lavish riches of the United States to teach high school in Belize. There he made very little money, and lived without modern conveniences like the fast-food restaurants, shopping malls, and paved roads that most Americans have come to know as second nature. Peter loved his life in Belize, and when he sent this story to me I looked at it and thought "Wow, that would make an excellent piece on consumer society." Peter's prose highlights the differences between living in cities and towns with an abundance of procurable ready-made goods, but it also makes one wonder what shopping means around the world. Are malls in Mexico any different than malls in Melbourne? How, and why, do people shop in different countries? Moreover, what do consumer goods, spending habits, and conspicuous consumption indicate about a culture, society, or generation?

The thrust of the literature on consumer space and society focuses on product labeling, marketing techniques and approaches to branding, as well as how mass consumer culture has reshaped individuals' interactions with needs and desires. *The Globetrotting Shopaholic* departs from this discourse by examining both consumption venues and the cultural, political, and social reasons why we consume. It elucidates international trends in consumption politics, and how they impact the creation of consumer spaces, which, in this book, take the form of numerous global loci including Canada's West Edmonton Mall, Japanese theme parks, shopping venues in the Philippines, and expat boutiques in Budapest. Using a wide range of epistemological frameworks including cultural ethnography, historical analysis, literary theory, sociological dissection, anthropological examination and philosophical ruminations, this multidisciplinary collection conveys how material objects and lifestyles are accumulated and represented internationally, and how consumer goods and spaces define who we are as human beings.

Consumer Spaces, Products, and their Cultural Meanings

No matter where they are located on the planet, all consumption venues exhibit the same goal: to lure consumers and provide them with goods—some necessary, others not—via the exchange of money. Scholars like Jackson Lears have remarked that consumption patterns are thus based on the simple premise of "lure and excitement." Under this configuration, the symbolic meanings of material goods often supersede their functional value.[2] Advertising entices the consumer, but peers, neighbors, and celebrities make products *desirable.* Advertising manipulates emotions and creates untapped desires: it suggests beauty through the hottest shade of eye shadow, attractiveness through the newest slimming corset, and envy through the glorification of the latest red sports car. Consequently, purchasing provides a sense of comfort—almost redemption—for the buyer because it reinforces one's social framework. Shopping provides an exploration of desire, and a fulfillment of responsibility; it commodifies our guilt and pride, as well as our successes and failures.[3]

While other works have addressed the rise of consumer society, the desires that drive conspicuous consumption, and the impact of factors such as class, ethnicity, and gender, very few have coupled their findings with a global perspective.[4] Earlier works, such as Tyler Cowen's *In Praise of Commercial Culture*, established the theoretical foundation of "capitalism as a legal framework based on private property and voluntary exchange," and made the connection between "commerce, industry, technology, and markets." Scholars have also revealed that the world's most affluent societies consume the largest amount of non-pecuniary enjoyments.[5] However, they very rarely ventured beyond the borders of North America in illustrating their observations. Susan Strasser, Charles McGovern, and

---

[2] Jackson Lears, *Fables of Abundance: A Cultural History of Advertising in America* (New York: Basic Books, 1994), 5.

[3] Ibid.; Jean Kilbourne, *How Advertising Changes the Way We Think and Feel* (New York, London, et al.: Touchstone, 1999); Thomas Hine, *I Want That!: How We All Became Shoppers (A Cultural History)* (New York: Harper Collins Publishers, 2002), ix–xv.

[4] These studies include: Juliet B. Schor and Douglas B. Holt, eds., *The Consumer Society Reader* (New York: The New Press, 2000); Don Slater, *Consumer Culture and Modernity* (New York: Polity Press, 1997); and Daniel Miller, et al. *Shopping, Place, and Identity* (New York: Routledge, 1998). Some of the prominent works on consumption and gender are: Roger Horowitz and Arwen Mohun, *His and Hers: Gender, Consumption, and Technology* (Charlottesville, VA and London: University of Virginia Press, 1998); Anne M. Cronin, *Advertising and Consumer Citizenship: Gender, Images, and Rights* (New York and London: Routledge, 2000); Kathy Peiss, *Hope in a Jar: The Making of America's Beauty Culture* (New York: Henry Holt and Company, 1998); and Jennifer Scanlon, *Inarticulate Longings: The Ladies Home Journal, Gender, and the Promises of Consumer Culture* (New York and London: Routledge, 1995).

[5] Robert Kuttner, *Everything For Sale: The Virtues and Limits of Markets* (New York: Alfred A. Knopf, 1998), 3; Tyler Cowen, *In Praise of Commercial Culture* (Cambridge, MA and London: Harvard University Press, 1998), 2.

Matthias Judt's *Getting and Spending: European and American Consumer Societies in the Twentieth Century* attempts to discuss consumption within a larger framework by examining consumer society from a variety of geographical and political standpoints. It also posits consumption as a social phenomenon that catalyzed the rise of capitalism in the West.[6] However, once again, the focus is mainly on the US and Western Europe.

Anthologies on consumption and gender have faired far better in terms of presenting a broad-based global perspective, yet they, like *Getting and Spending*, fall short of providing a true international survey. Jennifer Scanlon's *The Gender and Consumer Society Reader* critiques consumer culture by conceptualizing it as the "water we swim in," and conveys how consumption leads to a decline in social values.[7] Her work covers a wide breadth of topics, including the promotion of women's spheres and racialized commodities. However, it primarily focuses on the United States, Great Britain, and its former colonies.[8]

Other works dealing with gender have also made strides in exposing the role of niche consumerism, but have, like previous works, remained too narrow in their focus. Lawrence Glickman's *Consumer Society in American History* examines the attainment of status through political consumption (e.g., consumption and unions).[9] Similarly, Dana Frank's *Purchasing Power: Consumer Organizing, Gender, and the Seattle Labor Movement, 1919-1929* and Lizabeth Cohen's *Making a New Deal: Industrial Workers in Chicago, 1919-1939* also illustrate how consumption helped forge a political and social identity not only for male and female union workers, but also for immigrants.[10]

---

[6] Susan Strasser, Charles McGovern, and Matthias Judt, *Getting and Spending: European and American Consumer Societies in the Twentieth Century* (Cambridge and New York: Cambridge University Press 1998), 2, 5, 6.

[7] Jennifer Scanlon, ed. *The Gender and Consumer Society Reader* (New York and London: New York University Press, 2000), 1, 3.

[8] The anthology predominantly covers the United States with one article (each) on London, the British Commonwealth, Jamaica, and the Caribbean.

[9] Lawrence B. Glickman, *Consumer Society in American History: A Reader* (Ithaca, NY and London: Cornell University Press, 1999). Examples of works on niche/political consumption include: Arlene Dávila, *Latinos Inc.: The Marketing and Making of a People* (Berkley, Los Angeles, and London: University of California Press, 2001); and James B. Twitchell, *Branded Nation: The Marketing of Megachurch, College Inc., and Museumworld* (New York: Simon & Schuster, 2004).

[10] Dana Frank, *Purchasing Power: Consumer Organizing, Gender, and the Seattle Labor Movement, 1919–1929* (New York: Cambridge University Press, 1994); and

Nan Enstad's *Ladies of Labor, Girls of Adventure: Working Women, Popular Culture, and Labor Politics at the Turn of the Twentieth Century* is significant because it uses the lenses of class and gender to place working women in their social and political contexts as consumers. Her discussion highlights the central conflict of consumer culture: it promotes luxurious abundance, yet remains unaffordable to the average citizen-worker. Enstad's study, which focuses on American working girls during the turn-of-the-twentieth century, illustrates how young women "bought into" the myth of consumption—a trap which still exists today: many spent their wages on five dollar French heels and fashionable clothes instead of food and even shelter. Andrew Hurley also broaches the subject of class and consumption by showing how the rise of trailer parks, family-oriented and cost-conscious diners, and cheap entertainment venues, such as bowling alleys, allowed working-class individuals the opportunity to secure vestiges of the American Dream.[11]

Although Enstad's and Hurley's works, and those like them, continue to build upon the discourse of consumer culture, they still do not address the important issue of globality. Lizabeth Cohen probably provides the best attempt at approaching the subject of globalization in *A Consumer's Republic: The Politics of Mass Consumption in Postwar America* which, like Mark Gottdiener's *New Forms of Consumption: Consumers, Culture, and Commodification*, deciphers the cultural and social meanings behind mass consumption venues such as shopping malls.[12] As Cohen illustrates, the expansion of suburbia and the rise of democratized spending led to the spread of shopping malls, which, in the West, reconfigured residential landscapes and shifted consumption from urban centers to the local community. However, while this model may explain consumption habits in western industrialized nations, it does little to elucidate how, and why,

---

Lizabeth Cohen, *Making A New Deal: Industrial Workers in Chicago, 1919–1939* (New York: Cambridge University Press, 1990).

[11] Nan Enstad, *Ladies of Labor, Girls of Adventure: Working Women, Popular Culture, and Labor Politics at the Turn of the Twentieth Century* (New York: Columbia University Press, 1999) and Andrew Hurley, *Diners, Bowling Alleys, and Trailer Parks: Chasing the American Dream in Postwar Consumer Culture* (New York: Basic Books, 2001), 5, 9, 15–19. Also see Kathy Peiss, *Cheap Amusements: Working Women and Leisure in the Turn-of-the-Century New York* (Philadelphia: Temple University Press, 1986) for a study examining the rise of leisure culture in relation to consumption, gender, and labor.

[12] Lizabeth Cohen, *A Consumer's Republic: The Politics of Mass Consumption in Postwar America* (New York: Alfred A Knopf, 2003); Mark Gottdiener, *New Forms of Consumption: Consumers, Culture, and Commodification* (Lanham, MD: Rowman and Littlefield, 2000).

individuals spend their money elsewhere (in Nigeria, or the jungles of Ecuador, for example). Moreover, such a narrow focus on malls as "the" place to shop also marginalizes other culturally-important, alternative spaces such as flea markets, gay pride parades, tourist gift shops, or even megastores like Home Depot and Wal-Mart.[13]

Pursuing the Globetrotting Shopaholic

This anthology helps fill some of these scholarly voids by accentuating the important point that understanding international consumer spaces is essential to defining the culture of consumption. It reflects on the meaning of consumption in the age of globalization, and discusses, at great length, how elements of consumption (i.e., the ways in which we spend our money and the venues in which we consume) are internalized by societies, thus becoming cultural signifiers. Essays on topics such as patriotic products, gay and lesbian advertising campaigns, tourism and consumption, and maternity shopping not only convey how consumption has been manipulated for both personal and political reasons, but also illustrate that consumer space is continuously evolving and, as a result, defying standardization. For some, consumption may be a trip to the local mega mall; for others, it might be shopping at the local organic market or purchasing goods that are linked to a political cause. Either way, it is undeniable that consumption, especially in the twenty-first century, fills a multitude of niches, and is an integral part of identity politics. If, as Jon Goss contends, "you are what you buy," then to a certain extent we have all become globetrotting shopaholics, searching for the next object to buy, whether it be homegrown, or imported from half way around the world.[14]

This anthology is a welcome edition to the scholarly literature, especially given the current climate of eco-friendly living and shopping, and the trend of boycotting companies and products that support contentious political causes. Many works tell readers how to be eco-friendly, politically conscious, and cost efficient, but very few analyze how human actions impact, and are impacted by, global society. The Green Movement began in earnest in the early 1970s, and nearly forty years later, has become a part of our everyday consumer lives. Eco-

---

[13] Susan Strasser, "Woolworth to Wal-Mart." *Wal-Mart: The Face of Twenty-First Century Capitalism*, ed. Nelson Lichtenstein (New York: The New Press: 2006).

[14] Jon Goss, "The 'Magic of the Mall': An Analysis of Form, Function, and Meaning in the Contemporary Retail Built Environment." *Annals of the Association of American Geographers* 83: 18–47; Lane Crothers, Globalization and American Popular Culture (Lanham, MD: Rowman and Littlefield, 2007): 25.

friendly cars, hybrids, natural fibers, pesticide-free food, energy-saving appliances and light bulbs, handbags made from recycled license plates or candy wrappers, organic feminine hygiene products, and biodegradable condoms are just some examples of commonly known (and lesser known) green products currently on the market.[15] Why are these products so popular? The ecoist in us would like to say that we are becoming more and more aware of our carbon footprint and our impact on future generations. Unfortunately, however, this is not the case. Global human behavior (examples of which will be explored in this anthology) suggests that while some consumers are genuinely concerned about the environment, others are just "keeping up with the Joneses," mimicking a superstar, or simply indulging in the purchase of wants, rather than needs.

In her recent *Washington Post* article, writer Monica Hesse summarizes the tenuous place of eco-consumption in modern society in one sentence: "It's done with the best of intentions, but all that replacing is problematic."[16] Here, she refers to the new trend of replacing home goods that are not green with eco-friendly products. While many middle and upper-class Americans have embraced this new lifestyle (most working-class individuals cannot afford the higher priced merchandise sold by organic/green stores), many have done so without considering the waste that this transition is creating. Instead of using products until they break or wear out, or recycling them in multifunctional ways, Americans are continuing to participate in a new cycle of consumption. The only aspect that has changed is *what* they are consuming. A quick Amazon.com search for green living books will produce more than a thousand titles, while the term "eco chic" registers twelve pages of choices.[17] Al Gore's international environmental work has undoubtedly fueled the movement over the past decade, but it is clearly too early to become excited about green living since this new lifestyle choice is still in its infancy, and most likely to experience some bumps (and awful failures) along the way.

When Do-It-Yourself (DIY) hit the American market in the 1950s, most consumers did not know what to *do* with the products. Early critics said that DIY would fail, but mega stores like Home Depot and Lowes now dominate the American landscape. These stores provide tips, products, services to install items (usually when consumer attempts fail),

---

[15] There are lines of eco-friendly condoms (e.g., Naturalamb), lubricants, and even lingerie. www.greendaily.com has a list of eco-friendly sex products for sale around the globe. Last accessed August 4, 2008.

[16] Monica Hesse, "Greed in the Name of Green to Worshipers of Consumption: Spending Won't Save the Earth," *Washington Post,* March 5, 2008, C01.

[17] Test search performed on July 27, 2008.

and lists of local consultants. It is very possible that green consumption will also follow the same trajectory (especially as consumers become more invested in costly eco-friendly products, like Hybrid automobiles). As many of the chapters in this anthology illustrate, consumption is a continual process—one that is subject to trial and error, as well as success and failure. Thus, we should take the excitement about green living with a grain of salt (preferably organic).

This anthology is divided into three sections, each of which examines, in great detail, different aspects of global consumption. Part I, which focuses on fringe markets, politics, and identity, begins with Annessa Babic's discussion of patriotic consumption. In her chapter, she dissects numerous types of patriotic products and advertisements, and problematizes the meaning of patriotic merchandizing. Millie Creighton's chapter explores how the consumption of *Anne of Green Gables* products in Japan has framed Japanese perceptions of Canada. Daniel Farr and Gretchen Guenther's chapter on gay and lesbian marketing delves into the complex relationship between gender, sexuality and consumption. Brett Westbrook's chapter, which completes Part I, extends many of the same arguments made by Farr and Guenther by scrutinizing the normative femininity and consumer culture that pervades the reality television show "Tim Gunn's Guide to Style."

Part II expands on the theoretical framework outlined in Part I by providing readers with an intricate, global examination of consumer spaces and the culture of buying. These chapters, which range from personal reflections to ethnographic studies, compel the modern shopper to rethink how we create, perform, and internalize social signifiers through the goods we purchase. Tanfer Emin Tunc's chapter, which discusses consumption in the works of American writer F. Scott Fitzgerald, elucidates that the symbiotic relationship between the consumer and the consumed (i.e., "you are what you buy") serves as the foundation of the alienation, disillusionment and spiritual emptiness associated with modern materialism. Jennifer Le Zotte continues our foray into consumer spaces with her study of flea markets and their liminal place in American society. Robin O'Brian and Veronica Davidov critique consumption within the tourist industry, and problematize the commodification of native peoples in Mexico and Ecuador, respectively. Using fieldwork conducted in Budapest, Hungary, Brigette Thompson draws critical conclusions about gender, socio-economic status, and American expat consumption. Amparo Pamela H. Fabe, Peter Clandfield, and Michael Angelo Tata complete this section with their chapters on mall culture in the Philippines, Canada, and the United States.

The final segment of this anthology, Part III, takes a closer look at how, and why, products are consumed in various locations around the world. While Ayokunle Olumuyiwa Omobowale's chapter explores the social, economic, and cultural place that *tokunbo* (or imported second-hand vehicles) have in Nigeria, Africa, Elizabeth Johnson examines the African American hair care industry and the construction of race-identity in the United States. Through a series of fascinating interviews, Meredith Nash focuses on the burgeoning Australian maternity industry, while the final chapter in this anthology, written by Sara Stevens, dissects the logistical consumption junction that is Home Depot.

PART I:

FRINGE MARKETS: POLITICS, IDENTITY, AND CONSUMPTION

CHAPTER ONE

BUYING AND SELLING A PIECE OF THE AMERICAN PIE: THE USES, DISUSES, AND SPACES OF PATRIOTIC CONSUMPTION

ANNESSA ANN BABIC

Since the US flag's inception, it has been suffused with ambivalent sentiments, mystery, awe, reverence, and contempt. Political and legal debates have frequently shocked and divided the American public over uses concerning the national banner, and the US Congress has embarked on several failed attempts to amend the US Constitution with a flag protection amendment.[1] As congressional and media debates demonstrate, acceptable uses of the American flag are still socially and constitutionally contested and undefined. In times of war and national crisis, wearing and displaying the flag on one's person is acceptable, but defiling the flag in political protest is frequently scorned. Moreover, in 1907, the US Supreme Court declared that states have the right to prohibit using Old Glory in advertising. However, since World War II, there have been very few cases addressing uses of the American flag in marketing. Officially, commercial uses of the flag do not exist, but its likeness can be seen daily in the United States—in car lots encompassing their property with Old Glory, and in the fashion and home décor lines of Tommy Hilfiger and

---

[1] The text of the proposed amendment reads as follows: "The Congress and the States shall have the power to prohibit the physical desecration of the flag of the United States." Kenneth J. Cooper, "House Approves Amendment on Flag Desecration Measure Would Override High Court Rulings, Let States and Congress Outlaw the Act," *Washington Post*, June 29 1995, A7. The main reason that the amendment has not passed the US Senate is because many Senators feel that the language is too vague, leaving leeway for future disputes over its intended meaning and usage. In the Senate debates, legislators used examples of clothing and advertising to exemplify this point. Senators remarked that a small lapse in personal hygiene could make a flag bathing suit a form of desecration.

Ralph Lauren, both of whom regularly use the flag with respect to their products.[2]

This chapter examines various aspects of patriotic consumption, while critiquing the spaces in which the nation and flag are purchased. Aspects of the free market shape this discussion, particularly issues relating to how products find their market niche, and who enables items to become viable products—the consumer, creator, or advertiser. One of the key questions in this chapter asks if there a limit to patriotic commercialization. However, the central query looks for a sense of meaning (if any) for the uses of products celebrating the nation. More specifically, this chapter looks at advertisements, products, and museums that go beyond standard flag bumper stickers, decals, or purchasing campaigns to buy "Made in the USA" merchandise in order to examine how consumers, creators, and advertisers construct, and derive meaning from, spaces of patriotic consumption.

Columbia's Legacy

Popular examples of contemporary patriotic products are American flag bathing suits, cigar wrappers that reveal an American flag when unrolled, bumper stickers, and red, white, and blue fake eyelashes. Slogans like "Be Safe. Sleep with a Soldier" are sold on t-shirts, and nostalgic images like Rosie the Riveter abound. Little Earth Productions once sold a series of recycled belt buckles that used classic advertising and propaganda images. Some of these belt buckles had images of World War II factory workers, and slogans like "Built by Betty."[3] These products represent key aspects of consumer culture that require further examination, especially since national symbols in marketing function as familiar markers during the purchasing process. These gestures can appeal to the visual field, or one's sense of pride in the nation.[4] Patriotic consumption is a vast topic that can be dissected in many ways—from buying

---

[2] *Halter v. Nebraska*, 205 U.S. 34 (1907) and Carolyn Marvin and David W. Ingle, *Blood, Sacrifice, and the Nation: Totem Rituals and the American Flag* (Cambridge and New York: Cambridge University Press, 1999), 298. In this landmark case, the Court declared that state's rights prevailed over the individual. The case derived from Halter's use of flag imagery on beer bottles sold in Nebraska.

[3] Little Earth retired the line of belt buckles in 2005. See Figure 1.1. Little Earth specializes in making eco-friendly goods. Their products are made from a minimum of fifty percent post-consumer material.

[4] Marvin and Ingle, *Blood Sacrifice and Nation*, 299 and 302.

"American made" to purchasing, using, and displaying products with the American flag on them—but the meanings of patriotic buying are what makes it manifestations so intriguing.

Figure 1.1: Little Earth Productions
Belt buckle from Little Earth Productions, Circa 1995.
Photograph property of author. Used with permission.

Figure 1.2: Museum of Patriotism, Atlanta, GA
Display of patriotic items to purchase or collect.
Photograph property of author. Used with permission.

Lady Columbia's Continued Place

Lady Columbia, initially a symbol for the infant nation in the 1770s, is an appropriate symbol to begin this discussion of patriotic consumption. As one of the oldest national images in the United States, the figure of Columbia initially represented liberty and progress.[5] In 1792, the year of the Columbia tercentenary, British Americans sought to disassociate themselves from England, and used the Columbia image to represent their

[5] To see a depiction of Columbia see the logo for Columbia-Tri Star Pictures. The author does not have permission to reproduce it here.

division from Britannia and the Royal Crown.[6] She quickly became imbedded in US national iconography, alongside the American flag, the liberty pole and cap, the shield, the eagle, and a plethora of other depictions. Her image is still used in the present era, but appears in a drastically different manner. Columbia-Tristar Entertainment, a division of Sony Pictures, uses the Columbia image as part of its company's logo.[7] Many Americans, and film viewers, regularly see this image but do not associate it with patriotism. However, in this context, it is not intended to represent the United States. Rather, it is meant to symbolize Columbia-

[6] Thomas J. Schlereth, "Columbia, Columbus, and Columbianism," *Journal of American History* 79.3 (December 1992): 937–940. Also see David Ciarlo, "Consuming Race, Envisioning Empire: Colonialism and German Mass Culture, 1887–1914" (PhD Dissertation, University of Wisconsin-Madison, 2003). During the years of the Early Republic, Americans used Columbia as a representation for their expanding geography. Later her name was used for the first American vessel to circumnavigate the globe. The connection of Columbia to commercial culture is related to the rise of German mass culture. German mass culture coincided with the colonial subject, which helped reinforced the notion of the superiority of the German race and its concept of "the Nation." Moreover, it also provided the concrete context for the Other. For American colonists/revolutionaries, Columbia provided a concept of the Other in themselves. They were the Other that Great Britain sought—much like the Other that Germany desired to surpass—and Columbia provided the new Americans with a different and unique image, which was also within the European traditions of race and modernity.

[7] Sony Pictures Museum, email to the author "Re: Columbia Pictures Image," December 1, 2004 and Clive Hirschhorn, *The Columbia Story* (New York: Octopus Publishing Group Limited, distributed by Sterling Publishing Company, Inc., 1999), 7–9.

Tristar Entertainment's place in commercial market society.[8]

Other examples of Columbia's usage relate to her name. Products and companies like Columbia Batteries, Columbia Window Shades, Columbia Trust Company, and Columbia Records are just a few examples of her

[8] To date, I have been unable to secure a concrete meaning or intent for the utilization of the image from Columbia Pictures. However, it may be connected to the founders' heritage, and their desire to avoid racial stereotypes through Americanization. In the early twentieth century, Jack Cohen and Joe Brandt decided to expand their small film studio into a full-length production house, and brought on Cohen's younger brother Harry. In 1919 they formed CBC (Cohen-Brandt-Cohen) Productions, but the name quickly got dubbed Corned Beef and Cabbage. Harry Cohen took offense to the stereotype, particularly since he and his brother were the sons of a German-Jewish immigrant father and a Polish-Jewish immigrant mother. On January 10, 1924 the company officially changed its name to Columbia Pictures Corporation. Throughout the course of this project I have been attempting to find statistical evidence to support my claim that Columbia remains one of the most recognizable icons in US history. However, I have been unable to locate this information. In the meantime, I have relied upon informal surveying. I have questioned friends, relatives, colleagues, and strangers (the man next to me on the plane, the police officer examining my license and registration at a checkpoint, the person in front of me at the grocery store, and most humorously the bouncer at the bar…along with a few others). Each question has elicited nearly the same response. AB: "Do you know who Columbia is? Or, perhaps Lady Columbia?" Here, I frequently received a puzzled look. AB: "You know that woman shown above the credits, or at the start of the movie, for Columbia-Tristar Pictures?" Once prompted my respondents have nearly all given me the same response—a slow rising smile, gleam of recognition in their eyes (like they've just encountered an old toy or candy from childhood), or a nod of affirmation—that yes, they know her. Respondents have generally been slightly surprised to learn that Columbia was once a key component of the "national agenda" in World War I, and was used in patriotic posters of the era. A war veteran from the current Iraqi engagement was even stunned to learn the continued uses of Columbia, "Lady Columbia," and "Lady Liberty" (as my respondents have dubbed her). I feel this evidence is sufficient to surmise that Columbia retains a resilient place within the American psyche—even if her meaning and mainstream imagery have faded away and have been replaced by modern-day images like *Wonder Woman*. The Statue of Liberty also supersedes the image of Columbia in modern society because her name and figure are routinely recognized.

continual presence and discursive uses in US society.[9] Products, business names, and other uses for her male-counterpart, Columbus, are still prevalent, but their usage and meaning do not directly correlate to this story. The 1995 John Singleton film *Higher Learning* does recognize the Columbus legacy through the naming of the fictional Florida-based college "Columbus University." However, the premise of the movie centered not on exalting Columbus as a patriotic figure, but rather upon exposing, examining, and destroying prejudice in the sensitive atmosphere of the period. In the 1990s racially-divided culture of the US, the name Columbus acquired a dark overtone. Recently, academia, as well as the collective national memory, has begun to place Columbus in the category of "oppressor" over that of "explorer" and "saintly" discoverer of the New World.[10]

While Columbia symbolizes patriotism, her visual image has been used as a marketing tool. During World War I, Columbia's image was used to convey prosperity, progress, and the greatness of US society. Western Electric Company ran an ad campaign that played upon notions of national unity, patriotism, women's social/familial role, and the elusive (and often changing definition of) "The American Dream." In an advertisement entitled "The New Enlightenment," readers are first drawn toward the image of a woman vacuuming. However, this woman is not just *any* woman. She is dressed as the classic image of Columbia with her flowing gown draped over one shoulder. Her image does show signs of change—she has a blouse, with short, slightly puffed sleeves, on under her gown, and on her head she is wearing a Liberty cap. The young girl, with curled hair slightly protruding from underneath the cap, is looking at the viewer with her left arm slightly bent and extended, holding the cord of the vacuum her right hand is pushing. The text of the advertisement promotes the use of electricity in the home as "destined to fill a still larger sphere of domestic usefulness…[it adds] hours to the leisure, recreation, and broader interest that claim the modern woman's attention." The ad could thus be easily interpreted as conveying that any housewife/woman who uses

---

[9] Schlereth, "Columbia, Columbus, and Columbianism," 939–942; "Columbia Batteries," *The Saturday Evening Post*, April 14, 1917, 119; "Columbia Window Shades," *The Ladies Home Journal*, October 1917, 90; "Al Jolson, exclusive Columbia artist," Columbia Records, *Chicago Daily Tribune*, January 4, 1917, 4; and "Columbia Trust Company," *New York Times*, January 4, 1917, 18. The female name of "Columbia" was used for the proposed national name change because European tradition denotes countries as feminine.

[10] *Higher Learning*. 1995. 127 min. Los Angeles: Columbia/Tristar Studios.

electrical appliances promotes the nation.[11]

Selling War and Making Patriotic Spaces

This image of Columbia helping the middle class wife with her home duties becomes more poignant when placed alongside World War II advertisements proclaiming "There's a war job in my kitchen," "Who said this is a man's war?," "Wanted: Housekeepers to help the Army and Navy," and "Mother, keep house clean the way Uncle Sam does."[12] These titles appealed to female emotions, urging them to provide care for their families through cleanliness and well prepared meals, but the patriotic consumption campaign did not end here. Women were further told that mundane tasks like sewing a button onto a shirt when gripper fasteners could not be found, also served a patriotic purpose: mending of torn clothes reduced the waste inherent in purchasing new ones.[13] Lastly, the patriotic female could guide her family, and self, toward a patriotic life through her consumption habits, which took the role of "looking her best." This could be achieved by focusing on appearance (i.e., fashion, as discussed in the ads in this chapter). Tangee Lipsticks, for example, proclaimed that lipstick symbolized one of the reasons the US was fighting the war. "No lipstick—ours or anyone else's—will win the war," the ad declared. "But [lipstick] symbolizes one of the reasons why we are fighting...the precious right of women to be feminine and lovely—under any circumstances."[14]

During the Second World War, advertisers and copyeditors continually formed their publications around the war effort. Patriotic advertising was promoted during World War I, but it occurred on a larger scale during World War II. This large-scale mobilization partly occurred because of

[11] "The New Enlightenment," Western Electric Company, *Good Housekeeping*, October 1916: 149.

[12] "There's a war job in my kitchen," Nabisco, National Biscuit Company, *Good Housekeeping*, September 1942: 101; "Who said this is a man's war?," General Electric, *Good Housekeeping*, October 1942: 82; "Wanted: Housekeepers to help the Army and Navy," Pepperell Fabrics, *Ladies Home Journal*, August 1943: 66; and "Mother, keep house clean the way Uncle Sam does," Lysol Disinfectant, *Good Housekeeping*, April 1942: 69.

[13] "It's no fun . . . but it's patriotic!," Gripper Fasteners, Scovill Manufacturing Company, *Good Housekeeping*, March 1942: 175.

[14] "War, Women, and Lipstick," Tangee Lipsticks, *Ladies Home Journal*, August 1943, 73; and Anne McClintock, *Imperial Leather: Race, Gender, and Sexuality in the Colonial Contest* (New York and London: Routledge, 1995), 190, 196.

the duration of the war, but it also transpired because US territories had been attacked during the conflict. The magnitude of patriotic advertising, and its infiltration into the public arena, reached its peak on July 4, 1942. Magazines across the country joined in an unprecedented campaign to display American flags on their covers for Independence Day, with nearly three hundred publications participating in the patriotic measure. Paul MacNamara, a publicist for Hearst magazines, masterminded the idea because he believed the united display of patriotism would ignite buyers to spend more money on magazines and affiliated products. Additionally, half the magazine covers included the US flag juxtaposed with the words "United We Stand."[15]

Aside from displaying wartime advertisements promoting patriotic consumption, places like The National Museum of Patriotism in Atlanta, Georgia teaches and sells patriotism. The National Museum of Patriotism opened its doors on July 4, 2004, which coincided with the initial stages of the US occupation of Iraq and the War on Terror. Just like the aforementioned World War I and World War II advertisements, The Museum of Patriotism emerged during a time of heightened patriotism (or a perceived need for it). The museum states that its mission is "about educating our country's youth, celebrating personal achievement, motivating people to respect the rights of others, to help our neighbors, to inspire good, and to magnify love of one's country."[16]

---

[15] Smithsonian National Museum of History, *July 1942: United We Stand* (Behring Center, Smithsonian National Museum of History: Washington D.C., March 22–October 27, 2002); and Peter Gwillim Kreitler, *United We Stand: Flying the American Flag* (San Francisco: Chronicle Books, 2001). The Smithsonian's exhibit consisted of 103, of the original 300, covers, and the exhibit was planned in concurrence with the sixtieth anniversary of the patriotic campaign. It was merely coincidental that the exhibit occurred so closely after the events of September 11, 2001. The Kreitler book was published in conjunction with the exhibit.

[16] National Museum of Patriotism, *National Museum of Patriotism: Discover the Sprit of America* (Atlanta, GA: National Museum of Patriotism), 2004. The author viewed the National Museum of Patriotism in February 2005.

Figure 1.3: National Museum of Patriotism
Selection of items that can be purchased at the museum gift shop.
Photograph property of author. Used with permission.

Figure 1.4: 9-11 Room
Photograph property of author. Used with permission.

Figure 1.5: Ellis Island
Photograph property of author. Used with permission.

The museum showcases US patriotic culture throughout its various displays: the branches of the military are exhibited, patriotic jewelry is housed behind glass cases, patriotic magazine covers hang from the walls, and posters showing superheroes (or superhero-like characters) dominate the landscape. The museum even has Ellis Island and 9-11 rooms. The Ellis Island area resembles a condensed version of the exhibits at the Ellis Island Immigration Museum in New York. The displays, at both locations, briefly mention that immigration helped US domestic and international growth, and as the Museum of Patriotism conveys, immigrants acted patriotically by pledging allegiance to the United States through action, work, and family life. The 9-11 room at the museum portrays the firefighters and police personnel from 9-11 as heroes, and like the rest of the objects on display, focuses on the happy collective image of the nation. The museum does not breakdown elements of patriotism, and does not differentiate between male and female modes of patriotic expression.[17]

This museum, while attempting to educate the visitor on different acts of patriotism (e.g., serving in the military, voting, and supporting the

[17] National Museum of Patriotism: Atlanta, GA; and Ellis Island Immigration Museum: New York, NY.

nation during time of national crisis or war), also sells patriotism. Displays with comic book-type heroes, and replicas of the Twin Towers in New York, evoke nostalgia and community. The gift shop, which forces someone to leave the museum via the store, is not unusual. However, what *is* different about this store is that it only sells patriotic regalia. A visitor can purchase decals proclaiming "Patriotism Rocks," t-shirts declaring love for the United States, coffee cups with the Pledge of Allegiance, novelty pens with flags and other US symbols, and books entitled *Patriotism in America.*[18] The products for sale continue the agenda of the museum: imbuing the visitor with a sense of pride and love for country. Here, patriotism is literally taught and sold. Yet, not all acts and spaces of patriotic consumption perform the same function.

Radical Patriotism

A 1977 advertisement for US Bongs depicts an Uncle Sam-type image offering a bong to the viewer. Unlike the standard Uncle Sam with his stern facial expression, this Uncle Sam is smiling. The title of the ad reads "Strike A Blow For Freedom: Buy US Bongs."[19] An advertisement of this nature would have appeared in a niche magazine like *High Times*, which specialized in marijuana paraphernalia and culture. This ad, however, functions differently than other patriotic publications, namely because it merges illegal activity with a national image.[20] The fact that the ad was used during the Vietnam War era, which is known for its various

[18] National Museum of Patriotism: Atlanta, GA.

[19] "Strike A Blow For Freedom: Buy US Bongs," US Bongs, 1977. Reprinted in *The Golden Age of Advertising the 70s*, ed. Jim Heinmann (Köln, Germany: Taschen, 2006), 139 and Gerald Leinwand, *Patriotism in America: Democracy in Action* (New York and London: Franklin Watts, 1997), 65–66. The name "Uncle Sam" for the US government emerged during the War of 1812 when Sam Wilson and his brother Ebenezer became the head meat buyers for Elbert Anderson in Troy, NY, which supplied meat to troops in the local area. When a group of visitors asked a workman the meaning of the letters "EAUS" (which were stamped on the meat), he replied that "EA" was for Elbert Anderson, and "US" was for Uncle Sam (i.e., "Uncle" Sam Wilson). The name quickly caught on, and items supplied to troops were dubbed as coming from "Uncle Sam." The name evolved into a reference for the US government in much the same way that the words "government issue" were shorted to GI, and used to refer to soldiers in the military during World War II. In the present era, the term GI still refers to enlisted US troops.

[20] In 1933, the US government criminalized marijuana, however, it has remained in use throughout the United States.

(sometimes anti-American) protest movements, also suggests a satiric, tongue-in-cheek, play on patriotism. The ad critiques the First Amendment Rights of free speech and expression, and within the context of the 1970s, reaffirms Americans' ability to protest against US national and international policy. Thus it cleverly interweaves patriotism, democracy, the anti-war movement, and an illicit activity to make a profound commentary on the nature of freedom—in this case personal (the private choice to smoke marijuana) and political (the public right to voice personal opinions).

Recent products have also used patriotism in non-traditional ways to promote awareness and education. In 1990, Old Glory Condoms (OGC) debuted on the US consumer market, and almost immediately the product line encountered controversy. The condom's advertising campaign depicted an unfurled condom resembling an American flag flying from a flag pole, with a slogan proclaiming: "Worn with Pride, Country Wide." While OGC purposefully used American flag imagery to "catch" its viewing public and ignite a firestorm of support for its merchandise, the "Never Worn at Half Mast" product was not intended to offend or discredit the United States or one of its national symbols. Jay Critchley, the president of OGC, adamantly claims that the condoms were designed to promote AIDS education and research, and notes that OGC sought to utilize the rhetoric of war in an uplifting manner for domestic and health related issues. When OGC petitioned the US Patent and Trademark Office, a division of the Department of Treasury, for official recognition and protection of their product, the company's request was quickly denied. Statements from the DOT called this marketing technique "immoral and scandalous," and a three-year legal battle ensued on the validity of both claims. In 1993, OGC finally won its petition for trademark status, but the condoms were later pulled off the market because the FDA did not approve the use of colored ink in condoms. Critchley remarked that his goal was to "challenge the government's silence and redefine patriotism." He viewed saving lives as patriotic. His concern for patriotism and the AIDS epidemic finally won OGC its trademark approval.[21]

---

[21] Press Release. "Transamerica Building Re-Created by Old Glory Condoms: The Patriotic Safer Sex Corporation will Unveil Its Scale Model in San Francisco on March 30 at The Lab," Old Glory Condom Corporation. March 2007. Last accessed October 24, 2007: http://www.bigtwig.org/oldglory_pr.html and M. Christopher Bolen, Richard J. Caira, Jr. and Jason S. Wood, "When Scandal Becomes Vogue: The Registrability of Sexual References in Trademarks and Protection of Trademarks from Garnishment in Sexual Contexts," *Idea* 39.3 (1999): 448. Critchely has since moved onto other campaigns like "Latex is for

The OGC example reflects a trend in anti-advertising (to go against the standard grain of promotion), and conveys how non-traditional acts of patriotism are treated in US society. The controversy surrounding OGC also elucidates the discursive elements of patriotism since, clearly, not everyone views acts celebrating the nation and its symbols in the same light. In addition, this case illustrates what can occur when the personal (condom use) clashes with the political (patriotism) in the public arena. Unlike the OGC campaign, the 1977 Uncle Sam bong ad did not receive an outcry of opposition because it appeared in a niche publication, did not apply for trademark status, and was not exposed to the general public. OGC sought to reach a large community of viewers, and purchasers, namely due to its goal to spread AIDS awareness and education. While OGC undoubtedly succeeded in self-promotion, it is doubtful that OGC actually educated anyone about AIDS or safe sex.

The First Lady and the Military

Barbara Bush is known for wearing an American flag scarf during the 1988 Presidential Campaign, and her television advertisements denouncing flag desecration. Her actions captured the zeitgeist because they coincided with the Supreme Court controversy *Texas v Johnson*, which dealt with flag burning. Barbara Bush continued her television ads after her husband, George H. W. Bush, won the election in an attempt to promote the Flag Protection Act of 1989.[22] The FPA of 1989 was overruled by the US Supreme Court in 1990, but Bush's actions still fall into the category of "standard patriotism" because she was encouraging the protection of a national symbol.

Laura Bush, like her mother-in-law Barbara Bush, routinely campaigns for educational purposes. Laura Bush does public service announcements (PSA) for education, and actively promotes literacy and reading. A July 2003 PSA in *Cosmopolitan* showed Bush posing with a book entitled *Long May She Wave*. The ad says "First Lady Laura Bush Gets Caught Reading."[23] The cover of the book is covered in American flags, and the

---

Lovers." Recently he sponsored a reproduction of San Francisco's Transamerica Building from OGC boxes.

[22] *Flag Protection Act of 1989,* Public Law No. 101-131, 103 Stat. 777 (amending 18 U.S.C. § 700, a-c [1968]). The act banned physical flag desecration, and permitted up to a one-year imprisonment for such actions. It allowed individuals to dispose of soiled or worn flags.

[23] "First Lady Laura Bush Gets Caught Reading," Get Caught Reading. *Cosmopolitan,* July 2003.

open book shows other flag designs hidden in its pages. The ad looks like a normal PSA for literacy, with a little patriotic flare, but the book *Long May She Wave* is not a book of text. It is a two hundred plus page book filled with pictures of American flag artwork and designs. Most likely, this ad was strategically-designed to promote patriotism in the wake of the March 2003 US invasion of Iraq. In doing so, it fails to promote reading because the First Lady is not reading a book of text. Rather, she is looking at a book of pictures. Yet this ad campaign did not meet an outcry of opposition, and to my knowledge, no one wrote letters of protest. Instead, it appears to have faded away into the background of patriotic images and displays of patriotism.

The Potomac Mills Outlet Mall in Potomac Mills, Virginia showcases yet another brand of patriotic space and consumption. Potomac Mills Outlets, thirty miles south of Washington DC, has emerged as a prime tourist destination. It is estimated that out of its fifteen million annual shoppers, between four and six million are tourists. The enclosed mall has more than 225 shops, and boasts both high-end and low-end shopping venues.[24] This vibrant mall, with its tourist appeal, also hosts an Armed Forces Recruiting Center. The striking oddity about this patriotic example is not its perceived scandalous imagery, its misguided advertisement, or its promotion of goods. Instead, its peculiarity comes from the fact that you can buy your grandmother a birthday present, get your sister a prom dress, eat Chinese from the food court, drink a Starbucks Soy Caramel Macchiato, and sign up for military service all under the same roof.

---

[24] Edwin McDowell. "America's Hot Tourist Spot: The Outlet Mall," *The New York Times Online*, May 26, 1996. Last accessed July 27, 2008: query.nytimes.com/gst/fullpage.html?res=940CE1DA1139F935A15756C0A960958260

Figure 1.6: Potomac Mills Outlet Mall, Potomac Mills, VA, August 2007
Photograph Property of author. Used with permission.

Patriotic Meanings

While messages of patriotic consumption usually surface during wartime, the intertwining of patriotism with household appliances, or women's lipstick for that matter, illustrates its propensity to infiltrate mainstream, peacetime consumer society and its manifestations. Consumer society studies routinely note that the purchase, use, and display of products express social identities, and individuals frequently obtain identity through ownership. Carolyn Marvin and David Ingle remark that not only is the pursuit of consumption ritually obligatory, but individuals also act as "participating congregations" when buying goods.[25] The purchasing of patriotic goods, or goods that will promote patriotism, places the consumer within the national discourse of promoting the nation, but one must question how different patriotic purchases impact consumer identity. Gerald Leinwand denotes patriotism as asking individuals to place their needs aside so that the desires of the nation can take precedence.[26] Thus, when one purchases small totalities of the nation, does that mean that s/he is the nation?

The acts of patriotic consumption and space explored in this chapter reflect the changing spheres of US political, social, and consumer life.

---

[25] Anne M. Cronin, *Advertising and Consumer Citizenship: Gender, Images, and Rights* (London and New York: Routledge, 2000), 1, 13; Marvin and Ingle, *Blood, Sacrifice, and the Nation,* 301–302.
[26] Leinwand, *Patriotism in America,* 11–19.

Contemporary manifestations (and remanifestations) of patriotic images, like those in Little Earth products, reflect nostalgia and the idealization of mythic "Golden Ages." Consequently, purchasing these products, or viewing these displays, continues the well-established rite of incorporating popular memory and culture into the national discourse. The products and spaces mentioned here do not necessarily change national politics, or even completely reflect politics. Instead, they parallel public conversations about the image of the nation within American minds, homes, and communities.

CHAPTER TWO

JAPANESE JOURNEYS IN SEARCH OF A FICTIVE FOREIGN FRIEND: ASSUMING, CONSUMING AND SUBSUMING CANADA THROUGH *ANNE OF GREEN GABLES* TOURISM

MILLIE CREIGHTON

To honor the 100th anniversary of Lucy Maud Montgomery's novel *Anne of Green Gables* (1908), Canada Post issued a set of commemorative stamps. The set contains a stamp that depicts Anne as a young girl, with red braided hair, in a purple dress with a lavender pinafore amidst rolling hills, and another that showcases the Green Gables house. In keeping with Canadian bilingualism, the commentary that accompanies the stamps was printed in English and French. However, in an unusual twist, it also appears in a third language—Japanese. Additionally, Canada and Japan teamed up to simultaneously issue Anne stamps, so Japan Post also issued anniversary stamps in Japan, despite the fact that they commemorate a foreign book.

Anne of Green Gables, which is about an imaginative orphan girl who finds a home and family in a rural Canadian community on Prince Edward Island (PEI), has greatly influenced Japan and Japanese projections of Canada. Montgomery's novel was first translated into Japanese in 1952 during the post-World War II era when the Japanese were avidly consuming Western culture, much of which was restricted during the pre-World War II and war years.[1] Ever since, "*Akage no An,*" or "Carrot-Head

---

The research for this chapter has been made possible by a Humanities and Social Sciences Research Grant from the Social Sciences and Humanities Research Council of Canada (administered by the University of British Columbia).

[1] Millie Creighton, "Maintaining Cultural Boundaries in Retailing: How Japanese Department Stores Domesticate 'Things Foreign,'" *Modern Asian Studies* 25.4 (1991): 675–709.

Anne" as she is known to the Japanese, was introduced to Japan, the book and its heroine have been immensely popular, and have become nearly synonymous with Japanese perceptions of Canada. "Carrot-Head Anne" has not only inspired Japanese consumer fads and tourism to Canada, but has also inspired the Japanese to become globetrotting shopaholics—a people in search of Anne souvenirs and "Anne-like" experiences wherever possible.

In their quest for a connection with their beloved Anne, Japanese tourists have spent millions (if not billions) of dollars on Anne related items and experiences. For many Japanese, the most famous Canadian (and perhaps the only one they know) is the fictitious Anne. Moreover, the physical location they most strongly associate with Canada is Prince Edward Island, also known as "Anne's island home." Although many Canadians in the early twenty-first century think of PEI as a quaint but peripheral area of Canada where potatoes are grown, for the Japanese, PEI is Canada, and Anne is the ultimate Canadian. Thus Green Gables—Anne's "home" and a tourist destination on PEI (along with neighboring sites)—has become the fictive and physical geography where Canada is assumed, consumed, and subsumed by Japanese enthusiasts.

Japanese Women Encounter Anne: Meetings, Merchandising and the Media

Much of *Anne of Green Gables'* phenomenal success in Japan has been attributed to Hanako Muraoka, who translated the first Japanese-language version of the novel, which was published in 1952. Muraoka was given the book in 1939 by a teacher at a Canadian-run school she attended in Japan (*Tōyō Eiwa Jogakuin*) before Canadians were forced to leave the country due to the impending war.[2] The book's instant popularity in Japan was partly because the story of the orphan girl appealed to a nostalgic post-war population who had suffered the ravages of wartime violence and post-war poverty. The Japanese were eager to regress into an era where community, nature, and goodness defined human interaction, and where self-improvement could still be achieved. Moreover, Japanese girls and women were particularly enthusiastic about embracing a character who challenged the patriarchal social order that had been

[2] Yuka Kajihara, "An Influential Anne in Japan" (2001). Last accessed August 2008: www.yukazine.com/lmm/e/japanne.html

inscribed onto their lives.[3] In the novel, Anne's adoptive parents (brother and sister Matthew and Marilla Cuthbert) originally request a male child and are disappointed when they receive Anne, a girl. At the time, this paralleled the Japanese desire for boys and the idea that the primary goal of a household was to produce a male heir. Females were a "disappointment," and Japanese girls internalized this as they grew older. However, this parallelism is inverted when Matthew states to Anne—and by extension to all Japanese females—"*soosano, washi wal da-su no otoko no ko yori, an no hō ga ii yo–mashū.*" ("Well now, I'd rather have you than a dozen boys, Anne.") [4] By prioritizing female intelligence, friendship, and imagination, *Anne of Green Gables*, made the impossible possible for many young Japanese girls.

Consumer merchandising soon followed the novel's initial success. Early Anne products included dolls, comic books, and children's clothing patterns. Later, in the 1980s and 1990s, packages of "Anne" candy were sold which included plastic figurines of the characters from the novel. Even though these products were marketed at children, they became the basis of mother-daughter interactions—a material way for Japanese women to pass on their love of Anne to the next generation. Since one never knew which figurine would be in the box, girls and their mothers would make repeated purchases hoping for a different figurine (in many cases, the candy itself was irrelevant). *Anne of Green Gables* merchandising became a basis for "*shumi.*" *Shumi* is often erroneously translated into English as merely a "hobby," but implicit in the word is a dedicated involvement to continual learning and self-improvement. "Anne Study Clubs" (*An no benkyō kai*), or "Let's think about Anne Clubs" (*An o*

---

[3] Anne Allinson, "Japanese Mothers and Obentos: The Lunch Box as Ideological State Apparatus," *Anthropological Quarterly* 64.4: 195–208; Millie Creighton, "Edutaining Children: Consumer and Gender Socialization in Japanese Marketing," *Ethnology* 33.1 (1994): 35–52; Millie Creighton, "The Shifting Imagery of Childhood Amidst Japan's Consumer Affluence: The Birth of the '5 Pocket Child.'" In *Images of the Child*, ed. H. Eiss, 75–99. Bowling Green, Ohio: The Popular Press, 1994; Millie Creighton, "Marriage, Motherhood, and Career Management in a Japanese 'Counter Culture.'" In *Re-Imaging Japanese Women*, ed. Anne Imamura, 192–220. Berkeley: University of California Press, 1996; Mariko Fujita, "'It's All Mother's Fault': Childcare and the Socialization of Working Mothers in Japan," *The Journal of Japanese Studies* 15.1 (1989): 67–91; S. Vogel, "Professional Housewife: The Career of Urban Middle Class Japanese Women," *Japan Interpreter* 12 (1978): 16–43.

[4] This translation can be found in the May 2008 guidebook for the NHK (Nihon Hōsō Kyōkai) English language learning program "Akage no An' e no tabi" ("A Journey to Carrot-Head Anne's World").

kangaeru kai), became, and remain, popular among Japanese women. Such groups bring women together to read the book, talk about its themes, explore connections to their own lives, and discuss Anne products. Canada is often discussed at these club meetings, but knowledge about Canada generally focuses on the locations in the book and the important locales of Lucy Maud Montgomery's life. These Anne study clubs have not only shaped the experiences the Japanese seek when visiting Canada, but have also made substantial monetary contributions to the Montgomery legacy. One prominent club, the *Buttercups,* contributed $3000 CDN in 1988 towards the renovation of the Lower Bedeque, PEI school where Montgomery once taught. Moreover, in 1996, it donated $17,000 CDN to help convert the former Montgomery family dwelling in Leaksdale, Ontario into a museum.[5]

Visual and print media have also contributed to the ever-growing popularity of Anne. Beginning with a long run in Tokyo followed by other major Japanese cities, "The Musical, Carrot-Head Anne" ("*Mu-jikaru Akage no An*") was performed throughout 2008 to commemorate the novel's 100th anniversary. Advertisements and promotional material were posted all over the Internet including the Shiki Theatre Company's website, and the Canadian Embassy in Japan's on-line "Events Calendar."[6] Takashimaya Department Store in Nagoya staged the exhibit, "Anne of Green Gables Centennial Exhibition: The Prince Edward Island that Montgomery Loved," which also reinforced associations between the novel, Prince Edward Island and Canada. Meanwhile, the Japanese educational broadcasting channel NHK (*Nihon Hōsō Kyōkai*) screened an English language learning program called "*Akage no An' e no tabi*" ("A Journey to Carrot-Head Anne's World"). The show highlighted English phrases from the novel and featured segments about Canada. Of course keeping up with the television program required purchasing monthly magazine guides and CDs.

The immensely popular series helped many Japanese Anne fans learn English phrases that they thought were associated with life in Canada. One such phrase was "tempest in a teapot," which was used to describe the scene where Anne and her friend Diana become inebriated consuming what they believe is non-alcoholic raspberry cordial. Many Japanese fans can now reference raspberry cordial, perhaps thinking it is a Canadian

---

[5] Yuka Kajihara, "An Influential Anne in Japan" (2001). Last accessed August 2008: www.yukazine.com/lmm/e/japanne.html

[6] Shiki Theater Company, Shiki Group Japan (2008). Last accessed August 2008: http://www.shiki.gr.jp/applause/anne; Canadian Embassy, Japan (2008). Last accessed August 2008: http://www.canadanet.or.jp/p_c/event_e.shtml

drink when in reality many Canadians do not know what it is. The English drills even suggest traveling to Canada: "If I were you, I would go to Canada" ("*Moshi watakushi ga anata dattara, kanada e iku darō*"). The show's monthly viewing guide features detailed colored maps of PEI, showing precise locations such as Cavendish, Green Gables, Charlottetown, Lower Bedeque, and Park Corner, while the rest of Canada is largely an unmarked empty void. The May 2008 issue even featured photos of PEI, including the Green Gables house, the forests that were the inspiration for Anne's "haunted woods," the church Lucy Maud Montgomery attended, and her grave. Articles under the heading "*Purinsu Edowaado-Tō kikō: An no shima o tazunete*" ("Travel to Prince Edward Island: Visiting Anne's Island") included a short interview with one of Montgomery's living relatives, excerpts on berry picking, having tea, and making ice cream at Orwell Corner Heritage Village. Other articles focused on the two young female stars of the program as they traveled to Prince Edward Island, learned patchwork, and were taught how to craft Anne dolls.

Japanese Globe(s)hopping: Searching for Anne in Canada

A Japanese tourist can (and often does) buy plenty of Anne dolls and other *Anne of Green Gables* paraphernalia outside of PEI. Anne merchandise is usually featured in most downtown Canadian tourist shops geared towards globetrotting Japanese visitors. In fact in some Vancouver stores (which is thousands of kilometers away from PEI) Japanese is spoken and purchases—including Anne souvenirs—can be made in Yen. Moreover, in 2008, tourists can also buy official Anne stamps at any post office in the country. However, the first destination for many Japanese tourists is Green Gables itself. Situated on a PEI preserve operated by Parks Canada, it is the only Canadian national park dedicated to a literary theme. Brochures for visitors are printed in three languages: English, French (as required by official Canadian bilingualism statutes) and Japanese, which clearly illustrates the importance of Japanese consumption to the site. As one Parks Canada employee confirmed, Japanese tourists, and in particular Japanese women, visit in large numbers, have more knowledge of the area than visitors from other countries, and account for a significant percentage of souvenir sales.

After walking through rooms decorated in period style (many of which depict episodes from the book), tourists are encouraged to visit the Green Gables store, which adds to the notion that this national park is not merely a park, but rather a "theme park," complete with leisure opportunities (e.g., strolling down "Lover's Lane" or through the "Haunted Woods"), entertainment (e.g., taking a picture with an Anne look-alike), and shopping. Japanese tourists almost always purchase books, dolls, and other small trinkets onsite, often buying gifts for fellow Anne club members or others back home in Japan. They also shop at other sites near the theme park, making Japanese tourism and consumption important to PEI and neighboring Nova Scotia and New Brunswick. Organized tours of PEI are often run by Japanese expats or are directed at Japanese consumers, with tour brochures printed in both English and Japanese. Tourists participate in orchestrated consumer activities such as berry picking and ice cream making. Some even purchase wedding packages which arrange for Japanese couples to be married in the same parlor as Lucy Maud Montgomery. Many Japanese brides even wear an Anne wig. One PEI man involved in the tourism industry could not understand, as he expressed it, why "those pretty young Japanese women" want to get married wearing "those red braids." Perhaps such a wedding is one way of making the leap from "meeting Anne" to metaphorically "becoming Anne."

"Canadian World" in Japan

In 1991, Canada came to Japan in the form of Canadian World, built in Ashibetsu (Charlottetown, PEI's sister city), located on Japan's northern island of Hokkaido, whose wide open spaces, flora, and farmland is believed by some to resemble Canada. Billboards directing highway traffic towards Canadian World feature the image of a large red hat, with two red bows on each side, signifying Anne without the necessity for words. Outside the theme park is another billboard message, "Welcome to Canadian World," written in red in both English and Japanese. Attached to two pillars, the board is a portal marking a metaphoric spatial transition between Japan and Canada.

Although this theme park promises Canada, it is devoted to Prince Edward Island and Anne. However, here, Anne is no longer, "Anne of Green Gables," but "Anne of Canadian World." Gift stores sell T-shirts, handkerchiefs, and small hand towels emblazoned with Anne and the words "Anne of Canadian World" and "Hokkaiko, Japan." These goods often picture logos which include a spray of lavender, mainly because of the association between Anne, Canada and lavender fields. One popular item is a package of cookies in a container shaped like the Green Gables house. Anne's revised identity, which has been inscribed on souvenirs meant for the "folks back home" in local Japanese communities, is a clear indication of where the traveler/shopper has been—in this case Hokkaido, Japan, rather than PEI, Canada.

Before constructing the park, Japanese representatives visited the Cavendish, PEI site, consulted with Parks Canada representatives, and brought carpenters from PEI to build an "authentic" depiction of Green Gables. However, unlike the PEI site, Canadian World was built with the covert intention of being a themed shopping mall.[7] In addition to the Green Gables house, the theme park featured a post office, a school, a hilltop chapel, a train called the PEI Express, and plenty of consumer opportunities. During the heyday of Canadian World, the post office operated as an official Japanese postal outlet. Visitors could purchase stamps and mail letters from it, which would be post-marked "from Canadian World." Canadian World sought authenticity by hiring Canadians to dress like Anne and other characters from the novel. The park also offered other Anne experiences: visitors could take part in ice-cream making, patchwork quilting, or drying herbs for use in craft projects. Thus Canadian World's main attraction was the promise of a "real" encounter with Anne and engagement in an "Anne-like" lifestyle.

Canadian World was planned during the bubble economy of the late 1980s, when Japan's population had money to spend on leisure and domestic travel. Even though the Japanese economic bubble burst in the early 1990s, the Canadian World project proceeded as scheduled until the full impact of the economic downturn emerged around the middle of the decade. In the early 1990s, tallies of visitors, predominately Japanese, were listed as 11,000–14,000 per day, and still reached 9,000 per day in 1995.[8] However, shortly afterwards, numbers began to plummet. The recession meant that Japanese elsewhere in the country could not make leisure trips to Hokkaido. In 1999, Canadian World was recognized as a business failure, and, like the bubble economy, went bust.

Those involved were not sure what to do with the ghost town that was now Canadian World. There seemed a genuine sense that it would be regrettable ("*mottenai,*" or a "waste") to simply tear down the elaborate theme park. Ashibetsu chose a novel alternative: in one area of the compound, a few gift shops and eating stalls remained open because they were independently run by locals. Everyone else—ticket takers, guides, and "authentic Canadians"—departed. The main entrance gates were

---

[7] For more information on this phenomenon, see Susan Davis, "The Theme Park: Global Industry and Cultural Form," *Media, Culture & Society* 18.3 (1996): 399–422.

[8] Joy Hendry, "Foreign Country Theme Parks: A New Theme or an Old Japanese Pattern?" *Social Science Japan Journal* 3.2: 213.

simply left unlocked and open, as were all the buildings. One could still cross the boundary zone of national imaginaries, enter Canadian World, stroll the premises, view the lavender fields (or what remained of them), and peruse the post office, school, and the Green Gables house. However, now it was free to enter, and almost no one was around. Canadian World had gone from being the projection of a grand rural Canadian community to a ghost theme park, home to the specter of Canada.

My Canadian World

I knew about Canadian World's heyday in the early 1990s, and visited in 2000. I experienced the strangeness of passing the abandoned row of ticket booths leading to the main entrance gates, expecting to see ticket vendors who eerily were not there. Realizing I could just enter, I nonetheless paused, wondering if I should really go in. I entered and proceeded to "engage" with the theme site, strolling the lanes, viewing the lavender, and entering the buildings. The post office was still decorated with large framed photographs of Prince Edward Island fishing scenes, but some of them had been taken off the walls and were propped against the counters of the post office, with seemingly nothing but their size to prevent someone from taking them as souvenirs of the Canadian World that once was. I wondered if this could happen elsewhere. Would a major theme park no longer in operation somewhere else in the world simply leave its doors open with seemingly little fear of theft or vandalism? Perhaps the answer lies in Anne's sacred place in the hearts of the Japanese people.

After visiting the post office, I entered the house and walked to the dining room where the table was set with Victorian style china for Anne and Diana's special tea party. Although there were no staff members to maintain the premises, everything in Anne's bedroom was still in place, including the candle Anne used to signal her friend for their unauthorized rendezvous. The window was open. Clearly, it seemed, the fictitious Anne was "really" there, had just gone out the window, and was likely meeting her bosom friend Diana on one of their jaunts, while "real" people were no where to be encountered. Some non-Japanese who visit the now defunct Canadian World blog about it: some are fascinated by the ghost theme park, while others ridicule it severely. However, those criticizing the site and the idea of transporting "Canada" to Hokkaido most likely never knew Canadian World in its heyday, with the action, crowds, and festivities at their height—all of which provided Japanese who could not travel to the real PEI with the chance "to go to 'Canada' to visit 'Anne.'"

The Japanese association of *Anne of Green Gables* and her Prince Edward Island home with Canada has complicated the identity of Canadians attempting to interact with Japan. On one hand, these associations have produced a very positive image—Anne and PEI are usually coupled with compassion, nature, the Great Outdoors, and the quaint goodness of rural life. On the other hand, such associations elide a full understanding of the breadth, complexity, diversity, and modernity of contemporary Canada. They erase the contemporary reality of Canada as a developed, multicultural nation with major cities, a global stock exchange, advanced medical facilities, cutting edge research and technology, and a prominent performing and fine arts sector. Clearly, assumptions of an Anne-like existence in a simpler time and place subsume a broader understanding of Canada. Until some Japanese Anne-*otaku* (overzealous Anne fans) are able to transcend the grasp of Anne's touristic trap, they will continue to view the rest of Canada as the "blank void" on the map displayed in the viewing guide for "A Journey to Carrot-Head Anne's World."

CHAPTER THREE

SEEKING THE RAINBOW DOLLAR: GAY AND LESBIAN MARKETING AND CONSUMPTION

DANIEL FARR AND GRETCHEN GUENTHER[1]

The use of gay, lesbian, bisexual, and trans (GLBT) imagery in marketing suggests a mélange of inclusion, pandering, and irony.[2] Central to all advertising is the targeting of consumers. Traditionally, the "model" consumer has been the white, middle-class, heterosexual American, oftentimes gender segmented, depending on product. As this middle-class market has become flooded with consumer opportunities, we have seen increased efforts to access niche markets comprised of minority groups. This chapter seeks to explore the market's use of GLBT imagery in television commercials, and assess how this is experienced by gay and lesbian consumers.

The growth of a gay and lesbian consumer market has been noted in the marketing literature of the past several decades. Historic research demonstrates the existence of marketing to, and consumption by, gay men and lesbians throughout the early twentieth century.[3] However, it is only during the latter half of the twentieth century that these consumers became a particularly recognized force in the market. As this community gained visibility, it drew greater attention in advertising and marketing, thus becoming a desirable consumer population to court. The recognized financial strength of this consumer pool was accompanied by the integration of more identifiably gay men and lesbians into mainstream

---

[1] Daniel Farr (Lead Author); Gretchen Guenther (Secondary Author)

[2] Alexandra Chasin, *Selling Out: The Gay and Lesbian Movement Goes to Market* (New York: Palgrave, 2000).

[3] Blaine J. Branchik, "Out in the Market: A History of the Gay Market Segment in the United States." *Journal of Macromarketing* 22.1 (2002): 86–97.

culture. As these men and women gained increased access to positions of power, they were able to influence marketing strategies and company policies to foster visibility, support, and social change.

While the numbers vary, profit margins from the gay and lesbian market segment are substantial. Estimates show that about fifteen to twenty million American consumers comprise this market niche, having an annual purchasing power of $513 billion US. This minority consumer niche is second only to African Americans and Hispanics.[4] This group's importance in the market is further enforced by the characterization of gay men and lesbians as having higher levels of education and disposable incomes.[5] While some businesses may struggle with social or moral issues associated with marketing to the queer community, the potential fiscal gain is difficult to resist; therefore, more businesses have begun to address this market, regardless of their religious and social ideologies. An example of such a business is the global retail superpower Wal-Mart, a company notorious for its conservative, Christian values. Wal-Mart's recent association with the National Gay and Lesbian Chamber of Commerce exemplifies such a compromise.[6] Despite an affiliation with traditional Judeo-Christian family values, they have begun to offer gay and lesbian greeting cards in their United Kingdom subsidiary Asda.[7] Had Wal-Mart refused to make such a transition, it would have risked the alienation of a significant market segment. The company may not be prepared to support gay and lesbian rights, but it is not prepared to risk losing their business.

Attempting to appeal to gay and lesbian consumers without alienating the heterosexual consumer is a complicated and increasingly necessary advertising approach. A significant number of gay and lesbian consumers are conscientious enough to ascertain if a company is gay-friendly before purchasing products, and these consumers are more likely to purchase

---

[4] Justin Nelson, Chance Mitchell, and Walter Schubert, "National Gay and Lesbian Chamber of Commerce" (Testimony to the House Financial Services Oversight Subcommittee, Washington DC, July 14, 2004). Last accessed July 2008: http://www.nglcc.org/news/pressreleases/20040714

[5] Annette Pritchard, Nigel J. Morgan, Diane Sedgely, and Andrew Jenkins, "Reaching Out to the Gay Tourist: Opportunities and Threats in an Emerging Market Segment." *Tourism Management* 19.3 (1998): 275.

[6] William Henderson, "Wal-Mart Puts on a Gay-Friendly Face." *The Advocate*, September 26, 2006: 14.

[7] "Wal-Mart Courting Gays." *The Advocate*, January 31, 2006: 16.

products from companies that include gay themes in their marketing.[8] Moreover, their high level of brand loyalty makes gay and lesbian consumers a desirable customer segment to court.[9] Clearly, in a continually expanding world of market choice, companies must be cognizant about the messages they convey in their advertising and internal policies and practices.[10]

The gay and lesbian rights movement has resulted in an increasingly visible consumer market, forcing changes in media coverage of the gay and lesbian communities, marketing strategies, and product availability. Gay and lesbian consumers have achieved a critical mass, demanding consumer opportunities, recognition, and respect. While many gay and lesbian consumers do not feel it necessary to place their personal identity firmly in their wallets, there is an ever-increasing number who believe sexual identity is important and should receive consumer support. These products and services have taken off so well, that a queer consumer can even show his or her alignment with the GLBT movement through the use of the Rainbow Card from Bank of America.[11]

Historically, print advertisements were the primary method of approaching the GLBT consumer as queer magazines and newspapers were the only media sources available.[12] However, increasingly visible queer identities in television programming have transformed commercials into a powerful way to address the GLBT consumer. It is this emerging commercial presence on mainstream television that is of particular interest to this analysis.[13] These advertisements usually fall into one of three genres: "straight" advertisements with subtle gay referencing; advertisements that use GLBT identities and situations as camp humor;

---

[8] Opuscomm Group and GL Census (A Syracuse University and Opuscomm Group Partnership), *2006–2007 Gay/Lesbian Consumer Online Census.* Last accessed July 2008: http://www.GLCensus.org

[9] Brenda G. Pitts, "Sports Tourism and Niche Markets: Identification and Analysis of the Growing Lesbian and Gay Sports Tourism Industry." *Journal of Vacation Marketing* 5.1 (1999): 44.

[10] For example, the Adolph Coors Company experienced boycotts and strikes in the 1970s due to discriminatory policy and treatment of gay and lesbian employees. Steven Kates, *Twenty Million New Customers! Understanding Gay Men's Consumer Behavior* (New York: The Harrington Park Press, 1998), 157.

[11] Bank of America Rainbow Card. Last accessed July 2008: http://www.rainbowcard.com

[12] Branchik 90.

[13] There are numerous commercials that appear on the Logo Network, a gay and lesbian television network; however, they are clearly created under a different cultural context than ads intended for mass, mainstream, consumption.

and advertisements that seek to integrate visible homosexuality into mainstream society. These commercial techniques—the "invisible guise," "pinkface," and "normalized integration"—demonstrate the complex and diverse manners in which the queer niche is addressed, influenced, and explored by the television media.

A Queer Take on "Straight" Commercials: The Invisible Guise

Addressing sexual minorities in advertisements has historically occurred through subtle gay references. This "invisible guise" uses heteronormative constructs to present queer subtexts, while allowing a company or individual to deny association with GLBT. Such subtext is often invisible to the heterosexual consumer because he or she may not be aware of gay and lesbian iconography and/or cultural references. Audience variations that exist across class, race, and gender lines will inevitably impact the recognition of queer referencing. Thus, this is a complicated advertising tactic that permits both multiple interpretations and the reinforcement of hegemonic social ideology.

Given the subtlety of the references found in these types of commercials, in the face of protest, companies have been able to argue that they were unaware of the gay or lesbian content, and had inadvertently made a queer reference. However, the significant financial investment and effort put into the creation and placement of advertising campaigns makes the inadvertent argument increasingly difficult to comprehend. While this tactic offers a degree of safety for companies unwilling to publicly express and embrace a GLBT perspective, they also run the risk of alienating the queer consumer should they imply a negative connotation to a queer interpretation of a commercial.

While, in the past, the inclusion of GLBT content in advertising may have been unintentional, contemporary advertisements likely include "conscious" queer references under a guise of invisibility. A number of companies have used invisible guise campaigns. Volkswagen, Benetton, and Miller Lite demonstrate a particularly effective use of this technique because they were able to create commercials that could be read from both a straight and queer perspective. In the 1997 Volkswagen commercial *Sunday Afternoon* two young men, one black and one white, are seen driving around in a hatchback, picking up an easy chair found on the curb, and ultimately abandoning the chair again presumably due to its smell.[14] Over the course of the commercial, these men do not speak at all, but exchange ideas and make decisions based solely on eye contact and facial expression, which conveys a strong sense of ease and intimacy. While these men may be college roommates or friends, they may also be a gay couple. The interpretation of these men as a couple is reinforced by their ability to communicate non-verbally. A queer reading of the commercial is further enforced by the fact that it premiered during the coming-out episode of the 1990s sitcom *Ellen*.[15] Volkswagen denied that the men were a couple, and was publicly surprised at such an interpretation, but was unconcerned that the ad could receive a gay reading.[16]

Volkswagen's ad not only suggests a scenario with multiple interpretations, but also illustrates an instance where the denial of queer content has no negative repercussions. The company's response to the gay issue as a "non-issue" was smart in that it was able to avoid the potential alienation of queer consumers. The ad continued to run, receiving limited media attention despite its implicit acceptance of GLBT identities, families, and ultimately consumers.

A 1995 commercial from Benetton is one of the few ads referencing lesbianism. The commercial shows rapid shots of an Asian female model with a voice-over declaring your "best dress…you love more than your boyfriend—but let's not get started on that."[17] This ad easily can pass as a consumer joke involving the love of clothing. However, the model in this commercial, Jenny Shimizu, is an out lesbian. The use of an out lesbian model, and the accompanying voice-over, can be recognized as queer by those aware of gay icons, but these subtleties are unlikely to be read by many viewers. While there does not seem to have been much critique of the content at the time, Benetton could have made the argument that the personal identity of the model used was irrelevant to the campaign, thus deferring potential accountability.

While the invisible guise was a popular tactic in the 1990s, commercials still continue to use this strategy. The 2005 Miller Lite commercial *Unbeerman-like Conduct,* successfully created an ad open to

---

[14] Commercial Closet Association, *Sunday Afternoon*, 1997. Last accessed July 2008: http://www.commercialcloset.org

[15] *Ellen* ran on ABC from 1994 to 1998. The coming out episode, "The Puppy Episode," aired on April 30, 1997.

[16] Commercial Closet Association, "Editors Comments" *Sunday Afternoon*, 1997. Last accessed July 2008: http://www.commercialcloset.org

[17] Commercial Closet Association, *Best Dress—Jenny Shimizu,* 1995. Last accessed July 2008: http://www.commercialcloset.org

queer interpretation.[18] Since beer is often regarded as a consumer product for the heterosexual man, Miller Lite has a significant investment in maintaining the gendered, sexual status quo when approaching the advertising arena, which makes this ad all the more interesting. It depicts father and son (Timmy) fishing on a small lake in a rowboat. Timmy reaches into a cooler for beer and says “Pop, there’s something I gotta tell you.” He is suddenly interrupted by a referee standing in the pond critiquing the quality of the beer, and the loss of respect Timmy faces. He also notes the unoriginal tattoo on Timmy (a tribal armband). The consumer audience is left to conjure its own story about what Timmy wishes to tell his father and why he risks a loss of respect. While once popular primarily among gay men, the tribal arm band has become fashionable among both homosexuals and heterosexuals, rendering it a symbol that is open to interpretation. A straight consumer may view this ad and expect Timmy to discuss his girlfriend or his new tattoo; a gay viewer may believe that Timmy is about to come-out to his father. In this context, the possibility for multiple interpretations or narratives clearly fosters the invisible guise.

As seen through these three examples, the invisible guise is found particularly within the fluid interpretations of social symbols, situations, and language, all of which create a scenario of multiple-meanings when read from differing perspectives. While these commercials often do not convey a particular message about a company’s GLBT stance, they do offer the opportunity to appeal to a diverse consumer base. Usually, when a response is required about the potentially queer content of its commercials, a company’s (non)position becomes evident. If a positive, or even ambivalent, response is conveyed, the queer consumer may walk away with the impression the company is at the very least tolerant, if not supportive, of GLBT.

Camping Up the Commercial World: Pinkface and Homo-Humor

Another common form of GLBT inclusion is the use of queer and gender variant references as forms of deviance or as sources of camp humor. This heteronormative humor makes light of the possibility that one could or would want to be regarded as gay, lesbian, or trans. For example, the dressing of men in women’s clothing to obtain access to Ladies’ Night

---

[18] Commercial Closet Association, *Unbeerman-like Conduct,* 2004–2005. Last accessed July 2008: http://www.commercialcloset.org

at a bar is a source of ironic humor when enacted by a man with heavy facial hair. This portrayal might also be seen as a humorous take on transgenderism, which trivializes and stigmatizes trans-identities and social interactions. The use of non-traditional gender and sexual expressions serves to reinforce hegemonic heterosexual behavior, but also fosters a culture of discrimination where GLBT identities themselves are belittled and seen as humorous.

Commercials that use queer identities as a source of camp humor can be regarded as a modern form of blackface, or in this case, "pinkface." Blackface, a prevalent form of vaudeville entertainment between the 1830s and 1880s, created a caricature of black identities and social interactions through the use of white actors, wearing black makeup, and performing to a predominately white audience. By allowing the audience to simultaneously access the racial identity of the "other," while affirming that of its own, blackface created racial boundaries through performance and situational comedy. Blackface affirmed a hierarchical race system that not only posited white identities as preferred and privileged, but also stigmatized blacks as sexual, lascivious, and infantile.[19]

A similar configuration of social dynamics is used in many contemporary advertisements to make GLBT references. In ads, pinkface is conveyed through portrayals of gender variant or non-heterosexual individuals, situations, and/or behaviors which collectively create a humorous stigmatization of GLBT. While consumers usually regard these pinkface characterizations as simply amusing and ironic, they are in fact insidious in their content and underlying messages. Much like blackface, pinkface advertisements create a culture that posits the identities of GLBT persons as inferior, inappropriate, and ludicrous. The gendered components embedded within this commercial strategy are also important in that many only address masculinity. Very few, if any, advertisements include pinkface references to lesbians or women. This division is, perhaps, a reflection of the gendered hierarchical system that privileges men. While companies such as Dunkin Donuts, Snickers, and Bud Light may engage in the use of pinkface in their ad campaigns, they are careful to avoid racial references, using primarily white actors in these advertisements. The removal of race further enforces the sexist gender issues embedded in this practice.

A common form of pinkface occurs via men in drag, often in a manner that makes it apparent to the viewer that this individual's "true" sex does

---

[19] Sharon Kinsella, "Minstrelized Girls: Male Performers of Japan's Lolita Complex." *Japan Forum* 18.1 (2006): 65–87.

not match his external gender portrayal.[20] In the 1984 Dunkin Donuts commercial *Disguise* we see the "Dunkin Donut Man" dressed as a woman in order to investigate the doughnuts of a competing store.[21] This pudgy, middle-aged, balding white man with a full mustache and hairy arms is seen donning a flowery dress, blond wig, and white gloves. S/he inquiries about the quality and types of doughnuts available at a competing doughnut store, while the clerks stare in awe and confusion, with one even dropping doughnuts in shock. The Dunkin Donuts Man uses a feigned feminine voice and inadequately covers his mustache with his gloved hand during the interaction, suggesting a campy, stigmatized take on trans-women. This stigmatization is affirmed by the shocked, gaping stares of the clerks, and more poignantly, by a woman at the beginning of the commercial who turns her daughter's face away from this person, which confirms that s/he is an inappropriate subject for a child's gaze.

Bud Light's 2003 *Clown* commercial conveys another form of pinkface by addressing the perceived belief that homosexual men are perverse.[22] The viewer sees a man in a clown costume who appears as if he is walking on his hands.[23] At the bar, he orders a beer and drinks from the bottle, which visually appears to be inserted into the clown's anus. The other bar patrons look at this image in disgust. The derogatory humor of anal sex is reinforced as the clown leans over to the bartender and asks "Can I get one of those hotdogs?," to which the bartender responds with loathing "I don't think so." Bud Light's 2002 commercial, *Opener,* also references anal sex. The ad portrays a bartender popping the caps off beer bottles using the anus of a man hidden under the bar.[24] Clearly, both of these commercials demonstrate the degradation and perversion frequently associated with what might be construed as gay male sex. A distinction

---

[20] Drag, a complex social behavior engaging gender and social identity, is often constructed within these ads as dressing in clothing commonly affiliated with that of the other sex. Verta Taylor and Leila J. Rupp, "Chicks with Dicks, Men in Dresses: What It Means to Be a Drag Queen." *Journal of Homosexuality* 46, no. 3/4 (2004): 114–115.

[21] Commercial Closet Association, *Disguise*, 1984. Last accessed July 2008: http://www.commercialcloset.org

[22] Commercial Closet Association, *Clown*, 2003. Last accessed July 2008: http://www.commercialcloset.org

[23] The clown's feet function as his "hands," while his arms, which are raised in the air, appear to be the clown's legs and feet. Because he appears to be walking on his hands, the clown's face is positioned near the man's groin, while his buttocks are positioned over the man's face.

[24] Commercial Closet Association, *Opener*, 2003. Last accessed July 2008: http://www.commercialcloset.org

found in these commercials, however, is that the clown has a bar audience, while the hidden man in the *Opener* is known only to a friend sitting at the bar. The *Clown* reinforces the idea that anal sex is repulsive, which is affirmed by the numerous onlookers at the bar. On the other hand, the *Opener* conveys an implicit sense of disgust, which is tempered by a degree of sympathy for the presumed pain of anal sex.

Another form of pinkface is that of same-sex intimacy between "homosexual" men. One example is the 2007 Snickers commercial *Chest Hair*, which premiered during the Super Bowl, a stereotypically masculine television event.[25] In this commercial, the viewer sees two burly, white, male mechanics working on a car engine. One begins to eat a Snickers bar, allowing the end to hang from his mouth. The second man cannot resist the candy bar and begins to eat from the other end, which culminates in an accidental kiss. They recognize that they must quickly resolve this situation by doing something "manly," wherein they each rip out a patch of their own chest hair while screaming.[26] The ad conveys the idea that if two men accidentally engage in a homosexual act, it must be resolved through a campy enactment of hypermasculine behavior. An ironic aspect of this commercial, however, is the construction of body hair removal as masculine. Perhaps, in this context, true manhood involves the self-infliction of pain. In other words, it is preferable to physically harm one's self than to be identified as gay.

Penis-envy may also be regarded as a form of pinkface. Even though masculinity is symbolized by the phallus, "straight" men are told they should not look at other men's genitals. Doing so suggests the possibility of homosexual yearning, and the comparison of phalluses implies a questioning of one's masculinity. In the 2002 7-Eleven commercial *Big Gulp,* we observe two men in a car, one with a small drink, the other with a large one.[27] The man with the smaller drink places the cup between his legs and then looks down at his lap with a look of shame. As he looks at the larger drink between his companion's legs, he is given a slight nod and smile, which acknowledges his companion's larger "cup." This commercial demonstrates both the concerns of real manhood embodied within the phallus, as well as the competitive quality found in the

---

[25] Commercial Closet Association, *Chest Hair,* 2007. Last accessed July 2008: http://www.commercialcloset.org

[26] Several versions of this commercial were shot, all of which can found on www.youtube.com. Due to negative public response, this version was ultimately withdrawn from television airing.

[27] Commercial Closet Association, *Big Gulp*, 2002. Last accessed July 2008: http://www.commercialcloset.org

comparison of male bodies. It also suggests that comparing one's phallus may imply a questioning of one's heterosexual identity given the cultural mores that equate the intentional viewing of another man's phallus as a potentially homosexual act.

A final form of pinkface is the sexualization or objectification of the male body by other men. While we have, on occasion, observed the sexualization of the male body by women in commercials, it is far more common for men to objectify the bodies of women.[28] In a 2005 ad campaign, Arby's mocks this commercial format by depicting a group of male construction workers who neglect to catcall an attractive woman passing their site.[29] Instead, they catcall a man who walks by in slow-motion, accompanied by sexy music, carrying his Arby's lunch. The viewer observes what is really on the construction workers' minds, as an Arby's icon appears over each of their heads.[30] The idea that masculine construction workers would catcall another man is regarded as humorous and, quite frankly, ridiculous. It must be clearly articulated in the commercial that they are not homosexual. Rather, they simply have "food" on their minds. Thus, pinkface commercials not only reverse traditionally-held beliefs on sex, gender, and sexuality for a campy effect, but also confirm appropriate gender identities. Indeed, many pinkface commercials are resolved with an expression of appropriate masculinity/ (hetero)sexuality.

Welcome Home: Normalized Integration in the Mainstream

"Normalized integration" is the most clearly visible and identifiable queer advertising technique. Businesses that embrace this approach are seeking to court the queer consumer, though often tempering their advertisements to be socially acceptable to a broad audience. While the invisible guise offers a "safer" courting of the queer consumer, it also elides direct support. Pinkface, on the other hand, is the most destructive genre of queer commercials because it involves the manipulation of identities to create a campy brand of humor, irony, and stigmatization that

[28] Between the 1980s and 2000s, Diet Coke aired a series of commercial portraying the sexualization and objectification of a muscular man by women.

[29] Commercial Closet Association, *I'm Thinking Arby's*, 2005. Last accessed July 2008: http://www.commercialcloset.org

[30] One can also make the argument that the Arby's hat icon is a phallic symbol.

reinforces heteronormative standards, and ultimately alienates the GLBT consumer.

In more recent years, mainstream advertisers have moved beyond social taboos to incorporate clearly-identifiable queer iconography and GLBT identities. While some advertisers have been proactively seeking to attract gay and lesbian consumers through queer print materials, the mainstreaming of these identities in television is relatively new.[31] Today, gay men and lesbians are increasingly portrayed in commercials as "normal" people, not as points of humorous reference and deference. This integration of normalized queer identities is dominated by gay men, with few lesbian portrayals, taking various forms ranging from the "acceptable" gay, to the "gay flip"—an extreme, but rare, form of normalization which occurs when the same plot is used in two commercials but the gender of the sex object is switched, making a straight commercial gay.

In the 2005 Diet Pepsi commercial, *Guy Watcher*, an attractive, all-American, muscular man is seen walking down the street drinking a soda.[32] He is leered at by countless women as well as Carson Kressley, a modern gay icon. During the commercial, we see the women and Kressley follow the man, who appears oblivious and unthreatened by their gaze. Kressley, who found fame in the popular television series *Queer Eye for the Straight Guy* (2003–2007), is important because he is recognizable to both gay and straight consumers. Because his role in *Queer Eye* established him as a flirtatious, flamboyant, but innocuous, gay man, Kressley's inclusion in the advertisement is non-threatening. He represents an acceptable gay identity, one that is non-sexual and safe. While this ad clearly seeks to capitalize on the tremendous popularity of *Queer Eye*, it also is a transitional advertisement because it helped facilitate the normalization of queers in commercials. Even though Kressley may have catalyzed the acceptance of gay style as mainstream chic, his futile attempt to objectify the man in the Pepsi ad places limits on public homosexual expression: like the women, he is only allowed to follow the man, and is not allowed to speak to, or flirt with, him. Were Kressley to step over such a boundary, he would become a perceived threat, a predatory gay man seeking to corrupt the presumably heterosexual soda drinker.

As gay identities become further integrated into the commercial world, the acceptable, non-sexual, gay begins to be replaced by more realistic depictions of gay relationships and intimacy. In a 2001–2002 commercial

---

[31] Branchik 92.

[32] Commercial Closet Association, *Guy Watcher*, 2005. Last accessed July 2008: http://www.commercialcloset.org

featuring Bailey's Irish Cream, three men and a woman are seen in a bar playing pool.[33] After her turn, the woman discovers that her glass is empty. In order to discover who has stolen her drink, she approaches each man and smells his breath. The last man is the culprit, and she reacts by kissing him. The commercial ends as she and the "thief" wrap their arms around each other and lean in towards the other two men who have their arms around each other in a similar intimate embrace. In this case, the queer content is made evident by the intimate embrace between the two men, however it is so subtle and brief that it can be missed. In fact, the embracing men were later cut from some of the on-air versions.[34] Without the embrace, this commercial becomes an example of the invisible guise—an ad that is open to multiple queer interpretations about the identities of these two men.

While gay men's identities have begun to find a stronger hold in the commercial realm, lesbian commercial content is more difficult to locate. The 2007 Dolce & Gabbana commercial, *Meeting,* not only addresses gay men, but also lesbians, which is a rare occurrence.[35] In this commercial, a well-dressed man and woman are rushing to make a date, presumably with each other. As the man sits in a cab in traffic, a lesbian couple embraces outside his window. Meanwhile, as the woman waits for the subway train, a brief image of an embracing gay couple appears in the background. The commercial culminates with the two characters meeting their same-sex dates. This commercial, which highlights the fallacy of heteronormativity, functions as the opposite of the invisible guise because it misleads the audience to believe that the primary characters are heterosexual, when in reality, they are gay and lesbian. The ultimate message is that if viewers can mistake the couple as heterosexual, then gays and straights must be alike.

The idea that gay men and lesbians are like heterosexuals, except for their chosen partners, is an increasingly present message in commercials. This is particularly evident in advertisements for personal ads and social networking websites that have traditionally addressed only heterosexual couples. Chemistry.com's 2007 commercial series, *Rejected,* has broken

---

[33] Commercial Closet Association, *Thief,* 2001–2002. Last accessed July 2008: http://www.commercialcloset.org

[34] Commercial Closet Association "Editor's Comment," *Thief,* 2001–2002. Last accessed July 2008: http://www.commercialcloset.org

[35] Commercial Closet Association, *Meeting,* 2007. Last accessed July 2008: http://www.commercialcloset.org

this mold to include homosexuality.[36] The basic theme of the series is that for some reason or another, applicants have rejected by eHarmony.com, their most significant competitor, and have now found acceptance at Chemistry.com. In one commercial, a young man is looking at an adult magazine of presumably naked women remarking "Nope, still gay." This commercial actively portrays the normalization of homosexual identity as the voice-over comments "who knows why eHarmony has rejected over a million people…at Chemistry.com you can come as you are." Chemistry.com clearly posits its acceptance and support of gay clients. Moreover, it constructs gay men as the same as millions of others who have been rejected from competing dating sites for a myriad of unknown reasons.

The idea that sexuality makes no difference has gained such importance that in 2007 two Levis 501 Jeans commercials were able to use the same leading man and plot to create a straight and a gay version of the same commercial. In both commercials, the man is in his loft apartment, pulling up a pair of jeans with great difficulty. As he pulls the jeans up, a phone booth, complete with a seductive caller, breaks through the floor. The apartment is mysteriously transformed into a streetscape, and the man is shown walking away with this mystery person. In one version of the commercial, the caller is a beautiful woman, in the other, an attractive man.[37] The two versions of this commercial, including the body posture and reaction by the loft owner, are identical, except for the sex object. This advertisement is the most extreme form of normalization—the gay flip—because there is no distinction of scenario or primary character. The only notable difference is the substitution or "flip" of the sex object. These advertisers are clearly stating that sexuality makes no difference: you are literally the same person, and thus the same target market, regardless of your preferred romantic partner.

While these three forms of queer referencing (the invisible guise, pinkface, and normalized integration) in commercial advertising demonstrate overlap in timeframe, they also exemplify the evolution of advertiser engagement with the queer consumer. Over the course of the last two decades, advertisers have been forced to engage with the increasingly visible GLBT audience clearly and explicitly. While earlier campaigns were often vague and implicit in their acceptance of queer consumers, advertising tactics have evolved from the invisible guise to a

---

[36] Commercial Closet Association, *Rejected,* 2007. Last accessed July 2008: http://www.commercialcloset.org

[37] Commercial Closet Association, *Change,* 2007. Last accessed July 2008: http://www.commercialcloset.org

more obvious integration that reflects, and enforces, changing social norms and beliefs about the GLBT community.

We're Here, We're Queer, We're Shopping

In today's post-closeted society, gay men and lesbians desire the comfort to be "one's self" when engaging in the consumer world.[38] While the wish to support businesses that are gay-friendly may be part of the GLBT consumer consciousness, sexual identity may be superseded by fiscal considerations when making purchasing decisions.[39] Sexuality especially takes on meaning when an individual's homosexual identity is actively visible during consumption. Queer identity itself is being transformed into a commodity, as GLBT persons seek to purchase pride or rainbow products that convey or confirm their identities.

Recently, the travel and tourism industries have actively sought to court gay men and lesbians. These consumers account for an estimated $54 billion dollars in annual US travel and tourism revenue. While a significant portion of this revenue is affiliated with recreation, business travel accounts for a major segment of tourism profits. Statistics show that gay men and lesbians take three times as many business trips annually as their heterosexual counterparts.[40] Thus travel and tourism companies are paying more attention to the GLBT community. Queer travel has become so prevalent that PlanetOut.com was created specifically to provide GLBT consumers with reliable choices and tourism information. Additionally, many mainstream travel websites, such as Travelocity.com, now include gay and lesbian links. These links convey a sense of acceptance and respect for these travelers, and foster a sense of security and safety.[41] The integration of GLBT identities into the marketing and services provided by these companies further serves to demonstrate the normalization of these identities.

---

[38] Steven Seidman, *Beyond the Closet: The Transformation of Gay and Lesbian Life* (New York: Routledge, 2002).

[39] Tracy L. Tuten, "The Effect of Gay-Friendly and Non-Gay-Friendly Cues on Brand Attitudes: A Comparison of Heterosexual and Gay/Lesbian Reactions." *Journal of Marketing Management* 21 (2005): 442.

[40] Nelson Congressional Testimony. Last accessed July 2008: http://www.nglcc.org/ht/d/ReleaseDetails/i/602

[41] Some other examples include Orbitz.com, as well as Southwest and American Airlines.

Many travel companies now organize cruises and travel trips specifically intended for gay men and lesbians.[42] In 1990, Olivia Cruise line became the first, and remains the only, cruise line to cater specifically to lesbians, and R Family Vacations has recently been established to cater to gay and lesbian families. These gay and lesbian companies enable the queer traveler to avoid the apprehension often affiliated with hospitality and hotel interactions, especially the potential confrontation affiliated with bed choice. Will the clerk, informed by heteronormative concepts of couples, assume that two same-sexed persons checking into a hotel would want separate beds? Might the reservation for a single king-sized bed be assumed an error? Ultimately, many gay and lesbian travelers report that the manner in which bedroom choice is handled is usually representative of the gay-friendliness of a business.[43]

While the construct of gay men as stylish, well-groomed, and cultured has been perpetuated by the media, especially in *Queer Eye for the Straight Guy*, television has also reinforced the notion that homosexuals are obsessed with appearance and fitness. *WorkOut* (2006–) with out lesbian Jackie Warner, and *Will & Grace* (1998–2006), an iconic mainstream gay sitcom, both convey the centrality of fitness in queer culture, and even go as far as portraying the gym as the gay church.[44] Some gym chains have attempted to exploit this connection by courting the queer customer. Planet Fitness, as noted on their website, seeks to "provide a unique environment where anyone, and we mean anyone can be comfortable. A diverse and judgment free zone."[45] An example of the invisible guise, this mission statement allows the queer consumer to interpret this gym as gay-friendly and thus a comfortable environment for a workout. Similarly, the invisible guise is also apparent when looking at 24-Hour Fitness's "Top Ten Reasons to Join": it "is a club for every lifestyle."[46] A family member only needs to live at the same address to be added to one's membership, demonstrating the implicit acceptance of gay

[42] This type of special interest gay tour group was portrayed in the film *Under the Tuscan Sun* (2003).
[43] Yaniv Poria, "Assessing Gay Men and Lesbian Women's Hotel Experiences: An Exploratory Study of Sexual Orientation in the Travel Industry." *Journal of Travel Research* 44 (2006): 327.
[44] *Will & Grace*, episode 4.11, "Stakin' Care of Business." Air Date: December 6, 2001.
[45] Planet Fitness, The Judgment Free Zone. Last accessed July 2008: www.planetfitness.com
[46] 24 Hour Fitness, "Top Ten Reasons To Join." Last accessed July 2008: http://www.24hourfitness.com/membership/reasons/10_reasons_to_join.html

and lesbian members.[47] Through the use of language and policy, these gyms are able to cater to straight and queer consumers alike.

While travel and fitness are certainly aspects of queer culture and consumption, products affiliated with identity, such as pride and rainbow clothing, bumper stickers, jewelry, and flags are also a part of queer communities.[48] These products have become a staple of queer identification in the past few decades, with a significant portion of GLBT persons owning some sort of pride item.[49] These items convey the symbolic engagement of the consumer with a queer community as well as its commodification. Additionally, these items serve as symbolic markers of queer-owned or friendly businesses.[50] Ultimately however, the sales of these products raises the question whether these business are truly gay-friendly, or are merely seeking to exploit an untapped market.

The question of identity, community, and commercial profit is also demonstrated by the marketing of products that support social causes such as HIV/AIDS. The success of pink breast cancer awareness products has laid the ground work for the (PRODUCT) RED campaign in support of HIV research.[51] The Gap, Apple, Motorola, Converse and Emporio Armani have all participated in this campaign, marketing goods that reference this cause, with a portion of the proceeds going towards the Global Fund's fight against HIV/AIDS in Africa. This campaign not only bolsters company sales, but also enables consumers to demonstrate their support for a GLBT cause.

The ability of advertising to appeal to a broad and diverse market pool has become progressively more important as consumers engage with an ever-expanding world of identity, social causes, and consumer options. The ability to support a cause, such as GLBT rights, is not only grounded in the consumption of rainbow and red products, but also in the

---

[47] 24 Hour Fitness, "Membership." Last accessed July 2008: http://www.24hourfitness.com/AddFamilyMembers.do Family members are limited to two adults and up to eight children residing in the same household. Sex is not mentioned.

[48] Other common symbols in the gay and lesbian community might include pink or lavender triangles, interlocking sex symbols, and various pride flags for subcultural queer identities and behaviors.

[49] Jane Ward, "Producing 'Pride' in West Hollywood: A Queer Cultural Capital for Queers with Cultural Capital." *Sexualities* 6 (2003): 88.

[50] Stephen M. Kates, "Out of the Closet and Out on the Street!: Gay Men and Their Brand Relationships." *Psychology & Marketing* 17.6 (2000): 497.

[51] Laura Heller, "Think Pink. Shop RED. What's in a Cause?" *Retailing Today* 45.21 (2006): 4, 40.

incorporation of normalized gay and lesbian consumer portrayals. As companies seek to access the commercial power of the gay and lesbian dollar, they must increasingly display their social perspectives in the public arena. Despite the rising tide of support for GLBT, some companies continue to use discriminatory pinkface techniques, thus perpetuating destructive sexual and gender stereotypes. This continued marking of GLBT as the undesirable and unacceptable "other" clearly demonstrates the need to struggle for equity not only in the market, but also in society at large. We can only hope that as the rainbow dollar gains more financial influence, advertising and consumer habits will transform, along with society's understanding and acceptance of the GLBT community.

CHAPTER FOUR

SHRIVEN INTO SHAPE: FASHION MAKEOVERS AND REDEMPTIVE TRANSFORMATION THROUGH CONSUMERISM

BRETT WESTBROOK

The proliferation of reality shows on broadcast and cable television has included a raft of fashion makeover shows, almost exclusively about women, such as *How Do I Look?*, *What Not to Wear*, *Tim Gunn's Guide to Style*, *Fashion Emergency* and *Ambush Makeover*. The most well-known makeover show featuring men is *Queer Eye for the Straight Guy*, in which five queers groom a straight man, teach him a few tricks in the kitchen, and spruce up his decor. Another is the mercifully short-lived *Pimp My Trucker*, a spinoff of *Pimp My Truck,* on Country Music Television. An important difference between these two shows featuring men, and the many makeovers featuring women, is that the men's essential nature *as men* is never called into question. At worst, they lack couth, a cultural capital held in abundance by homosexual men. Women, on the other hand, apparently require a makeover at a far more essential and fundamental level. Focusing on *Tim Gunn's Guide to Style*, this chapter argues that the fashion makeover show co-opts the discourses of confession and therapy to produce a woman whose very sense of self is narrowly prescribed and inextricably tied to consumer culture. The argument here is not whether a particular garment, such as a dress, is "good or bad" in and of itself. It is that the makeover show is not absolutely benign, that its message is ultimately even more insidious, and complex, than either late nineteenth-century advertisements for corsets, or 1950s *Leave It To Beaver*-type momism.

In some of these shows, friends and family set up a loved one for a much-needed makeover (*Ambush Makeover* and *How Do I Look*), while on others, like *Tim Gunn's Guide to Style*, the makeover subjects volunteer themselves, often pleading on video for the fashion guru's help.

Regardless of the impetus for the makeover (intervention or self-initiated), these fashion makeovers appear, on the surface, to have advanced far beyond the overtly didactic language of earlier periods. Marsha F. Cassidy discusses the "Cinderella Makeover" shows of early television, noting that on *Glamour Girl*, for instance, "the story of each day's contestants stigmatized them as misfits within the gender structures of American life, their plain, bedraggled, or unconventional bodies confirmed their marginal position within the social word and supplied a reason for it." Women on these and similar programs focused on glamour as a means to attract or keep a husband. For example, Cassidy cites one *Glamour Girl* contestant who complains that "she had been unable to 'trap' a husband because 'glamour [is] floatin' one way and me floating' the other."[1]

However, with the emergence over the last twenty years or so of the self-actualized, empowered, modern woman (think *Oprah*), the didactics and overt tactics of these earlier periods now play like a parody. Women on twenty-first century makeover shows do not talk about "trapping" a husband. Often executives or doctors, they are much more empowered than the suburban housewife of the immediate post-WWII era. Nevertheless, despite this apparent de-emphasis on getting a man and earning "redemption from misery," an examination of *Tim Gunn's Guide to Style* reveals that, far from disappearing, the pressure on middle- and upper-middle class women to conform to a normative femininity acquired and displayed through consumption has merely gone into stealth mode.

Tim Gunn's Guide to Style: The Template

The first season of *Tim Gunn's Guide to Style* aired in 2007 on the cable channel Bravo and was comprised of eight episodes. Tim Gunn, former faculty member and Student Dean at Parsons The New School For Design in New York City, is currently the mother hen on the Bravo hit, *Project Runway*. He is also the Chief Creative Officer for Liz Claiborne, charged with returning the company's "culture to one that is friendlier to the creative process" and also with helping to "shape a more competitive, consistent, and compelling product."[2] His so-called "Fashion Accomplice"

---

[1] Marsha F. Cassidy, "The Cinderella Makeover: *Glamour Girl*, Television, Misery Shows, and 1950s Femininity." *The Great American Makeover: Television, History, Nation*, ed. Dana Heller (New York: Palgrave MacMillan, 2006), 129, 131.

[2] Liz Claiborne press release, February 1, 2007. Last accessed February 3, 2008: http://phx.corporate-ir.net/phoenix.zhtml?c=82611&p=irol-newsArticle&ID=956778.

is Veronica Webb, retired supermodel, and the first African-American woman to be offered a contract with a major cosmetics firm, Revlon, in 1992. All eight makeover subjects in the first season were heterosexual and middle- to upper-class; seven of them were white and one was African-American. All eight cried at some point during the show.

Like all makeovers, *Guide to Style* follows a template. Tim Gunn and Veronica Webb view a plea from a would-be makeover subject on Tim's laptop in his office. After meeting the subject in her home, they ask for a verbal "contract."[3] This contract requires active participation from the makeover subject: she cannot be merely a passive recipient of directions from the two fashion experts. She must not only provide in-put about the impending changes, but she must also have complete buy-in, so to speak. Gunn and Webb's motto is, "We can't want you to succeed more than you want you to succeed." In the first episode, Gunn even offers the resisting Karen Vito a way out: "You don't have to do this." She agrees to continue with the process of the makeover, expressing trepidation about the person she might become, particularly if they make her wear "granny underwear." Still, she, and all of the others, agree to participate whole-heartedly and in good faith, abiding by Gunn's rules as they acquire new skills that will last them a lifetime of shopping. They also promise not to backslide into former habits, making choices based on comfort, cost, and convenience rather than fit or fashion.

The next act is "Last Week's Outfits." Through Polaroids taken of the makeover subject, Tim and Veronica gain a sense of what the subject wears in everyday situations: going out, work-casual, work-fancy, running errands, etc. The critique of these outfits is often brutal, with criticisms focusing on how unflattering the clothes are in terms of fit, color, and pattern ("stripes are for prison"). Gina Scarda, the newly retired NYPD sergeant, for example, describes herself as a "New Jersey girl," which means she likes "embellishments" on her jeans. Gunn and Webb, however, are critical of these embellishments because they are "low-class" and "unsophisticated." The makeover subjects endure this scrutiny and criticism, sometimes with a grimace toward the camera, a sort of "ow, that stung!" reaction. Elena Frappier (Episode 8) even says to the camera, "I feel a little bit attacked" after Webb announces, "She has literally outgrown clothes in her adult life and is still wearing them." However, Gunn and Webb's status as fashion experts, combined with the "contract,"

---

[3] Only Gina Scarda, retired New York City Police Department sergeant, is exempt from this requirement. One wonders if it is out of respect for her former standing as an officer of the law, especially in post-9/11 New York City where the show is set.

means that there can be no argument from the women concerning the conclusions being reached about their wardrobes.

Next comes the "Closet Cleansing." In this segment, Gunn and Webb touch and comment on every single item in the subject's wardrobe, including her bras and panties. As part of her active participation in the process, each makeover subject gets to determine into which of the four piles each item of clothing will go: give-aways, throw-aways, menders, and keepers. The clothes the women are encouraged to discard are those that are old and worn-out, frayed, ill-fitting, poorly made, junky in some way, or too much of the same thing. For example, Gina Scarda wore a uniform throughout her school years and then went straight into a police uniform. Now that she's retired, according to her husband, she has a new "uniform": jeans and a T-shirt. Her daughter complains, "She just knows jeans and T-shirts. She doesn't, like, read the magazines, or, like, watch TV and see what the stars are wearing." Also subject to removal are those clothes deemed somehow inappropriate, such as Elena Frappier's too-youthful clothing, Gina Scarda's "low-class jeans," and Stephanie Lichten's Care Bear socks. The fact that she is a pediatrician does not redeem the socks. She must dress like a professional in order to be considered a *real* professional, the medical school diploma on her wall notwithstanding. Some clothes will be given to a women's shelter, while others are thrown away, too raggedy to wear or hopelessly out of style, such as Lori Jones' velour, one-piece jump suit. The "keeper" clothes, the ones that they "can't live without," go on a rack that accompanies Webb and Gunn to the subjects' homes. Gunn insists throughout the entire process that the women are making the choices. He has the women try on some of the keeper clothes to see how the outfits are "styled." However, this leads to more cleansing. Lori Jones has so much clothing on her keeper rack that Gunn declares, "I can't work with this" because the clothes are of such poor quality. At last, Gunn and Webb make off with their bundles, leaving the makeover subjects to contemplate an almost empty closet. This stripping bare of the wardrobe is an essential part of the makeover process. The women cannot be allowed to cling to remnants of their past as represented by clothes chosen for all the wrong reasons, like comfort or price.

After razing the closet, Veronica Webb segues into the next section, "Underwear: The Foundation of a Good Wardrobe." Six of the eight women are very busty, but, as Tim Gunn announces, "even petite women need to be fitted properly." From there, makeover subjects are shown their "true proportions" through a fashion application called "OptiTex." Before the women can go shopping armed with this new understanding of their specific "shape and silhouette," they receive "coaching," because "style comes from within." Three women are coached by Jared Weiss, a so-called "Life Stylist." Other coaches are: Benny Ninja, a runway expert; Laura Bennett, fashion designer and mother of six; Junes B. Zahdi, international Salsa master; and Greg Behrendt, co-author of *He's Just Not That Into You.*

After the coaching, the women are given Tim Gunn's "Essential List," which contains ten items every woman needs in her wardrobe: basic black dress, trench coat, classic dress pant, skirt, blazer, classic white shirt, day dress, cashmere sweater, jeans, and sweat suit alternative. Gunn insists that these are the items needed by *all* women. What is clear, however, is that these particular items help enforce a middle-class, almost preppy standard, that recognizes no other possibilities for presenting as "female" in American society. As an incentive, the women are all given a gift before the shopping spree: five receive designer handbags; one a set of belts; one a set of shoes; and one eyeglass frames. The women then shop with a friend or family member at Macy's. The store is featured prominently, usually with Veronica Webb gushing that "they have everything," while the makeover subjects themselves generally express trepidation for the same reason: too many choices. While Webb finds the oceans of options invigorating, the makeover subjects are daunted by thought of having to sort through all of these alternatives for just the right item, especially since the items will be subject to Gunn's scrutiny and criticism. The friend or family member is dismissed upon the arrival of Tim and Veronica, who critique the invariably inadequate choices. This further cements their status as experts despite the show's apparent emphasis on individual women. The trio then "hits the floor" and this time with expert help, the makeover subjects find suitable items.

The real treat comes after Macy's, when Gunn accompanies each of the women to a design studio, where they receive a special occasion dress to wear to a "special event," such as a wedding anniversary or bachelorette party. Most importantly, the gift proves to the women that they, too, can and should wear designer clothing. At each studio, Gunn punctuates this point by asking the women if they *ever* thought they would wear a designer dress. The consistent answer is no, of course. Each designer discusses fit, proportion, quality of fabric, and sophistication, with the goal of making the women "fashion forward," as Webb puts it. This serves as their introduction into the world of *haute couture*.

The wrap-up is comprised of new hair and make-up, a "fashion show," where the women try on their new outfits for a host of friends, family, Tim Gunn and Veronica Webb, and finally the "Postcard," a check-up to see if the subject has stayed true to her new regime. On more intrusive makeover shows such as *Extreme Makeover* or *The Swan*, the hair and makeup section (along with plastic surgery, dental work, and liposuction) receives the most screen time; on *Guide to Style*, this segment is relatively short. There are definite reaction shots, where Gunn and Webb express wonder and delight at the new look, which is generally achieved through a modern, updated hairstyle and more toned-down "natural" makeup. Gone are the bangs of the 1980s and the blue eye shadow of yesteryear. Today's modern woman is sleek and stylish. More screen time is given to the "Postcard" segment, where the makeover subjects send video to Gunn and Webb to prove that they are still styling their hair and clothes according to the rules, and that they are, unmonitored, sticking to the contract.

The Confession

On *Tim Gunn's Guide to Style*, the transformative process is jump-started with a modern confession. In "The Psychological and Spiritual Efficacy of Confession," Margaret Klenck describes four confessional categories: the church (this is what I believe); the heart (this is whom I love); the law (this is what I did) and the psyche (this is who I am).[4] Each type of confession opens the penitent to both risk and reconciliation. For example, in a church-style confession, Klenck argues that, "each time ones says a confessional statement, one reconnects to an essential experience of one's faith."[5] Confessions of crimes reconcile the confesser with the ethics of the community, usually mediated through punishment. The teleology of confession, from the perspective of all four categories, is reconciliation and forgiveness. "Confession from this prospective point of view," Klenck argues, "fosters union and reunion with another, with community and with the self."[6]

Confession, however, is never easy or simple. As Klenck notes, "part of the inner drama was the fear that by confessing you would be destroying something precious and necessary to your survival." The secret in the confession of the psyche is not even known at first, because the ego so vigorously defends itself against its emergence. For Klenck, confession is "not the purgative spewing of guilt that happens on shows like Jerry Springer." Nor is confession "merely the act of telling one's story," i.e.

---

[4] Margaret Klenck, "The Psychological and Spiritual Efficacy of Confession," *Journal of Religion and Health* 43.2 (June 2004): 139–142.

[5] Ibid., 140.

[6] Ibid., 142.

"here is the narrative of my life; isn't it sad?" The consequence of "our American penchant for self-humiliation and easy catharsis," according to Klenck, is the "dumbing down of what is truly a difficult and dangerous project."[7]

The confessions on *Tim Gunn's Guide to Style* exemplify the diminishing of the confession's danger and potential. All of the women confess to not understanding "fashion" as presented by Tim and Veronica. Individually, they confess to the kind of "sin" that is now the staple of daytime talk shows: a lack of confidence, the failure to prioritize the self, and the failure to appreciate one's body as is. Karen Vito (Episode 1) is not age-appropriate in her clothing choices; Stephanie Lichten (Episode 5) worries how to avoid being "too overstated or looking like a mess." Nicole Appelman (Episode 4) has "focused on [her] husband and [her] kids more than anything else."[8] Because the secret is always already known, there is no real exploring, no careful unearthing. The journey is not fraught with ego-struggles; no new self emerges, phoenix-like, out of the ashes. There is also no exploration of the self in relation to society, no examination of a sense of responsibility or moral culpability in terms of one's decisions. Instead, on *Tim Gunn's Guide to Style* confession is easy, even when there are tears. There is no punishment or atonement. There is only shopping.

The act of consumption, especially as shaped by Gunn and Webb, cannot be confused with atonement. True penitents seek to reconcile themselves with their communities by scrutinizing the self, and doing the emotional work and critical thinking necessary to understand one's obligations to society. Shopping, on the other hand, focuses entirely inward, on self- gratification without thinking how this choice affects others. This is why it cannot be considered cleansing. JeAnne Swinley glories in her new Isaac Mizrahi dress, but does not ask the designer where his clothes are made, and whether or not the clothes are stained with the sweat of children. In this way, the point of confession is subverted away from a resolution, away from the transformation and reconciliation Klenck describes, and away from the possibility of a substantive assessment of one's place in the world.

Of course, it is not reasonable to expect that confession should be meaningful on a makeover show. In fact, an actual confession—one that produces an epiphanic transformation—threatens the entire project of *Guide To Style*. The result of the confession must be carefully controlled

---

[7] Ibid., 142, 143.

[8] Veronica Webb sympathetically sees this particular confession as symptomatic of a larger issue: "Moms who lose their way fashion-wise is an epidemic problem."

so that the confesser associates redemption with consumerism, atonement with shopping, and counting off those ten essential wardrobe items with counting rosary beads. What if the makeover subject actually became a responsible consumer? It might be embarrassing if JeAnne Swinley suddenly asked Mizrahi about his labor practices. If Nicole Appelman (Episode 4) brought up the price of that designer bra, she might expose the fact that it is made from less than a yard of fabric and cannot possibly be worth its selling price. Women who ask these awkward questions do not make "good" consumers, at least not on fashion makeover shows.

On *Tim Gunn's Guide to Style,* confession and therapy are intimately linked. Whatever personal issue is raised during confession must be "fixed." For *Guide to Style*, this means that after the "confession" comes "coaching," another word for the therapy that has become embedded in the discourse of American television. In her discussion of *Tele-Advising*, Mimi White argues that "therapy is understood as a means of generating narrative by setting in place a sequence of symbolic interpersonal exchanges."[9] These "interpersonal narratives," however, do not take place privately between the makeover subject and a trained therapist like a "Dr. Phil" or "Dr. Ruth." Instead, they take place between the makeover subjects and an expert.[10] Three of the women are seen by Jared Weiss, a "Life Stylist." His first "client" is Karen Vito (Episode 1), who wears cleavage-baring outfits to the PTA, much to the embarrassment of her eight-year-old daughter. He encourages her to write down the plusses and minuses of turning forty and insists that she give up the clingy, now-too-small cocktail dress she wore when she was a partying, single, twenty-five year-old. She bargains to keep, just not wear, the dress. Eventually, she gives it up completely. His approach with Karen is typical of the way he "styles lives" in general. With the other two makeover subjects, Rebecca Pinnino (Episode 2) and Lori Jones (Episode 6), he also encourages a great deal of self-realism, using symbols like juggling too many balls at one time to illustrate how they cannot all be balanced at the same time.

Other coaches are experts in areas that seem more or less relevant to a makeover. JeAnne Swinley (Episode 3) sees Benny Ninja, a "Runway Expert," because she has expressed a desire to be more assertive in her walk, to have that "runway fierceness." Nicole Appelman is coached by

---

9 Mimi White, *Tele-Advising: Therapeutic Discourse in American Television* (Chapel Hill: University of North Carolina Press, 1992), 12.

10 Only one makeover subject does not receive coaching: Stephanie Lichten, a pediatrician. While this omission is not discussed during the episode, it might be a reflection of her standing as a doctor, an already-respected member of the community who probably does not "need" therapy.

Laura Bennett, a fashion designer, winner of *Project Runway*, and the mother of six children. Her advice to Nicole Appelman is to spend more time, and money, on herself. While she would have been considered a perfect "Angel of the Hearth" in the second half of the nineteenth century, now her self-sacrifice is chastised as "over-done," and duly corrected by a woman who clearly is able to combine her career with motherhood.

The least relevant coaching is provided to Gina Scarda (Episode 7), who gets a dance lesson from Junes B. Zahdi, "International Salsa Master." The connection between fashion and Salsa seems tenuous at best, and this proves to be the most unwieldy of segments. Gina is a native of the Bronx and retiring at the rank of sergeant from the New York City Police Department after twenty-one years of service. While she clearly enjoys dancing, its relevance to her sense of self seems remote. During the fashion show, Zahdi is trotted out once again to show Gina Scarda's husband that his wife now knows how to dance. The meeting is awkward and disconnected from the other aspects of her post-retirement life, such as her intention to get a college degree. A more helpful "coach" might have been an academic advisor.

Collectively, these coaches offer a brand of "therapy" that is as "easy" as the confessions made on the show. There are no big revelations that threaten to discombobulate the makeover subjects' worlds; egos are not challenged; there are no reflections on the past so that there might be a healthier future. The sessions are apparently quite effective: all the women talk about how much better they feel. Nicole learns to pay attention to herself, which of course means spending money on her body. Karen Vito learns to wear clothes that cover her bosom. Lori Jones accepts the scar that she has been hiding for six years. These sessions function in the same way that confession functions, which is to tie the consumption of high-end fashion to a sense of self, thus making it a necessity. Therapy is no longer dangerous, rewarding work; it is merely the act of finding the right dress.

Despite the lack of a "master position" to provide a "final, determinate meaning," the coaching on *Guide to Style* does take all of the makeover subjects in a clear direction.[11] They examine themselves inwardly and outwardly, as they are on public display. In his discussion of *Big Brother*, Gareth Palmer makes an argument for the "central role the therapeutic discourse plays in public life." Through this non-threatening therapy, "the individual becomes an entrepreneur of the self, seeking to maximize its own powers, its own happiness, its own quality of life, through enhancing its autonomy and then instrumentalizing its autonomous choices in the

---

[11] White, 21.

service of its lifestyle."[12] This kind of project is possible only when the self is conceived of as a *tabula rasa*. Tania Lewis, in her examination of *Queer Eye*, argues that:

> Central to the makeover-oriented culture of late modernity is the idea that we as individuals can be reduced down to a mapable set of "problems" that can be addressed through recourse to various types of expertise, and in turn can be made "better" through the makeover process. Our everyday lives thus becomes seen as a therapeutic self-help "project" to be worked on while enterprising individuals are exhorted to "empower" themselves by finding better and smarter ways of living.[13]

Better and smarter ways of living on *Guide to Style* include expensive handbags, shoes, and dresses all consumed without a thought given to "inconvenient truths" such as sweatshop labor either in the US, or abroad. On fashion makeover shows, confession and therapy chain together a "self" that *must* consume high-end goods in order to realize any sense of self at all.

Femininity

Confession and therapy further function to enforce a rigidified version of femininity. The enforcement of a gender regime through television is certainly not new. Cassidy, for example, notes that on *Queen for a Day*, "consumer excess reinscribed each winner into the imaginary realm of sanctioned femininity—both as idealized homemaker and beauty queen. Consumer goods become the curative."[14] In the current incarnation of a makeover show, *Guide to Style* is simply a continuation of these earlier programs. While all eight subjects are already on the femmy side of the butch/femme divide, each makeover subject's womanliness is called into question, either in that the "feminine" needs to be made more explicit, or needs to be contained in some way. For example, Karen Vito's expression of her female self must be contained and controlled if it is to be appropriate. The first step is to re-orient her sense of femininity. She sees herself as young and sexy, a self-image that must be punctured. This

---

[12] Gareth Palmer, "Big Brother: An Experiment in Governance," *Television and New Media* 3.2 (August 2002), 295, 306.

[13] Tania Lewis, "'He Needs to Face his Fears with these Five Queers!': *Queer Eye for the Straight Guy*, Makeover TV, and the Lifestyle Expert," *Television and New Media* 8.4 (2007): 287.

[14] Cassidy, 364.

process begins during the Closet Cleansing segment of the show. After looking through some of her clothes, Veronica Webb announces, "To be forty and dressing like you're twenty, you look like a desperate, old cougar." When Karen appears in white jeans and a see-through, midriff-baring white top and no bra, Webb explains to her: "Straight up, it's a stripper. The only thing you're missing is a pole." Alone with Gunn, she justifies the harshness of the comment: "Better me tell her to her face…what she was wearing said, 'slut.' And that's what all the men looking at her say and that's what all the moms at her kid's school say." Gunn agrees, "You're telling the truth and I need to get a little more comfortable about it myself." As they prowl through her closet, they find dozens of small handbags. Gunn asks the rhetorical question: "Who carries an evening bag during the day? I mean, I know the answer. I'm not going to say it." Karen next dons a black pants suit. She asks in a small voice, "This is not so bad, is it?" and gets the following reaction from Webb: "It's very Elvira." And from Gunn: "This is really vulgar."

As Karen Vito stands there, isolated in the frame against a blank wall, Gunn and Webb discuss her fur coat, which Gunn describes as "a lot of look." She still has on the too-tight white jeans and see-through top underneath the floor-length, shaggy fur coat. Gunn and Webb see this look, and thus Karen, as vulgar and unsophisticated. Moreover, her sexuality must be retrained and disciplined. They convey that through the makeover she will become a "grown-up," and therefore more acceptable to the other mothers in the PTA, which, they assume, is her goal. Even though Karen initially resists the wardrobe changes, she does not seek liberation from such cultural constraints because she has already accepted the premise that she, as a human being, is defined by her clothing. If she dresses differently, she will somehow be essentially different. As Angela McRobbie argues, choice "is surely, within lifestyle culture, a modality of constraint. The individual is compelled to be the kind of subject who can make the right choices."[15] By the end of the first episode, Karen is making the right choices. In the "Postcard" section after the fashion show, she lets Tim and Veronica know that: "Not only did you put me in appropriate clothes, you made me feel good about wearing them."

Tim Gunn represents this newly-dressed self as if it somehow always existed. He promises Karen Vito: "We're not going to turn you into anybody you're not." For Gunn, changing how Karen dresses means that "we just have to help her find her real style as a grown-up." Her *real*

---

[15] Angela McRobbie, "Post-feminism and Popular Culture," *Feminist Media Studies* 4.3 (2004): 261.

style, the one truly at the heart of her being, apparently uses more fabric than her inauthentic self. Of the timid Rebecca Pinnino, Gunn believes that "It was all inside her; we just helped it come out." While he calls Nicole's change "a transformation," he is quick to insist: "But it was all there. It just needed to come out." This attitude toward an already-existing essential, knowable, self that can be excavated is not limited to Tim Gunn and his fashion accomplice. As Stephanie Lichten's makeup artist conveys: "I want to work towards giving her confidence in the way she looks. I felt that it was in there somewhere; we just really needed to bring it out." Neglecting the self does have dire consequences: marriage itself can be threatened. As Greg Behrendt, Elena's coach in Episode 8, mournfully predicts: "If you don't become the central focus of your life then all the rest of it breaks down and suddenly you're wearing a maternity bra to bed."

Tim Gunn and his fashion accomplices insist on an abiding, inner, feminine core for each woman. Most of the makeover subjects embrace this new image of themselves, and claim their brand new identities. As Karen Vito's husband remarks: "She turned a corner. She actually changed her life." Nicole Appelman announces: "I feel totally like a new person." Former NYPD sergeant Gina Scarda notes: "This whole experience has totally transformed every aspect of my life." Only Lori Jones expresses resistance to the transformative power of fashion, adamantly stating: "That dress is going to have to be the most fabulous thing in the universe to make me not think about that scar." She comes around by the end, however, noting: "It sounds kind of cheesy, but you guys really did change my life." All of the makeover subjects feel fundamentally transformed in some way. After experiencing the wonders of a "plunge bra," for example, Gina Scarda makes a solemn vow never to shop for bras at the outlet mall again.

Despite this apparent emphasis on the individual, *Guide to Style* reinforces conformity—a rigidified notion of the feminine that operates as a powerfully coercive force. There is only one possible expression of femininity: dresses. On *Guide to Style*, a dress is essential for the makeover subject because it is clearly associated with self-confidence: in other words, non-traditionally feminine women and, especially, women who do not present as typically "female" can have no confidence. Rebecca Pinnino's husband remarks, for example, "I think it would make a big difference for her confidence…if she dresses up more feminine." The last time Rebecca wore a dress was two-and-a-half years ago at her engagement party. Nicole Appelman has not worn a dress in eight years because: "I just feel I'm not tall enough or thin enough to wear" one. By the end of the episode, she's crying, "I haven't been in a dress in so long and to have one that finally makes me feel good about myself is what I've been looking for this whole week." The last time Lori Jones wore a dress was before an accident in 2001 which left her leg with a large, jagged scar. When she models several knee-length dresses, her maid of honor notes: "Seeing her in that dress I could tell it was definitely a transformation; her confidence is coming back." Tim Gunn is absolutely determined about dresses. Of Rebecca Pinnino, he remarks: "I believe she is meant for a dress and we're going to get her into some." His comment about Lori Jones is even more authoritarian: "Until Lori can look at her leg the way that I do, she's not going to be comfortable wearing dresses. But I really believe we're going to get here there. I believe it." Thus, through the mechanics of the ten essential items list, and dresses that manufacture confidence, the makeover process makes the acts of confessing and therapy palatable, even benign. There is an integration of the makeover subject and the community; however, it derives from conformity to a norm, not from any kind of substantive exploration or rigorous interrogation of moral responsibility.

I Like to Watch

Makeover shows are enormously popular, which suggests that large audiences take pleasure in watching these "reality" programs. In her discussion of the "Cinderella Makeover," Marsha F. Cassidy notes that the 1950s "*Glamour Girl*, and its sobbing counterparts, authorized 'girl talk' on television, [or] what Mary Ellen Brown has called 'feminine discourse.'"[16] That girl talk is still pleasurable today is proven not only by fashion makeover shows, but also by the longevity of soap operas, and the ocean of women on daytime TV: the cast of *The View*, Tyra Banks, Ellen DeGeneres, the venerable Oprah, shows about the *Real Housewives* first of Orange County (CA) and now New York City, *Bridezillas*, and more. Girl talk is particularly important in the context of the makeover because its emphasis on (an apparent) self-empowerment removes any sense of the makeover subjects' exploitation. Because changes are always latent, emerging from within the subject herself, the transformation promises an authenticity that allows the audience to sympathize and root for each woman. There is also a genuine aesthetic in the pleasure of viewing. A well-made dress, tailored to fit a specific body type, simply does look better than a frumpy, shapeless T-shirt and nondescript jeans. Karen Vito

[16] Cassidy, 135.

really should not wear a blazer with no shirt underneath to a PTA meeting. The effrontery of her bosom at an event for eight-year olds, their parents, and teacher is frankly creepy. Who could be so pessimistic as to not cheer for Lori, commending her bravery for stepping out in a dress that reveals the scar she carefully hid for so many years?

Yet, it is vital to call into question that sense of pleasure, that audience culpability in the rigidification of femininity. According to Rosalind Gill in "Postfeminist Media Culture," a woman's body "is constructed as a window to the individual's interior life." On makeover shows, a woman's body "is presented as simultaneously a women's source of power and as always unruly, requiring constant monitoring, surveillance, discipline and remodeling (and consumer spending) in order to conform to ever-narrower judgments of female attractiveness."[17] *Guide to Style* does not seem as obviously controlling as say *Glamour Girl* or *Queen for a Day*, partly because of the (corrupted version of) self-empowerment, but also because its hegemony is not constituted through the colonizing male gaze. While Tim Gunn is a male host, he is so obviously queer that he does not represent any kind of threat to female identity. He even sends his female accomplice to do the underwear shopping, despite his pronounced opinions on every woman's need for a well-fitted (read "expensive") bra.

It is that very sense of "choice," which constitutes at least a partial justification of our viewing pleasure, that is profoundly problematic. Gill argues that a "grammar of individualism underpins all these notions [of choice, of an identifiable, essential self]—such that even experiences of racism, homophobia or domestic violence are framed in exclusively personal terms in a way that turns the idea of the persona-as-political on its head." For Gill, the exclusion of all connection with modes of production represents "the almost total evacuation of notions of politics."[18] Ultimately, the pleasure of makeover shows is the guiltless, non-substantive consumption of an outcome always already known—she's happier, prettier, sexier, better. There are no difficult choices. The audience functions as the interlocutor for a toothless confession and witnesses a "therapy" drained of potential.

According to James B. Twitchell, "modern consumerism is not a replacement of religion but a continuation, a secularizing, of a struggle for order." According to this view, "salvation through consumption is not a contradiction, but a necessity." Late capitalism "survives by encouraging us to be raving maniacs at the cash register, to be pagans at Saturnalian

[17] Rosalind Gill, "Postfeminist Media Culture: Elements of a Sensibility," *European Journal of Cultural Studies* 10.2 (May 2007): 150, 149.

[18] Ibid., 153.

events like Christmas, and to be woefully insecure about ourselves, especially about our body size, our odors, our face, and even about our gender."[19] The made-over woman is a "better" person on the inside, transcending those insecurities because she knows how to shop. Makeover shows reintegrate women into a world of very specific goods—high end, designer items—all without any consciousness or critical thought.

There are many sins of omission on *Guide to Style*. For example, no one mentions fair-trade goods or sweatshop labor. This is only natural since the show intends to flog high-end fashion, shoes, jewelry, and accessories, and hearing about children toiling away under lock and key is a downer. Displaying phrases like "juicy land" and "juicy bling" in large letters across the butt of a forty-one year old woman is not examined in terms of a feminist consciousness, but rather in terms of social conformity. Fashion makeover shows deliberately operate in a world that obscures all the inconvenient issues, such as clothes sewn by children, or the construction of a rigidified femininity joined at the hip with high-end consumerism. Moreover, despite its insistence on the needs of the individual, *Guide to Style* produces the same results in each of the eight makeover subjects in terms of style and "look." This uniformity is manufactured partly by Gunn's claim that all women need ten essential items in their wardrobes, and that all woman want the same "long, lean look." The sameness also comes from the choice of makeover subject: pretty, heterosexual, solidly middle or upper-middle class, and already convinced of the transformative power of fashion. Everything these women "learn" during the course of their transformations, however, cements the link between an essential femininity and fashion, which in turn reproduces an apparent need for consumer goods—clothes, shoes, accessories, makeup, and hair products.

The absolute association between the self and high-end consumer goods is a necessary condition for the makeover show. A program about women who discuss alternatives to sweat-free clothing, or who simply do not shop at all, is not going to be a hit or bring in much ad revenue. Therefore, the expectation that makeover shows themselves will change is unreasonable. The fashion world as a whole is also unlikely to whittle away their profits by ensuring a living wage, decent working conditions, health benefits, and worker's compensation to those who sew $50,000 dresses for pennies an hour. Given the politics of globalism and sweat-

---

[19] James B. Twitchell, *ADCULT USA: The Triumph of Advertising in American Culture* (NY: Columbia University Press, 1996), 110.

shop modes of production, however, linking the self to high-end fashion has implications far beyond ever-shifting hemlines and the latest styles. Alternatives to thoughtless consumerism are available. Don't shop, join the "Church of Stop Shopping" (www.revbilly.com/about_us/), or shop less. Try to make thoughtful choices: shop sweat-free, look for the union label and, if there are no union-made garments to be found, ask store managers why they do not carry union-made clothing. No longer an option, it is a moral imperative to exercise the power of consumerism with compassion.

PART II:

CONSUMER SPACES AND THE CULTURE OF BUYING

CHAPTER FIVE

SIN, SEX AND SHOPPING: CONSPICUOUS CONSUMPTION AND MODERN IDENTITY IN F. SCOTT FITZGERALD'S *THE GREAT GATSBY* AND *THIS SIDE OF PARADISE*

TANFER EMIN TUNC

Perceptions of consumer space and the impact of consumption on identity often bring forth images of the physical: malls, shopping centers, bazaars, and flea markets. However, consumer identity is not only shaped by material goods and where they are purchased, but is also influenced by what consumers *read* on the process of spending. Shopping, both a pasttime and as the basis of social, class, gender and racial identity, became a prominent theme in American literature during the Modernist era (c. 1914–1945). During this time period, authors such as Sinclair Lewis (*Main Street*; 1920) and Theodore Dreiser (*An American Tragedy;* 1925) used their writing as a metaphorical space to critique the impact that mass consumption and excessive, vacuous spending was having on American values. A popular target of these novelists became the turn-of-the-twentieth-century New Woman, whose lavish lifestyle, social progressivism, and "questionable" moral principles (e.g., smoking, drinking, and promiscuity) fueled the "evil" triumvirate of consumption: sin, sex and shopping.

This chapter will examine how conspicuous consumption shaped American identity during the Modernist period by focusing on two of F. Scott Fitzgerald's most popular novels: *The Great Gatsby* (1925) and *This Side of Paradise* (1920).[1] It will pay particular attention to the ways in

[1] F. Scott Fitzgerald, *The Great Gatsby,* Ed. Ruth Prigozy (New York: Oxford University Press, 1998); F. Scott Fitzgerald, *This Side of Paradise,* Ed. James L. W. West (New York: Cambridge University Press, 1995).

which Fitzgerald used consumption as a space to critique changing social values, including the rise of the *nouveau riche* and the new role of women in US society. Moreover, by focusing on the nature of consumption in both novels (i.e., the social and cultural meanings ascribed to the acquisition of material goods), this chapter will also elucidate Fitzgerald's contention that the symbiotic relationship between the consumer and the consumed (i.e., "you are what you buy") serves as the foundation of the alienation, disillusionment and spiritual emptiness associated with modern materialism.

Romance and Conspicuous Consumption on Long Island's Gold Coast

A member of the literary movement known as the *Lost Generation* (which included Modernists such as Gertrude Stein, T. S. Eliot, Ernest Hemmingway, and Ezra Pound), F. Scott Fitzgerald spent most of his life feeling alienated from, and disillusioned by, what he saw as the unprogressive "progress" of the United States during the post-World War I era. His works critique this shift in social values by exploring corrupt worlds in which success is measured through the empty pursuit of wealth, superficial status, and meaningless commodities, and not through the traditional tenets of the Puritan work ethic that had defined America since the Colonial Era: ingenuity, honesty, and determination. According to Quentin E. Martin,

> Fitzgerald...describes an America transformed—what with the avalanche of new, mass-produced consumer goods, the new advertising dedicated to selling them, the mushrooming newspapers and magazines designed largely to showcase and promote these products—into a society driven by consumption, images, and jingles, transfixed by the new...The new "culture of abundance," in which everywhere there was an...emphasis on buying, spending, and consuming, served to displace the older Puritan-based capitalist culture, with its emphasis on hard work, self-denial, and deferred gratification.[2]

For Fitzgerald, Long Island, New York, the setting of his chef d'oeuvre *The Great Gatsby,* embodied the spiritual desolation, moral decay, shallow materialism, and loss of idealism that characterized the opulent,

---

[2] Quentin E. Martin, "The First Emotional Bankrupt: F. Scott Fitzgerald's Josephine Perry." *The F. Scott Fitzgerald Review* 1.1 (2008): 185.

commercialized lifestyle of the Jazz Age.[3] With its soulless inhabitants and extravagant Gold Coast mansions, chateaux, castles and villas, Long Island was the quintessential fantasyland of illusion—a place somehow untouched by the horrors of war, and completely consumed with the activity of consumption. In other words, it was a geography where goods and people were purchased not because they were needed or even wanted, but simply because they could be bought.

The novel's protagonist, Jay Gatsby, functions as the culmination of this new consumer identity. He, like the environment he inhabits, is based on magical deception: he changes his name from the "Jewish-sounding" James Gatz to Jay Gatsby; is allegedly Oxford-educated (he actually dropped out of St. Olaf College in Minnesota); speaks in an exaggerated English accent (he is from rural North Dakota); and, like a member of the British aristocracy, addresses everyone as "old sport." Like the Long Island he inhabits, Gatsby is part of a pre-packaged world in which a wealth-based caste system replaces the meritocracy of democratic America. On the Gold Coast, emotions are reduced to superficial reactions to transient sentiments and extravagant luxuries to be purchased.

Gatsby inhabits West Egg (present-day Great Neck, Long Island), "one of those little towns [which sprang] up on all sides of New York, which [was] built especially for those who [had] money suddenly, but never had any money before."[4] Gatsby, who made his money through "sinful means" such as organized crime and distributing bootleg liquor, is part of this *nouveau riche* society. As such, he can never participate in the arrogant "old wealth" materialism of Tom and Daisy Buchanan, who live in East Egg (present-day Manhasset and Port Washington)—the playground of upper-class, old stock, white Anglo-Saxon Protestant Americans. He will forever be excluded from their social clubs where those with inherited wealth "played polo and were rich together."[5]

Gatsby, who lives like a Gilded Age robber baron, uses conspicuous consumption as a means to compensate for his social short-comings and escape his working-class identity. However, because he is a self-made man and only recently wealthy, he is unable to detect the subtle social signals conveyed by the "born" aristocracy, and his efforts to "Keep Up with the Joneses" translates as crude, garish, and flamboyant. Gatsby's house, for example, is "a colossal affair by any standard—it was a factual

[3] Roger Wunderlich, "The Great Gatsby as Long Island History." *The Long Island Historical Journal* 7.1 (Fall 1994): 120.
[4] Matthew J. Bruccoli, *Some Sort of Epic Grandeur: The Life of F. Scott Fitzgerald* (New York: Harcourt, Brace, Jovanovich, 1981), 176.
[5] Fitzgerald, *The Great Gatsby*, 9.

imitation of Hôtel de Ville in Normandy, with a tower on one side, spanking new under a thin beard of raw ivy, a marble swimming pool and more than forty acres of lawn and garden."[6] He bought the mansion from another *nouveau riche* family that was so tactless they sold the estate with their father's black funeral wreath "still [hanging] on the door."[7]

Gatsby indulges in the luxury commodities that are available on the postwar market because he genuinely believes that his social transformation (i.e., his identity) is predicated on the accumulation of material wealth and status symbols. However, his attempts at posing as "old wealth" are undermined by the class markers he chooses: his pink suits, gold ties, piles of flashy silk shirts, library full of unread books, and hydroplane are not the elegant and understated trophies of established money, but rather misguided *nouveau riche* attempts at imitating refined taste. Gatsby's ostentatious Rolls Royce—which contrasts markedly with Daisy's sophisticated white roadster—is arguably his greatest material offense: "It was a rich cream color, bright with nickel, swollen here and there in its monstrous length with triumphant hatboxes and supper-boxes and tool-boxes, and terraced with a labyrinth of windshields that mirrored a dozen suns."[8] While to those who possess inherited wealth these status symbols are merely objects, to Gatsby they are sacred shrines of worship in a world of spiritual vacuums.[9] They not only constitute his identity, but also serve as outward signals of who he is (or, in this case, who he would like to be) in post-war America:

> [Gatsby] opened for us two hulking patent cabinets which held his massed suits and dressing-gowns and ties, and his shirts, piled like bricks in stacks a dozen high...He took out a pile of shirts and began throwing them, one by one before us, shirts of sheer linen and thick silk and fine flannel which lost their folds as they fell and covered the table in many-colored disarray. While we admired [them] he brought more, and the soft rich heap mounted higher—shirts with stripes and scrolls and plaids in coral and apple-green and lavender and faint orange with monograms of Indian blue.[10]

When Daisy (Gatsby's love interest) realizes that the shirts represent Gatsby's self-destructive obsession with the accumulation of wealth and his futile attempts to refashion his identity, she begins to cry with a

[6] Ibid., 8.
[7] Ibid., 70.
[8] Ibid., 51.
[9] John S. Whitley, *F. Scott Fitzgerald: The Great Gatsby* (Southampton, England: The Camelot Press, Ltd., 1976), 23.
[10] Fitzgerald, *The Great Gatsby*, 73–74.

passion that foreshadows Gatsby's eventual demise: "'They're such beautiful shirts,' her voice muffled in the thick folds. 'It makes me sad because I've never seen such—such beautiful shirts before.'"[11] As someone who married for money and not love, she knows that Gatsby is doomed to a life of neither peace nor pleasure, for he perceives materialism as the culmination of romantic perfection in an imperfect world.[12]

Fitzgerald uses Gatsby's Saturday-night parties to critique the greed, material excessiveness, and hedonism that characterize modern America. Appropriately, these elaborate, theatrically-staged parties are not grounded in reality but are defined by frantic jazz music, bootleg liquor, optimistic laughter, enthusiasm among strangers, egotistical escapism, and Gatsby's pathetic attempt to attain Daisy's love through extravagant spectacle.[13] The guests, most of whom Gatsby has never met, are mostly *nouveau riche* freeloaders, vying for a slice of aristocratic power and status. "Conducting themselves according to the rules of behavior associated with amusement parks," they await the realization of their dreams in a perpetual state of drunkenness.[14] However, they are consistently disappointed when they sober up and discover that Gatsby's parties will never amount to more that a deceptive "illusion of grandeur."

Gatsby experiences his own status panic when he discovers that the facade of enchantment and mystery that he has constructed through the consumption of material objects will only last as long as his external appearance remains in tact. Gatsby's obsession with Daisy, whose voice is "full of money," thus functions as a form of self-serving chivalry: by protecting Daisy and the wealth she personifies, he is literally fighting for the survival of his own constructed identity.[15] If he does not maintain this golden illusion, he will amount to nothing more than failure, for despite all of their obvious wealth, the *nouveau riche* are imposters—cheap simulations of authentic taste.

---

[11] Ibid., 74.

[12] Marius Bewley, "Scott Fitzgerald's Criticism of America." *Twentieth Century Interpretations of F. Scott Fitzgerald's The Great Gatsby,* Ed. Ernest H. Lockridge (Englewood Cliffs, New Jersey: Prentice Hall, 1968), 39.

[13] Brian Way, "The Great Gatsby." *Modern Critical Interpretations of F. Scott Fitzgerald's The Great Gatsby*, Ed. Harold Bloom (New York: Chelsea House Publishers, 1986), 103.

[14] Fitzgerald, *The Great Gatsby*, 34

[15] Ibid., 96.

Consumer Culture and the New American Woman

Daisy Buchanan, Jordan Baker (Daisy's friend) and Myrtle Wilson (Tom Buchanan's mistress) epitomize yet another manifestation of the Roaring Twenties: the New Woman. The New Woman originally emerged in late-nineteenth century America as a reaction to the Cult of True Womanhood and the rigid, socially-constructed gender roles it proscribed for white Anglo-Saxon Protestant women of the middle and upper classes, especially within the private microcosm of the family unit. The Cult stressed purity, piety, *naïveté* (especially in sexual matters), a lack of female passion, domesticity (i.e., a dedication to the "female" private sphere of the home), an abhorrence for the "male" public sphere of the outside world, submission, and subservience to patriarchal figures (especially husbands and fathers).[16] New Women, therefore, represented everything that members of the Cult did not: namely, self-actualization and liberation. They participated in the public sphere, were well-educated (usually college-educated, often graduating from co-ed institutions) and politically-aware, many of them advocating female suffrage and other women's rights. Moreover, New Women chose whom they wanted to marry, practiced birth control without shame, and rejected the restrictive clothing of the Victorian Era (especially corsets) for more comfortable alternatives. Many also transgressed gender boundaries by engaging in traditionally "sinful" masculine activities such as smoking, drinking, and dancing. By the 1920s, the Flapper, a hedonistic version of the New Woman who bobbed her hair, wore cosmetics and short skirts, listened to Jazz, drove automobiles and engaged in casual sexual behavior (ranging from kissing, to "petting parties," to one-night stands), came to represent young middle and upper class womanhood.[17]

Although in theory, Fitzgerald, like many of his literary cohorts, approved of the rejection of Victorian values that accompanied New Women, he was clearly critical of their elitism and disillusioned by the vacuous consumer culture that sustained the Flapper lifestyle. Thus he often portrayed New Women not as heroines, but rather as capricious,

---

[16] Barbara Welter, "The Cult of True Womanhood, 1820–1860." *American Quarterly 18* (Summer 1966): 151–174; John D'Emilio and Estelle B. Freedman, *Intimate Matters: A History of Sexuality in America* (New York: Harper and Row Publishers, 1988), 265–271.

[17] Martha H. Patterson, *Beyond the Gibson Girl: Reimagining the American New Woman, 1895–1915* (Champaign, IL: University of Illinois Press, 2008); Nancy Woloch, *Women and the American Experience* (New York: McGraw-Hill Publishers, 2005), Chapter 12; Martin, 182–183.

destructive, egotistical and materialistic femme fatales. Daisy, for example, is not in love with Jay Gatsby the man, but rather the romantic material image that he conveys. Even though she does not share Gatsby's extravagant taste, she does admire his ability to acquire everything he desires, at least materially. She, on the other hand, is an illusive ideal to Gatsby—a "holy grail" or idyllic symbol of perfection in a world gone mad.[18] Despite the fact that they share strong emotional feelings for one another, inhabit the same geography, and live opulent lifestyles centered on consumption, Gatsby and Daisy will remain star-crossed lovers due to their class backgrounds. What Gatsby felt when they first met as young adults at a military base in Louisville, Kentucky during World War I would always elude him:

> However glorious might be his future as Jay Gatsby, he was at present a penniless young man without a past...He took what he could get, ravenously and unscrupulously—eventually he took Daisy one still October night, took her because he had no real right to touch her hand. He might have despised himself, for he had certainly taken her under false pretenses...he had deliberately given Daisy a sense of security; he let her believe that he was a person from much the same stratum as herself—that he was fully able to take care of her. As a matter of fact he had no such facilities—he had no comfortable family standing behind him and he was liable at the whim of an impersonal government to be blown anywhere about the world.[19]

Gatsby understands why Daisy abandoned him in order to marry the financially-stable and reliable Tom who, even during the war, could "take care of her," at least materialistically, by giving her a $350,000 string of pearls. However, he cannot acknowledge that for Daisy, one's class and social background is just as important, if not more important, than great wealth. Thus, even after he achieves financial success, Gatsby refuses to confront the fact that Daisy will never abandon Tom, her daughter Pammy (whom she treats like an amusing toy, rather than a child), and the comfort and security of old wealth for her former sweetheart.

Like Daisy, Jordan Baker has "been everywhere and seen everything and done everything."[20] She too represents the New Woman of the 1920s: independent, intelligent, and witty, yet cynical, elusive, and conniving. A

---

[18] D. G. Kehl, "Sangria in the Sangreal: *The Great Gatsby* as Grail Quest." *Rocky Mountain Review of Language and Literature* 47.4 (1993): 203.
[19] Fitzgerald, *The Great Gatsby*, 118.
[20] Paul L. MacKendrick, "The Great Gatsby and Trimalchio." *The Classical Journal* 45.7 (1950): 309.

well-known amateur golfer, Jordan suffers from spiritual emptiness (she is constantly yawning, signaling her empty life and adolescent ennui) and continually manipulates her surroundings in a childish effort to secure her empty aspirations. She detests the idea of losing, often cheating to secure victory.[21] The fact that this strategy has the net effect of devaluing her triumphs has little impact on Jordan, for she, like her career, is based on the consumption of images: "She was dressed to play golf…she looked like a good illustration…her hair the color of an autumn leaf, her face the same brown tint as the fingerless glove on her knee."[22] Jordan applies the same strategies to her romantic entanglements as she does to her career. She deceives Nick, who functions as the novel's narrator, into thinking they have a future together. When she realizes that he cannot secure her materialistic needs, she capriciously decides to marry someone who can. Unlike Gatsby, however, Nick is able to see through the charade of innocence feigned by the emotionally-bankrupt Daisy and Jordan, and saves himself from their self-destructive rampage.

Myrtle Wilson, Tom's mistress who lives "on the other side of town," is also consumed by the spiritual emptiness that accompanies her world of sin, sex and shopping. As a social-climbing working-class woman, she is privy to glimpses of opulence, but is always excluded from actually possessing them. Thus, it is not surprising that Tom's patent leather shoes and fashionable dress suit first compel her notice him on a trip into the city on the Long Island Rail Road. She endures Tom's constant stream of abuse and neglect because she is attracted to old wealth and the illusion of glamour emanated by the inhabitants of East Egg. Tom feeds into Myrtle's material attempts to reconstruct her identity by indulging her, even acquiring a small, over-decorated apartment in New York City for their romantic trysts, which she transforms into a miniature Versailles. Pathetically aspiring to join the ranks of old wealth aristocracy, she, like Gatsby, tries to transcend her working class roots by mimicking their nonchalant sophistication and superior manners (she allows four taxi cabs to pass by before summoning an elegant lavender one with grey upholstery, and even buys a puppy from a John D. Rockefeller look-alike). Moreover, she is perpetually compiling endless lists of goods that need to be purchased, most of which she has seen in fashion magazines: "a massage, and a wave, and a collar for the dog, and one of those cute little

---

[21] David Parker, "Two Versions of the Hero." *Modern Critical Interpretations of F. Scott Fitzgerald's The Great Gatsby*, Ed. Harold Bloom (New York: Chelsea House Publishers, 1986), 38.
[22] Fitzgerald, *The Great Gatsby*, 141.

ashtrays where you touch a spring, and a wreath with a black silk bow for mother's grave that'll last all summer."[23]

Like all performances, Myrtle's "class act" is inherently flawed because she does not possess the social skills that would allow her to detect the subtleties of her role. Myrtle naively believes that costuming (i.e., dressing like a member of the old wealth elite) will grant her instant admission into their exclusive world:

> Mrs. Wilson had changed her costume some time before and was now attired in an elaborate afternoon dress of cream colored chiffon, which gave out a continual rustle as she swept about the room. With the influence of the dress, her personality had also undergone a change. The intense vitality that had been so remarkable in the garage was converted into impressive hauteur…"It's just a crazy old thing," Myrtle said. "I just slip it on sometimes when I don't care what I look like"…Myrtle's countenance suddenly changed. "I knew right away I made a mistake. [My husband] borrowed somebody's best suit to get married in and never even told me about it, and the man came after it one day when he was out…'Oh, is that your suit?' I said. 'This is the first I ever heard about it.' But I gave it to him and then I lay down and cried…all afternoon."[24]

As illustrated by her account of her husband's attempt to transgress class boundaries by wearing a borrowed suit, Myrtle is conscious of the way in which clothing serves as a class marker. The irony is that she does not register the fact that she is also engaging in the same sort of identity construction when slipping into her elaborate disguise of cream-colored chiffon. Thus Myrtle and Gatsby ultimately share the same fate: both perish as a result of their misguided assumption that rebirth and renewal can be bought and displayed through conspicuous consumption.

This Side of Shopping: Escapism through Consumption

This Side of Paradise which, until the time of Fitzgerald's death in 1940 was his most popular and commercially-successful novel, centers on the loves, and losses, of Amory Blaine.[25] Amory travels the world with his wealthy, sophisticated, and over-protective mother Beatrice before settling down and pursuing an education at a fictitious New England private boy's school, St. Regis Prep. He then attends Princeton University, but enlists in WWI before completing his studies. His mother

---

[23] Ibid., 31.
[24] Ibid., 26, 30.
[25] Bruccoli, 158.

dies while he is stationed overseas, and with few personal connections and very little of his family fortune remaining, returns to the US, cynical about life. In the novel, most of Amory's pessimism derives from the horror and futility of war, as well as his numerous encounters with social-climbing, husband-seeking old and new wealth women, all of whom seem to be obsessed with consumption.

Beatrice, who lives well beyond her means and invests her wealth unwisely, is the first to educate Amory on the virtues of luxury living. Despite the fact that she is raised during the late-nineteenth century and retains a measure of its propriety, "Beatrice is paradigmatically modern; her identity finds its perfect expression in the trends of her time: alcohol; conspicuous consumption; travel by car, steamer, and train; and the glib exaggerations in which the moderns announced their arrival in the public sphere."[26] As Pearl James elucidates, "it is from his mother that Amory learns to navigate the modern world. She teaches him to manipulate social expectations and their idioms," all of which, in some form or another, involve sin (drinking bootleg alcohol, frequenting speakeasies, gambling, and engaging in other illicit activities), sex (or at least romance), and, of course, shopping.[27]

Beatrice O'Hara Blaine, like Daisy, is raised with all the luxuries of Victorian America, including connections to old wealth European aristocracy. As Fitzgerald describes: "Pictures taken…in Rome at the Sacred Heart Convent—an educational extravagance that in her youth was only for the daughters of the exceptionally wealthy—[convey that]…her youth passed in renaissance glory, she was versed in the latest gossip of the Older Roman Families…She learned in England to prefer whiskey and soda to wine, and her small talk was broadened…during a winter in Vienna."[28] As someone educated in all the fineries of old world taste, Beatrice proves to be an excellent tutor for Amory, who spends his childhood traveling, with an entourage, from "fashionable hotel to fashionable hotel" in Grandfather O'Hara's private car. By the age of eleven, he is able to speak French, converse about the world's great composers, and appreciate fine European cuisine, thus exhibiting all the social markers of inherited wealth, despite the fact that he had never been abroad.

Eventually, the Blaines settle down in Minneapolis, Minnesota (Beatrice's health, and their dwindling funds end their extravagant road

---

[26] Pearl James, "History and Masculinity in F. Scott Fitzgerald's *This Side of Paradise*." *Modern Fiction Studies* 51.1 (2005): 6.
[27] Ibid.
[28] Fitzgerald, *This Side of Paradise*, 11.

trip). After attending the local school for a while, Amory is sent to a private boy's prep school in Connecticut, followed by a few years at Princeton University. While enrolled at Princeton, Amory receives a letter from a family advisor, Monsignor Darcy, asking him to visit his third cousin, a poor, widowed relation in her twenties living in Philadelphia. As a favor to the Monsignor, Amory makes the trip to Philadelphia, where he encounters a "golden goddess": "She was immemorial…Amory wasn't good enough for Clara, Clara of ripply golden hair, but then no man was. Her goodness was above the prosy morals of the husband-seeker, apart from the dull literature of female virtue."[29]

Amory quickly becomes enraptured with his cousin, and despite their mutual lack of money, uses their shopping excursions as a means of distinguishing himself from the masses, both in terms of his social status (for Clara is known for her former wealth), and his ability to attract beautiful women (on-lookers are not aware of the fact that they are cousins):

> How he loved to do any sort of thing with Clara! Shopping with her was a rare, epicurean dream. In every store…she was whispered about as the beautiful Mrs. Page…"I'll bet she won't stay single long"…"Society person, ain't she?" "Yeah, but poor now, I guess; so they say"… And Clara beamed…Amory believed that tradespeople gave her discounts, sometimes to her knowledge and sometimes without it. He knew she dressed very well, always had the best of everything in the house, and was inevitably waited upon by the head floor-walker at the very least.[30]

Much like Jay Gatsby, Amory Blaine is unable to sustain a long-term relationship in this new modern world, where worth is determined based on one's value as a commodity. When Clara explains to him that she has no intention of remarrying, or at least not marrying him (the reader is not told if money is a factor in her decision, but can certainly speculate it might be), Amory becomes disillusioned with love. He escapes this failed romantic attempt, college life, and the snobbery of his classmates, through war, only to return to a United States that is far more materialistically superficial and "uncultured" than the one he leaves behind.

---

[29] Ibid., 130–131.
[30] Ibid., 136.

Consumption and its Discontents

With the war over, his mother gone, and no financial prospects to speak of, Amory accepts an invitation to Rosalind Connage's coming-out party in New York. He is instantly fascinated with the debutante, who, like Daisy, is the epitome of the materialist youth culture of the 1920s. As Rosalind's sister, Cecelia Connage, reveals in a conversation with their brother, Amory's college friend Alec Connage,

> Rosalind has still to meet the man she can't outdistance. Honestly, Alec, she treats men terribly. She abuses them and cuts them and breaks dates with them and yawns in their faces—and they come back for more...She's a—she's a sort of vampire, I think—and she can make girls do what she wants usually—only she hates girls...Does Rosalind behave herself? Not particularly well. Oh, she's average—smokes sometimes, drinks punch, frequently kissed—Oh, yes—common knowledge—[loose morals is] one of the effects of the war, you know.[31]

Like Jay Gatsby, Amory is drawn to this destructive, cruel, vampiric New Woman, who hates other women (because they represent competition), is obsessed with men (because they symbolize wealth, strength and power), and sucks the lifeblood (money) out of all her suitors. Amory soon falls in love with Rosalind, who, at least physically, reciprocates his advances. When he broaches the subject of marriage, the reader is reminded, once again, that a prerequisite of a successful post-war "high-society" marriage is not simply money, but *old* money, which will guarantee security, respectability, and an unending flow of material goods and shopping sprees. As Rosalind explains to her mother: "He has a little income—and...he's earning thirty-five dollars a week in advertising," to which Mrs. Connage replies, "and it wouldn't buy your clothes...I have your best interests at heart when I tell you not to take a step you'll spend your days regretting. It's not as if your father could help you. Things have been hard for him lately and he's an old man. You'd be dependent absolutely on a dreamer, a nice, well-born boy, but a dreamer."[32] In this case, Amory is not rejected because of his social background, but because he does not have the financial means to sustain Rosalind's lifestyle. His status as "a dreamer, a nice, well-born boy" may be acceptable in certain social circles, but holds no currency for the Connages.

---

[31] Ibid., 159–160.
[32] Ibid., 178.

While the reader is left with the impression that Rosalind is materialistic, it is not completely confirmed until she rejects Amory's proposal (complete with racist Native American remarks), and considers marrying an old wealth acquaintance, Dawson Ryder, instead:

> Oh, we can't. I'd be your squaw—in some horrible place...Darling, I don't even do my own hair...Well—here's one little thing. There was a little poor boy we met in Rye Tuesday afternoon—and, oh, Dawson took him on his lap and talked to him and promised him an Indian suit—and [the] next day, he remembered and bought it—and, oh, it was so sweet and I couldn't help thinking he'd be so nice to—to our children—take care of them—and I wouldn't have to worry...I like sunshine and pretty things and cheerfulness—and I dread responsibility. I don't want to think about pots and kitchens and brooms. I want to worry whether my legs will get slick and brown when I swim in the summer.[33]

Clearly, Dawson will not only provide Rosalind with a lifestyle that will keep her out of the kitchen and allow her to pursue the perfect tan (a marker of the leisured class), but will also be able to "take care of" their children—at least materially. She is left with no option but to return Amory's ring, proving that only "the richest man gets the most beautiful girl."[34] Unlike Beatrice who married the impoverished Stephen Blaine out of boredom, and paid the price, Rosalind marries for money, not love, and Amory can do nothing to change her mind. Like Gatsby's Daisy, she will always represent the unattainable—a golden dream that constantly eludes Amory's reach.

Out of pride (he comments that they are "both high-strung"), Amory decides not to pursue Rosalind, and lapses into a depression fueled by memories of the war, drinking himself into a haze for weeks until Prohibition becomes federal law in January, 1920.[35] In this context, "disillusionment as a result of the war is a mythic and fraudulent explanation offered for emasculation at the hands of a materialistic, 'hard,' New Woman. Talking about history becomes a way of both leaving the New Woman out, and of implicating her in the traumas that modern history seemed to visit on men."[36]

Like Gatsby, Amory is unable to reconcile his identity as a "modern" American, mainly because of the fact that by the 1920s, modernity had become inextricably linked with money, status, and conspicuous

[33] Ibid., 180, 181, 183.
[34] Ibid., 256.
[35] Ibid., 182.
[36] James, 23.

consumption. The reader is thus left with a disillusioned picture of human progress, one in which "a new generation, [is] shouting the old cries, learning the old creeds, through a reverie of long days and nights; destined finally to go out into that dirty gray turmoil to follow love and pride; a new generation dedicated more than the last to the fear of poverty and the worship of success; grown up to find all Gods dead, all wars fought, all faiths in man shaken."[37] Both men spend their lives searching for their place in the world, and share similar fates—they become victims of the destructive nature of materialism and the unprogressive nature of American progress.

As Fitzgerald illustrates, the conspicuous consumption of the 1920s sounded the death-knell of traditional values such as the Puritan work ethic and the notion of a democratic American meritocracy, and transformed the United States into a landscape of hopelessly decaying despair and commodified identities. While Gatsby attempts to participate in this new society by acquiring the artificial security of wealth, he can never have the respectability required by the New Women who inhabit his social circle. On the other hand, even though Amory is able to grow from a naïve child into a mature young man, he realizes that for this new generation of emotionally-bankrupt Americans, money, and not morals, will be the measure of success. He, like Gatsby, is destined remain in a constant state of alienation: "'It's all a poor substitute at best,' he said sadly…He stretched out his arms to the crystalline, radiant sky. 'I know myself,' he cried, 'but that is all.'"[38] Their tales thus represent far more than the tragic fate of two naïve Midwestern boys. Their stories are the story of modern America—the tragic conflict between illusion and reality, the ethereal and the material, class status and absolute wealth—the latter of which, in the end, possesses its possessors.[39]

---

[37] Fitzgerald, *This Side of Paradise*, 260.
[38] Ibid., 260.
[39] Lionel Trilling, *The Liberal Imagination* (Garden City, NY: Doubleday, 1953), 244; Broccoli, 161.

Select excerpts on *The Great Gatsby* were taken from Tanfer Emin Tunc, "The Great Gatsby: The Withering of the American Dream on Long Island's Gold Coast." *Bloom's Literary Themes: The American Dream*, Ed. Blake G. Hobby (New York: Chelsea House Publishers, 2009). Used with permission.

CHAPTER SIX

UNITED STATES FLEA MARKETS AS BORDER PHENOMENA

JENNIFER LE ZOTTE

In San Jose, California, five days a week, thousands of people gather to buy, sell, barter, haggle over, or just peruse more than eight miles worth of goods and services. Mariachi bands and acapella singers, restaurants, snack bars, fish markets, spice shops, a quarter mile of produce, a carousel, playgrounds, and an arcade all contribute to the family-friendly, carnivalesque, multi-cultural feel of a large, twenty-first century flea market in the United States. At least seventeen different languages are spoken here, which often requires the use of the universal language of economic transaction.[1] Two pairs of socks? One open hand, fingers splayed.

Fifty years ago, much of this space was cattle land. Partly inspired by landowners using the lots of drive-in theaters (whose popularity had waned) for similar endeavors, in 1960 George Bumb decided to convert the lot into a flea market. In 2008, the San Jose Flea Market is still run by the Bumb family, and is one of several claiming to be America's largest. Dispelling the image of a flea market as a disarrayed hodge-podge of messy junk, the owners provide visitors with a neat and easy-to-read map of the premises, which outlines the locations of the vendors as well as the numerous sit-down restaurants. On the other hand, the alleys of unorthodox consumer items, new and used, commercial and homemade, counter any expectation of shopping-mall predictability. The market's location at the center of California's Silicon Valley at first seems to be a blatant contradiction of the area's slick, high-tech image. In reality, however, flea markets reflect a great deal about consumer life in the

[1] Rick Sebak, "A Flea Market Documentary." Pittsburgh: WQED Pittsburgh, Public Broadcasting System, 2001.

globalized information age, and thus represent the ultimate border between "high" and "low" consumption.

Flea markets are semi-permanent sites of consumer transactions, historically dealing in used and homemade goods. The exchanges are often open to haggling, as opposed to more conventional forms of consumption, such as department stores, where the prices are generally nonnegotiable. Despite their clear ethnographic potential, these markets have, for the most part, gone unexamined. Those anthropologists and sociologists who have studied flea markets have categorized them as "functional anachronisms," likening them to feudal markets and medieval fairs.[2] This depiction of flea markets misses the significance of the venues as adaptable sites of global commerce, and overlooks the complexity of their multi-tiered organizational structure. Rather than considering flea markets as either pre-modern marketplaces or as a subcategory of institutionalized commerce, this chapter theorizes flea markets as border phenomena, or fluid networks of cultural interaction. This conceptualization of flea markets not only exposes their potential as sites of social negotiation, but also helps bridge the artificial divisions that exist in contemporary consumer studies.[3]

The questions raised by consumer scholars are not fully answered when alternative modes of exchange are ignored. Binaries such as abundance/scarcity, public/private, formal/informal economy, gift/ purchase, production/consumption, work/leisure, local/global, and business/home have restricted the scope of consumer studies. Consumer historian Susan Strasser suggests examining "the relationships between oppositional tendencies and forces," instead of choosing a single vantage

---

[2] Russell W. Belk, John F. Sherry, Jr., and Melanie Wallendorf, "A Naturalistic Inquiry into Buyer and Seller Behavior at a Swap Meet," *The Journal of Consumer Research* 14.4 (1988); Nabil Razzouk and David Gourley, "Swap Meets: A Profile of Shoppers," *Arizona Business* 29.2 (1982); Cree McCree, "Flea Market," *Psychology Today* 18 (June 1986); Max H. Miller, "Patterns of Exchange in the Rural Sector: Flea Markets Along the Highway," *Journal of American Culture* 2.3 (1988); John F Sherry, Jr., "A Sociological Analysis of a Midwestern American Flea Market," *The Journal of Consumer Research* 17.1 (June 1990). Almost all studies of flea markets were conducted in the 1980s, with very little being published over the past twenty years. A recent work on the Washington, D. C. Eastern Market, a crafts, produce, and flea market, offers a more sophisticated anthropological analysis of the phenomenon: Robert J. Shepard, *When Culture Goes to Market: Space, Place, and Identity in an Urban Marketplace* (New York: Peter Lang, 2008).

[3] David Newman, "Borders and Bordering: Towards an Interdisciplinary Dialogue," *European Journal of Social Theory* 9 (2006): 171–186.

point.[4] Thus, a study of flea markets, arguably the most accessible and visible mode of alternative consumption, is a step towards transcending such constructed binaries and the institutionalized forms of retail that reify them.

Production of the "Real"

The institutionalization of retail sales began in the nineteenth century. Innovations in managerial and production methods followed the changes in agriculture, manufacturing, and transportation that defined the industrial revolution. In parts of Europe and the United States, giant department stores were built, and new methods of advertising were used to create a market for mass-produced goods. Over the past thirty years, scholars of consumption have assessed the institutionalized side of commerce, especially as it appeared in France, Great Britain, and the United States.[5] However, sites of less formalized, alternative consumer transactions have not been thoroughly analyzed. Such venues are important because they retain elements of pre-industrial commerce while incorporating aspects of contemporary consumption. Flea markets, for example, straddle various cultural, social, economic, and geographical territories, both responding to, and thwarting, expectations established by institutionalized retail sales.

US flea markets of the late twentieth and early twenty-first centuries are a blend of the intentionally produced and the unavoidably spontaneous. Flea market owners and promoters often wish to portray their venue as

---

[4] Susan Strasser, "Making Consumption Conspicuous: Transgressive Topics Go Mainstream," *Technology and Culture* 43 (2002): 671–672.

[5] Michael B. Miller, *The Bon Marché: Bourgeois Culture and the Department Story, 1869–1920* (Princeton: Princeton University Press, 1981); Bill Lancaster, *The Department Store: A Social History* (London and New York: Leicester University Press, 1995); Stuart Blumin, *The Emergence of the Middle Class: Social Experience in the American City, 1760–1900* (Cambridge, Cambridge University Press, 1989); Stuart Ewen, *Captains of Consciousness: Advertising and the Social Roots of Consumer Culture* (New York: McGraw-Hill, 1976); Jackson Lears, *Fables of Abundance: A Cultural History of Advertising in America* (New York: Basic Book, 1994); Roland Marchand, *Advertising the American Dream: Making Way for Modernity, 1920–1940* (Berkeley and Los Angeles: University of California Press, 1985); Lizabeth Cohen, *A Consumers' Republic: The Politics of Mass Consumption in Postwar America* (New York: Knopf, 2003); Robert E. Weems Jr, *Desegregating the Dollar: African American Consumerism in the Twentieth Century* (New York and London: New York University Press, 1998); and Jennifer Scanlon, *The Gender and Consumer Culture Reader* (New York and London: New York University Press, 2001).

being an "authentic" and, at the same time, unthreatening space, yet owners and advertisers are not fully able to control how transactions between buyers and sellers are conducted on their property. Throughout their existence, US flea markets have reflected this tension between the planned and the unprompted, and thus serve as examples of commercially contrived realities that often transgress preordained parameters.[6]

In the US, owners of open-air markets selling mostly used and homemade goods began to use the term "flea market" to describe their venues in the early twentieth century. Often, such markets were adaptations of other commercial ventures. For instance, many rural flea markets began as appendages to existing farmers markets. "First Monday Trade Days" in Canton, Texas, began as a trading market decades before the term "flea market" was in use. In the 1850s, the circuit judge came to Canton to hold court and conduct legal business the first Monday of every month, a practice common in rural areas at this time, particularly in the American South. These "Court Days" commonly did double duty as market and town meeting days.[7] In Canton, the first Monday of the month was thus designated as the day for townspeople to trade livestock, and sell and buy produce and other goods in the town square—and perhaps stop to watch a murder trial or hanging. Other county seats in the South such as Maysville, Kentucky, and Emporia, Virginia, underwent a similar consumer evolution, except their Court Days, and consequently *de facto* market days, fell on Wednesdays. The oldest operating flea market in Florida, the Monday Market in Webster (established in 1938), originated in much the same way.[8]

In the late twentieth century, the advertisers of First Monday Trade Days in Canton boasted that the venue was the largest flea market in the country—vying for that distinction with the aforementioned San Jose Flea Market. In order to attract crowds, the trade days were extended to the four days before the first Monday of each month. This strategy succeeded: in 2005, Canton had a population of 5,147 and hosted about 300,000 visitors during its First Monday Trade Days.[9] Moreover, the market itself

---

[6] Shepard, 7.

[7] Allan Kulikoff, "Households and Markets: Toward a New Synthesis of American Agrarian History," *The William and Mary Quarterly*, Third Series, 1.1 (April 1993): 342–355.

[8] Based on author's personal observations; also see websterwestside.com; Terry Goodson (Webster Westside Market vendor). Interview with author, September 9, 2005.

[9] Several flea markets claim to be the largest market in the country, or even the world. Sebak, "A Flea Market Documentary"; Sally Blakewood (WFFM owner).

became a "festival marketplace": a space that makes visitors "vaguely and generically happy…[an] entertainment space that offers an 'edginess' in which, paradoxically, the edge itself is part of the design and not an expected outcome of social reality."[10] Thus, the site itself became something to be consumed.

However, the intentions of owners and organizers are not the only factors that determine the public image and communicated (or perceived) style of flea markets. Because the individual vendors are able to determine, in conjunction with consumer demand, what is sold and how, the appearance of the site, and the manner of exchange, are constantly being negotiated. This built-in fluidity sometimes conflicts with the agendas of local bureaucrats. For instance, at the Eastern Market in Washington, DC, for decades city planners, independent vendors, local politicians, land owners, leasers, area business owners, and city residents have battled over differing visions of what a public market space should contain and represent. The Eastern Market originally began as part of late-nineteenth-century urban renewal efforts. The nation-wide City Beautiful Movement—loosely a product of the Progressive Era—established new city marketplaces as part of a belief in urban planning's ability to mold the increasing number of new immigrants into "Americans."[11] In the 1970s, the nearly abandoned Eastern Market was gentrified, and transformed into a self-conscious "festival marketplace" in order to attract affluent DC residents. The market's intended image was soon threatened by booth renters and vendors, who joined together to counter pressures to control the appearance and material content of the market. The city planners' vision of an "Old World" marketplace conflicted with those mini-entrepreneurs whose printed tee-shirts, imported trinkets, and diabetic socks served to bring the festival atmosphere "to the level of a flea market."[12]

Interview with author, July 10, 2005; "First Monday of Canton, TX." Last accessed May 6, 2008: http://www.firstmondaycanton.com/index.html ; Pamela Klaffke, *Spree: A Cultural History of Shopping* (Vancouver: Arsenal Pulp Press, 2003), 112–114; Gary McKenchnie and Nancy Howell, "The Flea Market Bug in Florida; It's Peak Season for Fencing Masks, Deer Heads, and Maybe a Classic Triumph." *The Washington Post,* February 19, 1995, E5.

[10] Shepard, 7.

[11] Ibid., 21; Katherine Tehranian, *Modernity, Space, and Power: The American City in Discourse and Practice* (Cresskill, NJ: Hampton Press, 1995), 83–87; M. Christine Boyer, "Critics for Sale: Merchandising History at South Street Seaport," Michael Sorkin, ed. *Variations on a Them Park: The New American City and the End of Public Space* (New York: Hill and Wang, 1992), 181–204.

[12] Shepard, 36.

In the late 1980s, the owner of the Eastern Market attempted to play down the flea market image by dividing the space based on the day of the week. Saturdays at the Eastern Market was billed a "Market Festival," intended to highlight "artists, craftsmen, or vendors of handmade items or merchandise." The "flea market"—basically days when anything was sold by anyone—was relegated to Sundays. This segregation failed because "in practice, both days attract the same types of vendors, and indeed often the same vendors."[13] The organizers' inability to control space designed to appear spontaneous and authentic actually encouraged a certain degree of genuine spontaneity. According to anthropologist Robert J. Shepard, this fluidity may have ultimately saved the market. The Eastern Market's popularity began to decline within a few decades of its 1874 opening, and the resurgent popularity of the market in the late twentieth century is "arguably a result of the success of the flea market vendors, [whom] many local residents...blame for 'ruining' the market."[14]

Regulation and Organization

Such conflicts ultimately highlighted the need for formal organizations which would help legitimate and protect flea markets as they grew in popularity and visibility. The National Flea Market Association (NFMA), and other state-wide flea market associations that employ public relations managers and state and federal lobbyists, are just one way in which late-twentieth-century flea markets have adopted formal commercial structures. The NFMA calls itself the largest association for free enterprise in North America, and actively portrays the markets as reflective of the American entrepreneurial spirit.[15]

With this entrepreneurial spirit comes a certain amount of market flexibility and informality. Requirements for tax numbers vary depending on the types of goods sold (whether new or used, for example) and state and county regulations. However, even where tax numbers are a legal requisite, enforcement is uneven at best. As with much informal-economy work—work that goes untaxed, unmeasured, or both—the cost of enforcing tax laws on individuals making very little profit far outweighs

---

[13] Ibid., 31, 33–45.

[14] Ibid., 159.

[15] Jerry Stokes, (National Flea Market Association founder). Interview with author, November 25, 2006; Gail Barron, Executive Director of the National Flea Market Association. Interview with author, October 30, 2006.

any resulting remuneration.[16] In other words, independent peddlers of cheaply printed tee-shirts, electric cords, and old Disneyland souvenirs are small fry. The success and growth of flea markets nationwide, however, has recently garnered the attention of competing retail interests. According to one flea market lobbyist, almost every year since the early 1990s, state and federal retail associations have tried to pass legislation concerning flea markets.[17] Citing the claim—which has some merit—that flea markets traffic in stolen, counterfeit, and illegally transported goods (and often without the required tax ID numbers), the bills usually include measures requiring stringent record-keeping on the part of individual dealers. So far none of these bills has passed.

While some flea markets did evolve as relatively spontaneous gatherings of dealers wishing to sell or trade mostly used and homemade goods in any space available, many US flea markets were established by independent business owners looking to make low-hassle profits. Thus, some of these flea markets serve as models of improvisational integrated economies. Many daytime and/or weekend flea markets were used as a way to offset the decline in profits which came with the slump in drive-in theater attendance in the 1950s and 1960s. Other drive-in theater owners abandoned the theaters, simply shifting to the business of flea market management.[18] Landowners looking to use large, open lots without the cost of converting them into expensive shopping malls found the flea market idea a quick fix.

Attempts to regulate these spaces lagged behind their growth. By the 1980s, thousands of permanent flea market sites were established in the United States, and many of the vendors sold and traded both new and used

---

[16] Alejandro Portes, Manuel Castells, and Lauren A. Benton, eds., *The Informal Economy: Studies in Advanced and Less Developed Countries* (Baltimore and London: The Johns Hopkins University Press, 1989); Alejandro Portes, "The Informal Sector: Definition, Controversy, and Relation to National Development," *Review* 7.1 (1983): 151–174; Alejandro Portes and Saskia Sassen-Koob, "Making it Underground: Comparative Material on the Informal Sector in Western Market Economies," *American Journal of Sociology* 93.1 (1987).

[17] Ed Collins, Florida flea market lobbyist. Interview with author, November 4, 2006. For an example of a bill presented before the Florida House of Representatives, see Florida House of Representatives, *An Act Relating to Flea Markets.* 189-853a-99 (1999).

[18] Gail Barron, Executive Director of National Flea Market Association. Interview with author, October 30, 2006; Kerry Segrave. *Drive-in Theaters: A History from Their Inception in 1933* (North Carolina: McFarland & Company, Inc. Publishers, 1992); John Leonard, "Handcraft Swapping at Drive-Ins: A Bit of California Dreaming." *The New York Times,* January 17, 1976, 44.

goods on a consistent, weekly basis. In 1991, the owners organized, establishing the NFMA in order to protect their business interests and promote a positive public image. State and federal lobbyists were hired by the NFMA and other statewide flea market associations to counter legislative bills proposed by primary retail interests wishing to limit the competitive force of flea markets.[19] By establishing their own professional standards and promoting a positive image, flea market owners managed to avoid formal restrictions which would reduce profits and compromise the formation of a stable clientele.

Geopolitical and Economic Borders

Flea markets in America operate along and across the borders of regulated and unregulated economic exchange, and formal and informal policies and organizations. US flea markets are also often positioned on or near literal borders, such as along the geopolitical border between the US and Mexico. Since the 1960s, the US-Mexico border has been an indicator of global economic change. Mexico's Border Industrialization Program of 1965 began the process, but the North American Free Trade Agreement (NAFTA) in 1994 ensured that region's economic importance.[20] Over the past fifteen years, both formal and informal economic exchange across the border has increased. Political scientist Kathleen Staudt's study of informal-economy work on the border demonstrates that increased exchange across the political boundary was not limited to government-sanctioned business. According to Staudt, informal workers living in Mexico made a living buying and reselling used goods, crossing to the United States to sell their merchandise at flea markets or regularly-held garage sales. In the 1990s, this became such a recognized practice that the city of El Paso, Texas, passed a law limiting the number of garage sales allowed yearly.[21]

---

[19] Gail Barron, Interview with author; Florida House of Representatives, *An Act Relating to Flea Markets* (1999).

[20] Kathleen Staudt, *Free Trade? Informal Economies at the U. S.-Mexico Border* (Philadelphia: Temple University Press, 1998); Kathleen Staudt, "Informality Knows No Borders? Perspectives from El Paso-Juarez," *SAIS Review* XXI, no. 1 (2001); Alexis McCrossen, ed. "Introduction," *Disrupting Boundaries: Consumer Culture in the U.S.-Mexico Borderlands* (Durham, NC: Duke University Press, forthcoming), 2–6.

[21] Staudt, "Informality Knows No Borders? Perspectives from El Paso-Juarez," 125. Although there are legal restrictions in place, it is unlikely the law is being enforced because financially, it is not worth the expenditure of enforcement. For

Recent scholars contend that an absolute distinction between so-called formal and informal economy work is not so easy to establish.[22] In major Latin American cities and among Latino/a immigrants in the United States, many workers with taxed employment supplement their income with informal work. A 2001 study of flea markets conducted by the National Flea Market Association (NFMA) concluded that new immigrants to the United States accounted for most of the flea market industry's growth in the 1980s and 1990s. An NFMA survey, also from 2001, indicates that flea market vendors in California came from at least thirty-six different countries and spoke at least nineteen different languages.[23] Thus border crossings enabled by government policies such as NAFTA have not only changed the landscape of production and consumption in the United States, but have also transformed the culture of shopping into a more fluid and multi-cultural process that seeks to transgress the boundaries of formal exchange that were established during the second half of the nineteenth century.

At the huge, urban San Jose Flea Market in California, one can find some of the same products sold at the Waldo Farmer and Flea Market in rural north-central Florida: Chinese-made novelty toys, inexpensive tools, electrical chords, incense, and native-American dream catchers. However, if one digs deeper, it becomes clear that the style of exchange at flea markets vary widely. One week, a consumer might find a pair of false teeth made in 1919 for sale alongside an image of a docile Florida panther soliciting donations for the National Wildlife Federation. In keeping with Arjun Appadurai's apt definition of commodities (as opposed to products or goods), what is for sale, barter, exchange, or even free at flea markets are "things with a particular type of social potential," whose social value and use is highly subjective and malleable.[24]

Critiques of consumption often bemoan the homogenization and standardization of mass-produced consumption, assuming a division between authentic and creative on the one hand, and contrived and banal on the other. Understanding bargain-oriented consumption such as flea

---

more information on informal economies, please see Bill Jordan and Andrew Travers, "The Informal Economy: A Case of Unrestrained Competition," *Social Policy and Administration* 32.3: 292–307.

[22] Basudeb Guha-Khasnobis, Ravi Kanbur, and Elinor Ostrom, *Linking the Formal and Informal Economy* (New York: Oxford University Press, 2006), 1–5.

[23] Gail Barron, Interview with author; Gail Barron, email correspondence, July 27, 2005.

[24] Arjun Appadurai, ed. *The Social Life of Things: Commodities in Cultural Perspective* (Cambridge, UK: Cambridge University Press, 1986), 6.

market shopping as border phenomena highlights the inaccuracy of seeing consumption as fully institutionalized and homogenized. The spaces themselves, while they may be intentionally designed to be flea markets, defy stasis and predictability. This is contrary to Henri LeFebvre's assertion that "repetition has everywhere defeated uniqueness, that the artificial and contrived have driven all spontaneity and naturalness from the field, and…that products have vanquished works."[25] Flea markets demonstrate that consumption does not necessarily choose between products and works, formal and informal, local and global, or social and commercial. Like the people involved in the selling, haggling, gifting, exchanging, buying, and stealing of commodities, consumption itself is adaptable.

[25] Henri LeFebvre, *The Production of Space*, trans. Donald Nicholson-Smith (Oxford, UK: Basil Blackwell, 1991 [1974]), 75.

CHAPTER SEVEN

BRINGING THE MALL HOME: PERFORMING "AUTHENTIC" CULTURE IN NEOLIBERAL MEXICO

ROBIN O'BRIAN

For tourists seeking an "authentic" alternative to the shopping mall, the open-air market found in many societies takes on the role of a "cultural mall," and markets itself to serve a tourist clientele so that it may perform this role exclusively.[1] The idea of traveling to encounter the "exotic other" is well known, but in contemporary neoliberal Mexico, different niches abound. Tourists seek a range of experiences.[2] The tourist who visits Cancún will have an entirely different encounter than one who travels to highland Chiapas. The latter is a more self-consciously sophisticated tourist looking for an experience that is simultaneously more "authentic" and "exotic." Perhaps this sought experience is one that even contains a whiff of revolutionary fervor, as Chiapas Mayas are usually associated with the 1994 Zapatista uprising that still permeates the region.[3]

---

[1] Dean McCannell, *Empty Meeting Grounds: The Tourist Papers* (New York: Routledge, 1992).

[2] Quetzil Castenada, *In the Museum of Maya Culture: Touring Chichen Itza* (Minneapolis: University of Minnesota Press, 1996); Pierre van den Berghe, *The Quest for the "Other": Tourism and Ethnicity in San Cristóbal de las Casas* (Seattle: University of Washington Press, 1994).

[3] Victor Azarya, "Globalization and International Tourism in Developing Countries: Marginality as a Commercial Commodity." *Current Sociology* 52.6 (2004): 949–967; Clifford Bob, *The Marketing of Rebellion: Insurgents, Media, and International Activism* (New York: Cambridge University Press, 2005); Desiree Martin, "'Excuse the Inconvenience, But This is A Revolution': Zapatista Paradox and the Rhetoric of Tourism." *South Central Review* 21.3 (Fall 2004): 107–128.

The artesanía market in San Cristóbal de las Casas, the urban center of the Chiapas highlands, is colorful, busy, and filled with people. As a visitor makes his or her way through the narrow paths created by the crowded booths, brightly woven blankets, blouses, shawls, and jackets catch the eye. People are calling to each other in Spanish, and in the unfamiliar languages of Tzotzil and Tzeltal. A man approaches, waving a bundle of rope: "Hammocks, hammocks! Want to buy a hammock?" Small children are everywhere, playing, running errands for parents, and trying their hand at vending.

A small boy, followed at a short distance by two others, stops to investigate a shopper's shoes. "Shoeshine, shoeshine. Your shoes are dirty. You should have a shoeshine. Do you live in a hotel? Do you have a helicopter?" He and his companions drift off in search of other dirty shoes. A middle-aged Maya woman, dressed in the clothing of Chamula, sits by her small stacks of weaving, watching an Evangelical preacher on her portable television. Many vendors have televisions or radios in their stalls, and catch up on sports and local events, or enjoy religious or entertainment programming between sales. If a tourist approaches a stall looking for an unavailable item, an enterprising vendor may use her cell phone to make inquiries in staccato Tzotzil. Soon, a small child appears with the desired item, brought from a nearby stall. It feels ethnic, contemporary, modern, yet timeless, as traditionally-dressed Maya women spin wool or embroider blouses.

The rise in tourism, which has been driven by the development of the so-called "Ruta Maya" (Mayan Route) in southern Mexico, has increased competition and creativity in drawing tourists. The marketing of the Ruta Maya has drawn a more self-consciously sophisticated tourist looking for an experience that is simultaneously more "authentic" and "exotic." While members of the nearby indigenous community of Zinacantán have long been economically active in their local communities and in the highland city of San Cristóbal de las Casas, in the past, they have been reluctant to pose for photographs, or interact at length with outsiders whom they viewed with suspicion.[4] However, recently, this has changed. Now Maya women frequently invite tourists to their homes, where they weave, pose for photographs in traditional clothing, prepare tortillas, sell handicrafts, and re-enact weddings in traditional dress. Zinacantecas thus

---

[4] In the past, most Maya women were very suspicious of outsiders, believing that photographs could steal one's soul or a vital essence, and that "gringo" outsiders were benefiting somehow from these pictures. Most had seen picture postcards locally, and assumed tourists were taking photographs home and profiting from them by making them into postcards.

market or perform indigenous culture in small vignettes for consumption by tourists, while enjoying the safety and control of their home communities. In this context, they market intimacy and familiarity as enacted in the home, thus transforming the home, a site that has traditionally been separate from the marketplace, into a market space itself.[5] However, there are limits to these encounters. Some experiences remain inaccessible to tourists: a visitor may not remain over night, must leave when asked, and is not privy to the private quarters of the home.

This chapter argues that the growth of neoliberalism in Mexico has penetrated the home, turning it, in part, into a commodified space, managed and performed by its residents. It will contrast the locations in which different tourists consume "authenticity" as they seek varying degrees of familiar contact with Maya vendors. While visitors certainly enjoy "interacting with the natives," the central component of this experience has become the acquisition of the "novel souvenir," which functions as physical proof of the encounter. In order to ensure that the treasure they purchase is as genuinely Mayan as possible, tourists visit street vendors and the booths of the artesenía market described above. Yet, ironically, the products they consume can range from the "authentic" (local hand-made goods), to the "inauthentic" (mass-produced souvenirs from as far away as India and Pakistan), suggesting that commercial value lies somewhere between the real and the "imagined" exotic.

Locating Chiapas

Highland Chiapas, in southernmost Mexico, is a starkly beautiful rural region, anchored by the city of San Cristóbal de las Casas. Reminiscent of Guatemala, there are numerous traditional Maya communities, most still farming corn, beans, and squash, and many following a syncretic Catholicism that combines pre-Hispanic elements with Catholic liturgy. Communities maintain a fairly strict gendered division of labor with women caring for children, producing tortillas, beans and corn drink, herding sheep (if they keep them), and making traditional Maya clothing. In contrast, men farm or seek manual labor as migrant workers. Together, men and women organize and finance fiestas for particular saints.[6]

---

[5] Christine E. Eber, "'That They Be In The Middle, Lord:' Women, Weaving and Cultural Survival In Highland Chiapas, Mexico." *Artisans and Cooperatives: Developing Alternative Trade for the Global Economy*, eds. Kimberly M. Grimes and B. Lynne Milgram (Tucson: University of Arizona Press, 2000), 45–63.

[6] Frank Cancian, *Economics and Prestige in a Maya Community: The Religious Cargo System in Zinacantán* (Stanford, CA: Stanford University Press, 1965);

While many Mayas wish to maintain their traditional way of life, economic and political factors have shaped and altered their communities for much of the past twenty years. Increasing indigenous populations, and the desire of large landowners to put their land into pasture, have steadily decreased the farmland available to Maya farmers. Few men can provide sufficient food and income for a family solely through farming. Moreover, Maya farmers are dependent on chemical fertilizers in the fields they do farm, further embedding them in the cash economy.[7]

These economic and social changes originated in the Mexican debt crisis of the 1980s. In the late 1970s, global recession prompted the Mexican federal government to support failing private businesses in an effort to keep the population employed, and it borrowed from foreign investment banks to do so. In 1982, Mexico was unable to meet its debt payments. The value of the peso dropped, capital flight rose dramatically, and in August of that year, the government declared bankruptcy. The Mexican government turned to the International Monetary Fund and the World Bank for assistance. In 1984, Mexico accepted loans premised on neoliberal restructuring, including wide-ranging privatization, the relaxation of labor laws, the elimination/lowering of tariff barriers, and the elimination of restrictions on foreign investments.[8] These factors hit Mexico's poor particularly hard. Subsidies for corn vanished. Urban work became unavailable, sending unemployed men back to their highland farms. Real wages dropped, and inflation increased dramatically, squeezing Mayas in multiple ways. Mayas sought a range of solutions, including entering the tourism industry as informal vendors, becoming unskilled workers in hotels and restaurants, and producing crafts.[9]

During this same period, the highland region became the locus of Protestant evangelizing. While Evangelists had long been present in Chiapas, Mayas suddenly became enthusiastic converts, perceiving

---

Evon Z. Vogt, *Zinacantán: A Maya Community in the Highlands of Chiapas* (Cambridge, MA: Belknap Press, 1969).

[7] Frank Cancian, *The Decline of Community in Zinacantán: Economy, Public Life, and Social Stratification, 1960–1987*. (Stanford, CA: Stanford University Press, 1992).

[8] David Harvey, *A Brief History of Neoliberalism* (New York: Oxford University Press, 2005), 98–104.

[9] Christine E. Eber and Brenda Rosenbaum, "'That We May Serve Beneath Your Hands and Feet': Women Weavers in Highland Chiapas, Mexico." *Crafts in the World Market: The Impact of Global Exchange on Middle American Artisans*, ed. June Nash (Albany, NY: SUNY Press, 1993), 155–179; Robin O'Brian, "The Peso and the Loom: The Political Economy of Women's Work in Highland Chiapas." PhD Dissertation (University of California, Los Angeles, 1994).

Protestantism as an avenue out of poverty.[10] Many left their traditional Catholic faith to become *Evangelistas*, some actually leaving their original communities to form new Evangelical towns.[11] These changes ended tragically in the community of San Juan Chamula, where, after much inter-religious hostility, several men were murdered and the community government expelled the Protestants. Many *Expulsados* now live in settlements around San Cristóbal, and where are entirely dependent on the cash economy. Many *Expulsada* women have been able to earn a small income through the sale of weavings, tourist items, or domestic work.

The most notorious change in the region was, of course, the Zapatista rebellion, an armed uprising that began on January 1, 1994. Partly the outcome of numerous long-simmering conflicts between Mayas and the dominant Mexican population, the rebellion was a violent response to the enactment of the North American Free Trade Agreement (NAFTA), which poor Mexican farmers perceived as a threat to their way of life.[12] While the conflict drew attention to this unfamiliar part of Mexico, it also dramatically affected tourism, reducing needed income for those who relied upon this industry.

Perhaps the most dramatic change in the region is the completion of the Ruta Maya, a major development by the Mexican government to increase tourism throughout southern Mexico.[13] While Zinacantecos had

---

[10] David Stoll, *Fishers of Men or Founders of Empire? The Wycliffe Bible Translators in Latin America* (London: Zed Press, 1983).

[11] Carolyn Gallaher, "The Role of Protestant Missionaries in Mexico's Indigenous Awakening," *Bulletin of Latin American Research* 26.1 (January 2007): 88–111; Gary Gossen, "Life, Death, and Apotheosis of a Chamula Protestant Leader: Biography as Social History." *Ethnographic Encounters in Southern Mesoamerica: Essays in Honor of Evon Zartman Vogt*, eds. Victoria R. Bricker and Gary H. Gossen (Albany, NY: Institute for Mesoamerican Studies, SUNY Press, 1989), 217–229; Sarah Washbrook, "The Chiapas Uprising of 1994: Historical Antecedents and Political Consequences," *Journal of Peasant Studies* 32.3 (Fall 2005): 417–449.

[12] George A. Collier with Elizabeth Lowery Quaratiello, *¡Basta! Land and the Zapatista Rebellion in Chiapas* (Oakland, CA: Institute for Food and Development Policy, 1994); Shannan Mattiace, *To See With Two Eyes: Peasant Activism & Indian Autonomy in Chiapas, Mexico* (Albuquerque: University of New Mexico Press, 2003).

[13] Aline Magnoni, Traci Ardren & Scott Hutson, "Tourism in the Mundo Maya: Inventions and (Mis)Representations of Maya Identities and Heritage," *Archaeologies* 3.3 (2007): 353–383; Lucero Cano and Avis Mysyk, "Cultural Tourism, the State, and the Day of the Dead," *Annals of Tourism Research* 31.4 (October 2004): 879–898.

certainly encountered tourists for a number of years, the impact of the Ruta Maya, and its more self-consciously sophisticated tourists, have changed women's experiences. In earlier years, women had participated in artesanía production and weaving cooperatives in their own communities, and did not frequently encounter tourists.[14] Now they eagerly invite tourists to their homes, where they display their textiles and stage "mock weddings."[15] Such strategies are not uncommon in other regions, but are a fairly recent innovation in Zinacantán.

The Ruta Maya was originally conceived as a grand experiment designed to encourage tourists to travel the regions of Chiapas, Campeche, Tabasco, Yucatán, and parts of Central America. *National Geographic* editor Wilbur E. Garrett outlined his concept of the Ruta Maya in October, 1989.[16] He described it as "a carefully groomed tourist route connecting important Mayan archaeological sites and nature preserves scattered throughout southern Mexico and three Central American countries."[17] It was also hoped that proceeds would provide income for the impoverished contemporary Mayas of the region. While development grew slowly in the post-Zapatista era, it generally led to improvements in the city of San Cristóbal, where a vast expansion of tourist-friendly shops provide further opportunities for local Mayas to encounter tourists.[18]

Shopping the Town: Artesanía Stores and Street Vendors

San Cristóbal Center features dozens of boutique-style stores selling indigenous craftwork and woven clothing. Often decorated in a way to suggest rural indigeneity (i.e. tortilla griddles, small chairs, and primitive paintings), such shops are often a favorite with tourists with limited time.

---

[14] Marielle K. Flood, "Changing Patterns of Interdependence: The Effects of Increasing Monetization on Gender Relations in Zinacantán, Mexico," *Research in Economic Anthropology* 15 (1994): 145–173.

[15] Carol Hendrickson, *Weaving Identities: Construction of Dress and Self in a Highland Guatemala Town.* (Austin: University of Texas Press, 1995); Walter E. Little, *Mayas in the Marketplace: Tourism, Globalization, and Cultural Identity* (Austin: University of Texas Press, 2004).

[16] Wilbur E. Garrett, "La Ruta Maya," *National Geographic* 176.4: 424–479.

[17] Carl Franz and Lorena Havens, "The Ruta Maya," *The People's Guide to Mexico.* Last accessed March 17, 2008: http://www.peoplesguide.com/1pages/best/maya/mayawhat.htm

[18] I will not address the development of what might be called "Zapatismo tourism," an important tourist segment that deserves further study but is beyond the scope of this chapter.

Many of these stores buy goods from Maya producers, and some even maintain long-term ties with them, although Maya women themselves sometimes regard the store owners as exploitive. Store owners will gouge women on prices, and then mark up the products because most tourists do not have time to comparison shop, and cannot speak the language. "It's exploitation," said one weaver. "They exploit us because we are poor."

A visitor can also stay in the city center and interact with artesanía vendors themselves. Many vendors sell in the main plaza in town (the zócalo), and by the restaurants and hotels frequented by tourists. Although women will sometimes solicit anyone who might be a tourist (anyone "European" in appearance or well-dressed), they are most heavily concentrated in this area where they compete with stores. Street vendors carry their goods with them and stroll through the streets, although sometimes they might sit briefly on the sidewalk and lay a few items out on a shawl or blanket. Women usually work in groups. Maya women rarely, if ever, travel unaccompanied, even if their companion is a child. When a single woman approaches a customer, her companions are usually not far away, selling to other tourists or laughing from a bench nearby. Most groups are comprised of two to four women, but one occasionally sees groups of eight or ten. In these latter instances, two or three sellers will approach customers and then return to the larger group. If a customer approaches the group, every seller will display her products and attempt to persuade the customer to buy from her.

The zócalo is a stop for most taxis, public transit, and tourist buses. Various up-scale tourist hotels are located across the street from the zócalo, making it a strategic location for sellers. Groups of women and girls begin arriving between 7:30 and 8:00 am, as tourists appear on the streets looking for restaurants or tour groups. The sellers circulate through the zócalo, often using a bench or a corner as a home base. Sellers will move slowly around the plaza seeking customers and chatting amongst themselves. When a potential customer appears, sellers will descend, sometimes in several groups at once. Sellers range from girls as young as five, to elderly women whose ages are unknown. Sellers can be aggressive, waving a variety of shawls, belts, cotton bracelets, and cloth purses at customers. Some sellers will attempt to tie a belt or a bracelet on a tourist. A seller also may attempt to braid or tie woven bands into a female tourist's long hair.

Most independent street vendors speak some Spanish, and the younger women and girls often speak it fluently. By the early 1990s, some women had learned a few English phrases ("Please, please! Buy it, buy it!"). By 2006, a number of women had learned phrases in English, French, and

German, and would even seek out opportunities to practice what they knew. When a vendor encounters someone obviously neither Mexican nor Maya, she asks simple questions, such as "What is your name?," "What is your country?," in these languages. The practice extends the vendor's interaction with a possible buyer, and some tourists are more likely to make a purchase from these multilingual vendors.

The Life of a Vendedora

When women are not actively soliciting sales, they produce macramé belts, hair bands, and bracelets. A work in progress is usually pinned to a vendedora's belt and tucked in under her skirt when she is not working on it. Women make the products when they are eating, nursing infants, resting or when business is slow. Sellers begin to leave the zócalo in the late afternoon to return to their nearby homes, or to catch buses or trucks to outlying communities. However, some women and girls are still at work into the night, and do not leave the zócalo before 8:00 or 8:30 pm.

Albertina, a vendedora from the community of Chamula, comes to the zócalo two or three times a week, walking from her *paraje* for two hours to save on transportation. While at the zócalo, she sells macramé *pulseras* and *cinturones* that she describes as "hand-woven" (*tejer de mano*) and a few traditional Chamula belts that are loom-woven. These latter items are much more difficult to make, requiring wool-processing as well as weaving time, so she rarely has more than two or three to sell. The macramé goods can be manufactured while she sits on a zócalo bench, or walks around soliciting sales. On the days she stays in the paraje, Albertina herds sheep and works in her house, washing and cooking. "There is always work to do," she says, "Here or in the paraje."

A few women maintain permanent locations in the doorways, or adjacent to tourist restaurants in San Cristóbal. One elderly woman sells elaborate macramé bracelets in front of a busy tourist restaurant located between the zócalo and the bus station. This woman speaks basic Spanish, only enough to conduct simple sales transactions, and sometimes her granddaughter will help with sales. This woman sells bracelets almost exclusively. Her bracelets are wider, have more colors, more elaborate designs and more openwork than those sold by most vendedoras, and are more expensive than usual, ranging from $ .50 to $3.00 US. Other women and girls also sell wares in front of the tourist restaurants lining the streets off the zócalo. These women sell a wider range of goods, including macramé belts and bracelets, Chamula and Zapatista dolls, small woven purses, and some machine-made Guatemalan goods.

Artesanía Markets

The artesanía market in San Cristóbal occupies the courtyards of the former Santo Domingo Convent and Church, and the smaller Church of La Caridad, just south of the former Convent. Women pay a small daily rental fee to a representative of the municipal government in to occupy a space in the yard. Spaces have evolved dramatically over the years. In the early 1990s, spaces were generally designated by lengths of plastic that each vendor would lay out. In the 2000s, vending locations have become plastic covered booths with roofs, shelving for products, and electrical outlets. Each day women begin arriving at 6:00 am, and continue to arrive until 9:30 am. Some women carry their goods from home, while others store locally for a fee. Whether brought by tumpline or cart from home, or stuffed into an empty room nearby, products are much the same, ranging from locally woven goods, to those purchased from Guatemalan vendors, to materials imported from as far away as India and Pakistan.

Most women work in small groups of relatives—daughters, sisters and mothers—though with the decline of available land and labor options it has expanded to include all members of the family, including men and boys. Vendors from different indigenous communities sell both their own craft items, and tourist items imported from all over Latin America. Goods produced in India and Pakistan are distinctly different from locally produced or even locally imported products. However they too convey the novel and exotic, and are thus popular with tourists. Women from the community of Chamula and from the various Protestant communities surrounding San Cristóbal predominate, but there are groups of women from a range of rural communities, including Zinacantán, Tenejapa, Oxchuc, San Pedro Chenalhó, San Andrés Larrainzar and Amatenango del Valle.

There is a distinct cycle to the Santo Domingo tourism market. During the peak tourist season in July and August, the patios and lawns in front of churches are crowded with women, each displaying items and hanging clothing on the front of the small plastic booths that protect vendors from rain. Merchandise fluctuates with the season. While there are always a few a non-regional items, these increase dramatically during the tourist season. The Guatemalan goods offered include machine-made skirts, vests, shirts, jackets, pants and tablecloths of Guatemalan cloth, as well as small coin purses and bags. Other non-regional items include hair bands, small wall hangings and eyeglass cases. A number of women have begun carrying commercially produced shawls from the Andes (usually Ecuador), purses, and decorative wall-hangings from India and Pakistan, and T-shirts ranging from a typical tourist shirt, to those with familiar cartoon characters. Most vendors sell small clay pots and figurines from the Tzeltal potting village of Amatenango. Chamula and Protestant women also sell clothing from Zinacantán and traditional blouses from Pantelhó and El Bosque. Zinacantecas, on the other hand, rarely, if ever, sell goods from other communities, specializing in their own artesanías.

Vendedoras also buy artesanías from women who do not sell wares to tourists. Zinacantecas are more apt to pursue this strategy. While, as noted above, some Zinacantecas sell in the churchyard, they represent only a small percentage of participants. It is more common to see Zinacanteca women carrying the typical servilletas, rebozos and ponchos, traveling from market spot to market spot, and offering these products to vendedoras. Before purchasing, women check the quality of the goods, measuring length using their arms, and the tightness of the weave by pulling fabric taut. Some women visit the market several days each week to sell their artesanías; other women will only visit occasionally, sometimes with only one or two items to sell. They circulate through the church offering the items to each stall. Vendedoras buy these items cheap, and sell them to tourists at a substantial mark up, which perpetuates the exploitation of indigenous women.

There is also a group of food sellers who move through the market at various times of day selling food to vendors. In the early morning (between 7:30 and 9:00 am) women pass through the market selling tortillas, hot corn porridge, and hot corn drink. Sellers and their children can purchase a bowl of cereal or a glass of corn drink served in a dish. When the woman is finished with her meal, she returns the dish to the food seller, who places it in a pail of water. Later in the day, between 10:00 and 11:30 am, women with buckets of chicken soup circulate amongst the sellers, offering bowls of soup for sale. In the afternoon, soup sellers sometimes return, joining women with large baskets of tamales. These food sellers market food only to the vendedoras and do not sell to tourists. In addition, there are snack sellers who peddle *helados* (ice cream), *elotes* (roasted corn ears), and other local delicacies. Vendedoras usually purchase these food products, however snack sellers also sell to local Ladinos and tourists.

Churchyard vendedoras generally remain at their selling locations throughout the day, with only brief trips to the bathroom, food vendors, or another nearby vendedora. Women typically perform many tasks while waiting to make a sale. Meals are eaten, children are groomed, and artesanías are made while tending one's place in the churchyard. In the morning, time is spent cleaning one's selling space and setting up wares, but because this is also an active selling time, women must constantly interrupt their activities to cater to interested tourists. Later in the day, when the weather may become more unpredictable and when tourists are eating, foot-traffic in the churchyard diminishes, and women nap, eat, visit, and produce macramé crafts for sale.

The artesanía market has been the province of tourists for at least thirty years, and its strong indigenous presence contrasts dramatically with stores. However, when questioned by a knowledgeable customer, vendors will readily admit that their crafts are commercially produced. Some customers cannot recognize mass-produced goods, and sellers habitually maintain that, for example, machine-made Guatemalan skirts with zippers are hand-woven, hand-sewn Chiapan articles. Young girls adopt this approach most often, telling customers that every item was woven by their mamá at home. Bargaining is still common, but many women have a base price below which they will not go, and most will want to make a small profit above the production cost of the item, explaining that they need to be compensated for their labor.

Seeking the "Authentic Exotic"

At the market, consumers find "timeless" indigenous women dressed in hand-woven clothing, pleasant interactions, and the experience of bargaining—all still exciting, even if some young women are talking on their cell phones or listening to iPods between sales. For the visitor who seeks a more "authentic experience" than that found among the artesanía vendors, a visit to one of the local indigenous communities is in order. Tourists can travel to the nearby community of Zinacantán, where they are met by girls and young women who invite them to their nearby homes. Once there, the women pose for pictures, invite tourists to try on and buy clothing, and cook tortillas for them. Women also stage "Maya weddings" for couples, dressing them in appropriate local wedding clothes.[19]

Generally, such visits begin with young women asking the tourists if they would like to take photos. If this encounter is successful, an invitation is extended: "Would you like to see what weaving is like in a real home?" The willing visitor is escorted to the home by one or more of the young women. Such homes are near the central plaza of the town,

[19] Wedding garments, traditionally made by Zinacantán, are customarily rented by the wedding couple and returned to the owner. See Patricia M. Greenfield, *Weaving Generations Together: Evolving Creativity in the Maya of Chiapas* (Santa Fe: School of American Research Press, 2004), 90; Walter F. Morris, Jr., *Living Maya* (New York: Harry F. Abrams, 1987), 105.

within easy walking distance of tourist buses. The tourist is invited to examine clothing for purchase, to receive weaving lessons, or to eat tortillas with the residents.

What does this visit provide the consumer, the tourist seeking the authentic encounter? Tourists who visit Chiapas (or similarly other regions of the Global South) are seeking an unusual experience. Consequently, the visitor to a traditional community believes that the encounter is more "real" and "authentic" than a stop on a preprogrammed tour: the opportunity to converse with individuals in their homes, eat with them, and interact with their family and friends allows the visitor to imagine that s/he has a deeper and more intimate relationship with "the natives" than a typical tourist.

Azarya has argued that such productions, found throughout the Global South, "freeze [participants] at the margin of society because it is their marginality that they exhibit and sell for profit."[20] While Azarya's point is true, one must also consider how the entire process of neoliberalization prompts individuals to exhibit their homes production for profit, thus moving the private (the key site of neoliberalism) into direct commodification. The agency of those who make this decision must also be examined. Azarya's argument partially erases, or minimizes, the degree to which "marginalized people" can control their own lives. While Maya women may be "frozen" in the tourist's gaze, they return this gaze with an oppositional stare, and control the tourist through a series of activities in which they are dominant: *they* invite the tourist, *they* sell to the tourist, *they* dress the tourist. Moreover, the touristic gaze is limited to public space—namely, the patio upon which women weave and the griddle from which they serve tortillas. Private space—farms, sleeping houses and storage sheds—are off limits, unless an invitation is proffered by a Maya woman. The producer of the scene, the resident of the community, knows full well that she performs for outsiders, but recognizes the advantages: staying at home among her kin and friends, demonstrating weaving for a fee, or selling old or worn clothes that the women themselves no longer wear.[21] Thus she may also convert unused items into income rather than having them go to waste.

While the tourist may see the community as "timeless" and authentic—indeed any of the clichés that scholars of tourism have noted—the

[20] Azarya, 961–962.

[21] The author bought two huipiles, or traditional woven blouses, as part of a research project on design and color change in traditional clothing. Both garments were grimy and worn, unlike the neatly stacked and wrapped items available in town.

community itself, managed by its inhabitants, is narrowly shaped and staged for touristic consumption. Its members commodify culture; however, they do maintain some semblance of autonomy and identity. The touristic consumer, wandering among the rural streets, feels a part of the indigenous scene. Community residents sell this sense of authenticity, while protecting what is most sacred to them: the non-material world of life among kin and friends.

CHAPTER EIGHT

INDIGENOUS COMMUNITIES AS SPACES FOR THE TRANSGLOBAL CONSUMPTION OF ALTERITY IN ECUADOR

VERONICA DAVIDOV

In the global marketplace, commodified culture is widely available, ambivalently desired, and suspiciously consumed. It is an industry of production, one in which the consumption of fantasies commingle with stereotypes, archetypes, histories, mythologies, cultural selfhood and alterity. One of the primary ironies of these fantasies, which are often as self-defeating as they are self-fulfilling, is the search for "authenticity" in the cultural products that flood the global marketplace of capitalist exchange. This elusive "authenticity" is at the core of the fantasies associated with cultural tourism in its various forms, especially heritage tourism, ecotourism, and ethnographic tourism.

The products themselves run the gamut from all-inclusive cultural tours aggressively marketed in travel brochures and in cyberspace, to word-of-mouth tips among "alternative" backpacker tourists. They may be "spontaneous" (but in reality contrived) encounters of the Masai warriors in their "natural habitat" in Kenya, or lodgings in *tonkogans*—traditional Toraja ancestor houses—in Sulawesi, Indonesia, or the marked, articulated distinctions between "the touristy" and "the authentic" in San Cristobal, Mexico.[1] In my field site, Ecuador, these products generally include rainforest trips with indigenous guides, traditional cleansing ceremonies performed by shamans, and physical objects, such as berry

[1] Edward Bruner, Culture on Tour: Ethnographies of Travel (Chicago: University of Chicago Press, 2005); Toby Alice Volkman, "Visions and Revisions: Toraja Culture and the Tourist Gaze," *American Ethnologist* 17(1990): 91; Pierre van den Berge, *The Quest for the Other: Ethnic Tourism in San Cristobal, Mexico* (Seattle: University of Washington Press, 1994).

bead necklaces and riverbed clay bowls crafted by Quichua women. The authenticity, and consequently value, of these experiences or objects is contingent upon the consumer's impression that they have been produced spontaneously, and with no preconceived plans, for intracultural consumption. As more and more communities in Ecuador become involved with tourism, this process, in a sense, is increasingly becoming recursive, with communities seeking to differentiate themselves from the "typical" tourist experience, which has come to be associated with compromised authenticity.

The "ethnographic" forms of tourism discussed in this chapter are a part of the transnational retrocolonial industry in which consumers of the exotic export themselves to the location where the production of the "primitive" takes place. Because they are aware of the fact that "the exotic" loses its luster once it enters the daily realities of the industrialized world via capitalist processes, consumers often search for the last vestiges of untainted cultural alterity, the last places on the map "untouched by civilization." Ironically, in doing so, they consume an "ethnographic present" produced to conform to postcolonial consumers' fantasies of the "authentic past."

The synthesis of ethnographic observations and anthropological analysis offered in this chapter centers around the Napo Quichua communities in the Ecuadorian Amazon which host tour groups in the Ecuadorian lowlands. This chapter will examine the ways in which ethnographic tourism in these locations enables a particular sort of consumption, one in which the capitalist exchange at the core of organized tourism is downplayed in order to effectively preserve the fantasy of an encounter with an "exotic" pre-capitalist culture. The cultural experiences these communities offer to the tourists/consumers exemplify "the marketable exotic," a phenomenon that is proliferating worldwide, creating instances of cultural consumption through a web of commodification that connects indigenous producers with Western consumers who come in search of their fantasies, externalized against a dramatically exotic geographic landscape. The data and analyses in this article are based on my fieldwork in Ecuador in 2004 and 2005. The ethnographic data featured herein was collected through a mixture of participant-observation, life history interviews, topical interviews, and informal interviews. Historical data was compiled using secondary sources and archival material.

An Industry of Alterity

In the 1950s the Ecuadorian government launched initiatives to promote tourism, which was becoming globally touted as the new path to development. Ecuador's geography (which includes topographic offerings as diverse as a massive shoreline, a mountain terrain, and the rainforest, not to mention the Galapagos Islands) was perfectly suited for a certain type of niche tourism, the sort that eventually grew into adventure tourism (including, but not limited to, hiking, whitewater rafting, mountain-climbing, diving and snorkeling, and horseback riding). Adventure tourism was subsequently integrated into ecotourism, which is at times a subcategory of, and at other times a synonym for, ethnographic tourism.

In recent decades, cultural tourism in Ecuador fell into two distinct trajectories of marketing and consumption. The first type of ethnographic tourism stemmed directly from the government's first attempts at promoting the Otavaleños—denizens of the picturesque, predominantly indigenous town of Otavalo in the highlands of Imbabura—and their weekly market where "ethnic" textiles were sold. The market is still advertised as one of the "must-see" attractions of Ecuador, but is promoted in tandem with other activities such as visits to highland villages, highland arts and crafts, folk festivals and other local cultural attractions. On the other hand, visits to the Indian communities located in the rainforest lowlands of the Amazon basin are arranged as a part of ecotours that emphasize such adventures as opportunities to observe the last vestiges of "pure," "untouched" nature.[2] Community visits are often incorporated into multi-day rainforest visits, along with other standardized fare: a stay in a jungle lodge, whitewater rafting, a canoe trip, hiking, and piranha fishing in a lagoon. Community visits are also largely standardized, and include some combination of the following: a traditional Indian meal, a crafts lesson, a *selva* (jungle) trip featuring a lesson in healing, edible plants and bird/animal calls, and a *limpiada* (cleansing) with the community shaman. The *limpiada* may or may not include the consumption of a hallucinogenic brew made from the local plant *ayahuasca* by the tourists themselves.

Tour guides assume that tourists interested in "community visits" will also be drawn to maximum radical alterity. At Amazonia Tours in La Mariscal district of Quito, I spoke with a tour guide named Oscar. After he gave up on talking me into the inner tube river trip that was commencing

---

[2] It is in such instances that ethnographic tourism is integrated with, if not subsumed by, the flourishing industry of ecotourism.

the following day, Oscar and I discussed the large map of Ecuador on display in his office. While I was inquiring about the different communities that could be visited by tourists, he showed me which indigenous groups lived where, first suggesting that I would be interested in a trip to the Yasuni National Park where the Huaorani Indian communities are located. He then actively marketed a tour scheduled for the following Monday that included an overnight stay in a Siona community. When I pointed to the Upper Napo and asked about the Quichua, he said, "*No son interesantes.*" He proceeded to explain that "[The Quichua] are too close to the cities." He showed with his hands how the Napo Quichua live "too close to civilization." He summed it up: "they are civilized, they all have cell phones; The Siona, they are primitive, they are interesting."

Based on this conversation and similar ones that followed, it would be safe to assume that in the tourist industry, there is a hierarchy of "wildness" among indigenous groups, with the Quichua occupying a position low on the "primitive" pyramid. The fact that the Quichua are not the "wildest" marketable group does not prevent people form marketing their alterity—if anything, in some ways they are considered the most "user-friendly" in terms of physical access and travel logistics. While visiting some of the other groups requires days of traveling by car, kayak, or even airplane, Quichua communities are located within two to five hours from tourist hubs in the Napo (like Tena and Puyo, and even Baños, which is a small town lying halfway between Quito and the lowlands, popular with the backpacker crowd for its hot streams and horseback volcano tours). For some tourists, their accessibility and proximity to urban centers makes them less primitive, and therefore less desirable, than more remote groups.

In some ways the Quichua compete with other groups for tourist business. Apart from their location (situated deep in the jungle), they also offer other signifiers of exotic alterity that satisfy Western fantasies of "the primeval forest." From the first moments of his/her visit, the tourist is immediately interpolated into a paradigm akin to Fabian's notion of "time and the Other."[3] That is, the marketed subject is positioned in the present via his/her geographical (and consequently temporal) proximity to "modern" things. The perfect pastoral geographies they inhabit in travel brochures and in the minds of the tourists are metonymically dependent upon effectively splitting the modern contingent from the ersatz

[3] Johannes Fabian, *Time and the Other* (New York: Columbia University Press, 2002).

"premodern" people. Whereas the very remoteness of certain indigenous groups, such as the Huaorani, is enough to render them "authentic," peoples, such as the Quichua, whose "authenticity" is compromised by their location and technology use, must offer tourists activities like traditional cleansings and traditional pottery lessons to compensate for their proximity to "civilization." In this context, traditional practices that evoke pre-modern living conditions replace the "authenticity" that the tourists expect from their visits. Even the technology used to reach these communities is framed within this discourse of creating a "bridge to the past": the canoes are "primitive" and "old-fashioned" means of transportation. When airplanes are used, tour guides recreate a colonial "first-contact" narrative to accompany the ride. As Carmen, a tourist from Spain, described her visit: "The plane just skidded to a halt in the middle of the forest [laughs]. I think we hit some branches on the way. I am never again flying in one of those airplanes. But it was just like in one of those old movies, you know!"

By aesthetically and performatively reverting to the colonial categories of primitivism vs. progress, the "other" is able to exist in the virgin rainforests, deeply and seductively entrenched in Western mythological fantasy. This myth becomes a product to be consumed, a contemporary iteration of colonial geotemporality that in the context of globalized capitalism facilitates the demand, and supply, of retrocolonial fantasies. It is important to note that these fantasies can reify divergent and even opposite goals and agencies. After all, the paradoxes and ironies that surface when tourism ventures attempt to materialize the fantasies of the exotic and primitive stem from the fact that the "tourees" are not blank slates passively reflecting colonial fantasies. Moreover, for communities involved in ecotourism, the production of a "pre-capitalist" cross-cultural encounter is a conscious choice made by actors who are participating in the global economy with their own agencies and agendas, whether they be investments in the cultural capital associated with hosting tourists, or a concrete plan to market videos and brochures of shamanic rituals via the Internet.[4]

---

[4] In many Quichua communities in Ecuadorian lowlands, tourism is associated with being "modern." In fact, some of the communities involved with tourism perceive communities that do not participate in tourism as being "backwards." Several of my informants, when asked about neighboring communities that chose to not work with tourists, bluntly attributed that choice to ignorance. At the same time, several of the community leaders I consulted associated the advent of tourism with their own "education." So in a sense, participation in tourism has become a marker of cultural capital in the Amazon.

Salvaging the Ethnographic Present

For Western tourists, the consumption that structures visits to indigenous villages is rarely processed as a naked capitalist encounter. Rather, it treated as a self-betterment project, a throwback to the antiquated-yet-current "salvage" paradigm popularized by Edward Curtis and Robert Flaherty. This sort of consumption, with its emphasis on capturing a "vanishing" way of life on film for posterity's sake, transpires without the tourists' awareness of their own complicity in the cultural transformation they are reifying as loss. The definitive mode of representation within the salvage paradigm locates the subject in the ethnographic present. In its present-day incarnation, global capitalism and postcolonialism add layers of ambiguity and irony to this already paradoxical predicament: the ethnographic present has now become truly eternal and self-reproducing due to its status as a lucrative product. However, its self-conscious performative nature also renders it a subject of deconstruction, and a tool of representation.

These acts of representation and the consumption of the indigenous "tourees" are no longer simply concentrated in Curtis' staged ritual footage, or the intertext of "Nanook of the North" that spoke of the "brave simple Eskimos." Rather, they are decentered and enacted in multiple locations, through innumerable instances of capitalist exchange in the marketplace of globalized multiculturalism.[5] They comprise a network of tours, indigenous exports, commemorative gifts, galleries of photographs, and memories narrated in anthologies and in cyberspace, where all items are equalized by their status as objects that can be circulated in a market system of exchange.

In *The Arcades Project*, Benjamin suggests that the past persists in the present in the form of a collective dream, often commodified as a wish-image, rich in symbols and promises which are encoded in those symbols.[6] As Susan Buck-Morss writes, this wish-image "break[s] from the recent past by evoking a cultural memory reservoir of myths and utopian symbols from a more distant ur-past."[7] This model serves as a useful allegory of the transformative process from the "ethnographic past," and colonial nostalgia, to the "ethnographic present"—the latter of which is

---

[5] "Nanook of the North." Directed by Robert Flaherty (1922). The DVD is available through *The Criterion Collection*, South Burlington, VT (1999).

[6] Walter Benjamin, *The Arcades Project*, ed. Rolf Tiedemann (Cambridge, MA: Harvard University/Belknap Press, 2002), 905.

[7] Susan Buck-Morss, *The Dialectics of Seeing: Walter Benjamin and The Arcades Project* (Cambridge, MA: MIT Press, 1991), 116.

characterized by the consumption of products. The Western wish-image of the "native" tourees marginalizes the transformations in indigenous communities which have occurred as the result of decades of missionary presence, and in effect ignores the local repercussions of globalization. Instead, the wish-image reproduces the fantasies of the precapitalist pastoral, in a sense recreating the "first contact" trope time and time again, mainly as a means to recapture the lost authenticity of the "ethnographic past."

In the global capitalist marketplace, the desire to possess and experience "the lost" (the value of which, like any other fetish object, is constituted by "the loss") presents as the "salvage paradigm."[8] Ethnographic tourism has been, and will be, informed by the idea of "disappearing cultures" and "the last of such people"—in other words, the tension that arises out of the desire to "rescue 'authenticity' out of destructive historical change"—in this case for Western consumption.[9] This discourse, in turn, is framed by the notion of cultural preservation and revivification, a project which can be catalyzed by tourists, and historically criticized as contributing to the adulteration and destruction of indigenous cultures. It is entirely consistent with the salvage paradigm in which the Western consumer is positioned as an altruist interloper, helping natives salvage their culture through Western patronage and money. This is particularly evident in the example of luxury ecolodges, as demonstrated through the mission statements and advertising semiotics of the lodges discussed in the next section.

Jungle Lodges as Sites of Virtuous Tourism

En route to the communities, but just before crossing the river to the "Quichua side," visitors of the Ecuadorian lowlands stay in cabins or "jungle lodges" on the "Mestizo" side of the river.[10] These are gateways into the rainforest, built especially to receive tourists. "Jungle lodge" visits serve as precursors to actual community visits, and range from inexpensive to luxurious, with the latter featuring conveniences such as

[8] James Clifford, "Of Other Peoples: Beyond the 'Salvage' Paradigm." *Discussions in Contemporary Culture,* ed. Hal Foster (Seattle: Bay Press, 1987), 21.

[9] Ibid.

[10] One side of the Napo River has officially been designated as indigenous land. Local communities hold titles to the land, which cannot be sold to or bought by non-indigenous parties. The other side of the river is informally called "the Mestizo side," and land there can be purchased by farmers or tourism entrepreneurs.

solar-heated showers, private bathrooms, wild herb massages, medicinal tonics with "native infusions" and other elements reminiscent of upscale spas.[11] The lodges generally feature a "primitivist" aesthetic, and in their advertising emphasize the exotic nature of the location and the ecologic sustainability of the enterprise (i.e. cabins constructed of natural materials and the use of solar energy).

The geographical positioning of rainforest lodges is often described in poetic language that aestheticizes and romanticizes the experience. As Prins writes, "indigenous websites are usually designed to publicly articulate the particular cultural identities of their owners…typically, they feature primitivist images."[12] Rainforest lodge websites are no exception, featuring "primitivist" rhetoric as part of their self-representation and marketing:

> Deep within the Ecuadorian Amazon you will find a mysterious lake called Challuacocha, where floating water hyacinths and grasses obscure the shores. And if you venture out on this lagoon in a dug out canoe early in the morning when it is quiet and the light is still low, you just might see, somewhere out there, lying hidden in the vegetation a rare and wild Manatee or Anaconda. Float here for a while, scanning the horizon and you would probably notice the yellow, banded chest of an Aracari or hear the hoarse whisper of the Hoatzin. Eventually, the day would pass and you could peer out across the shimmering, black water towards the setting sun, and almost certainly see the gleaming orange eyes of the Black Caiman. Come to Challuacocha and feel the mystery. Come to Challuacocha and experience the world of Sani Lodge.[13]

In similar fashion, the Napo Wildlife Center Lodge promotes itself through strategic descriptions designed to emphasize both eco-friendliness and luxury. The traditional nature of the materials and lodge design is mentioned in the same sentence as the promise of privacy and comfort. The assurance of comfort is made possible by electricity (i.e., a ceiling fan,

---

[11] Luxury lodge rates are very expensive by Ecuadorian standards, but quite reasonable for Western tourists. For example, the Napo Wildlife Center Amazon Lodge on the South Bank of the Napo River, a business that describes itself as a "luxury ecolodge," charges $795 for a 5-day stay in a double room. This includes all meals and activities.

[12] Harold Prins, "Visual Media and Primitivist Perplex: Colonial Fantasies, Indigenous Imagination, and Advocacy in North America." *Media Worlds: Anthropology on New Terrain*, eds. Faye Ginsburg, Lila Abu-Lughod and Brian Larkin (Berkeley: University of California Press, 2002), 71.

[13] "Sani Lodge Ecuador Jungle." Last accessed June 2008: www.sanilodge.com

lights, and power outlets) and is mediated by the description of silent solar-powered generators. Potential guests are assured that they can experience both luxury and the virtually-unmediated natural experience of the surrounding rainforest while staying in a private bungalow: "Even from your rooms you may see a group of giant otters investigating near the lodge dock or a large...black caiman crossing the lake or a capybara rummaging around by the waters' edge."[14] Clearly, the emphasis of representations crafted by ecotourism enterprises is on the materials and surroundings that metonymically provide an organic, healthy "alternative" to industrial capitalism—a haven with black caimans and a side of adventure that creates an immediate, visceral world which is specifically marketed to tourists.

Virtually every lodge portrays itself as "unique" or "one of a kind." This characterization is sustained by the desire to attract tourists, and by the need to maintain a cooperative relationship between the lodge and community. Businesses like the Anangucocha Lake Lodge frequently emphasize their location within the ancestral lands of the indigenous Quichua community (their collaboration with Non-Governmental Organizations, or NGOs, only exists to conserve the local forests). While most jungle lodges have established relationships with local indigenous communities, often these relationships are purely contractual and plagued with anxieties about exploitation. True community-based ecotourism is still rare in Ecuador. Consequently, lodges associated with such projects are unique, and thus do not hesitate to present their collaboration with the local community as a distinguishing characteristic. The Anangu Lake Lodge website, for example, emphasizes the fact that the local Quichua "are active participants in the conservation and management of over 52,000 acres within the Yasunì National Park as well as partners in the lodge."[15] "Virtuous" tourism is another element promoted by these websites, especially in cases when the community itself runs the lodge, as is the case with the Sani Lodge. What makes this lodge "truly one of a kind" is its dedication to "ecotourism, environmental conservation, and [the] community." Its literature emphasizes the fact that "profits from the jungle lodge are reinvested into the community, *improving the lives of all who live there* [emphasis mine]."[16]

---

[14] "Napo Wildlife Center Lodge Information." Last accessed June 2008: www.napowildlifecenter.com/open.html

[15] "Staff, Napo Amazon Jungle Eco Lodge." Last accessed June 2008: http://www.andeantrails.co.uk/napo-dos.htm

[16] "Staff, Sani Lodge Ecuador Jungle." Last accessed June 2008: http://www.sanilodge.com

(Micro)managing the Tourist Experience

The real-time lodge experience is typically micromanaged to sustain the experience of authenticity and alterity. Even though food is specially prepared for tourists using purified water, with vegetarian options, visitors are also offered "traditional" meals that imitate the "raw jungle experience": during the course of the visit they are presented with dishes that include snails, grubs, and bread tree fruit. Although monkey meat is not a traditional food staple, straight-faced lodge staff may refer to beef dishes as "mono," or monkey meat, to scare unsuspecting tourists. Lodges also house either a pet monkey or colorful parrot which has been trained to pose for pictures with tourists.

As these examples illustrate, the ecopositive/natural aspects of the lodge are simultaneously presented as "luxuries" *and* as implicit mission statements, enabling the ethos of virtuous tourism, which usually obfuscates the complex layers of relationships between consumers and producers. This effectively eclipses the issues of Western complicity in the processes of globalization and development to which these sustainable survival strategies aim to serve as alternatives. Tourists are made to feel that when patronizing such establishments, they are helping to preserve or revivify indigenous traditions. The consumer appeal that results from this exchange stems from metacolonial fantasies comprised equally of colonial desire, guilt, and reflexivity.

Convinced that they are salvaging cultures in danger of extinction (or at least vulgarization through modernity), Western tourists' sense of loss is mediated, if not resolved, through a capitalist encounter where culture is performed as labor. This assessment is analytical rather than judgmental. As co-reproducers of a capitalist encounter, consumers are alienated from the goods they purchase, and always remain detached from the all-inclusive prepackaged tours with their contrived itineraries. In effect, these tours:

> Constitut[e] a single unified commodity which integrates a number of diverse commodities. In the expanding economy of "services" and leisure, this gives rise to the formula of calculated payment in which "everything's included": spectacular environment, the collective pseudo-displacement of vacations, [and] subscriptions to cultural consumption.[17]

---

[17] Guy Debord, *Society of the Spectacle* (Cambridge, MA: Zone Books, 1995).

As Debord illustrates, such commodities can "circulate only because of the increased poverty of corresponding realities."[18] Yet this facet of the Western desire for alterity is downplayed in the discomfort voiced by tourists whose experiences are "not authentic enough" or "too commercial." These disappointments are all the more ironic because these tourists often lack self-awareness about his/her complicity in the consumer encounter. Despite copious evidence to the contrary (such as the proliferation of the archetypal tourist-in-a-canoe image), tourists seem to fashion a narrative for themselves in which they are the only ones within their community to undertake such a wild adventure (the phenomenon noted by Jedrej and Nuttall, of tourists feeling embarrassed by the presence of other tourists, comes to mind).[19]

Production and Consumption of Alterity

From the first moment that the capitalist transaction is enacted (i.e. tour arrangements are made, the itinerary is set, and money is exchanged), service providers (tour agencies and guides) micromanage the tourist experience to maximize the "exotic." Tour guides are usually liaisons who have relatives in the community. Sometimes they are even involved in the family tourism business (e.g., running a jungle lodge near an Indian community). In order to obtain their tourist guide certification, they attend a four or five-year university tourism program, where they study a wide variety of subjects, including business management, sustainable development, ecology, botany, history and anthropology. Their practical on-the-job skills largely consist of presenting information about everything that transpires during a tour in a way that highlights and emphasizes the exotic factor. Tour guides can also row tourists across the river in traditional canoes, even when a bridge exists only several hundred feet away. Canoe rides always include jokes about the canoe capsizing, and alligators and anacondas lurking in the river, waiting for their tourist "dinner." The guides are adept at taking group photos in the unstable canoe, and getting the tourists to "fan out" in a particular formation so that everyone is included in the picture. The guides row with one hand and take pictures with the other, while also balancing precariously at the tip of the canoe.

---

[18] Ibid.

[19] Charles Jedrej and Mark Nuttall, *White Settlers: The Impact of Rural Repopulation in Scotland* (London: Routledge, 1996).

During the journey, tourists receive background information about the community they are about to visit. This "briefing" usually emphasizes the ways in which tourism helps the community, which not only confers gravitas on the impending visit, but also implicitly frames consumption as a form of humanitarian aid. Naturally absent in this scenario is any interrogation of the tourists' complicity in colonial history, and the subsequent travails of globalization that have affected the communities, either directly or indirectly. Instead, the tourists are constructed as patrons of the conservation movement, with an unambiguous positive value assigned to that position. Guides also discuss their credentials, education, and commitment to ecological sustainability. This commitment is presented as directly arising from concrete contemporary initiatives, ideologically linked to historical notions of "our people" living in harmony with nature. This strategy clearly grounds the experience in an imagined, pre-capitalist, "authentic" fantasy world.

Once the tourists arrive at the communities themselves, they experience another important stage in the production and consumption of alterity: the sale of objects crafted by their indigenous hosts. These objects, both in their creation and destiny, are a testament to a new cultural category that has emerged in the space between tourists and hosts, one in which material artifacts and cultural knowledge intended exclusively for export are presented to tourists through a series of unique exchanges that appear spontaneous and organic.[20] The sale of these objects realizes both the economic dimension of this new cultural category, and the new rituals of production and exchange that accompany tourist visits. As Grant McCracken writes in *Culture and Consumption*, "one of the most important ways in which cultural categories are substantiated is through the material objects of a culture."[21] Material objects that are mass-crafted in anticipation of the next batch of tourists are no exception. Souvenirs that are crafted for tourists in their presence are especially transparent in their embodiment of the cultural conditions of their production.

---

[20] This is a phenomenon frequently found in ethnographic tourism around the globe. One notable example is found in the writings of Kirshenblatt-Gimblett and Bruner: Masai warriors appear to spontaneously cross paths with tourists and perform an equally spontaneous ritualistic dance. Edward Bruner and Barbara Kirshenblatt-Gimblett "Maasai on the Lawn: Tourism Realism in East Africa," *Cultural Anthropology* 9 (1994): 435.

[21] Grant McCracken, *Culture and Consumption: New Approaches to the Symbolic Character of Goods and Activities* (Bloomington: University of Indiana Press, 2005).

Indeed, I would argue that Mary Douglas' observation that material goods make "visible and stable" the categories of culture could be extended to a reproduction of intercultural fantasies, one in which the expectations of the "tourees" are reproduced and fulfilled through an exchange of objects for currency (a ritual and script belonging to the cultural space of capitalism).[22] The ritual is situated in a designated location: the tourists congregate in an area devoted to commerce. Sometimes the products are already displayed when the tourists arrive; at other times, they are brought in by the women. Often, the sale is preceded by a crafts demonstration by a Quichua woman, who makes a clay dish or a jewelry item as the guide explains the process to the tourists in English. Whatever communication he has with the women is in Spanish; often the women remain silent. The women are spoken for, and about, in the discourse between the guides and the tourists, and the only actual interaction they have with the tourists is an explicit physical exchange of products for money. Occasionally, the price is negotiated directly between the tourists and the community women, but usually the guides handle that aspect of the sale. There are variations on this exchange model. Sometimes the sale is preceded by an interactive "community activity" where tourists learn how to make clay dishes and necklaces from seeds and berries. This is more likely to occur on "educational" tours.

In instances where souvenirs are acquired through an educational experience (i.e. the tourists make their own memento, usually a ceramic decoration), the capitalist aspect of the interaction is covert, as no money overtly exchanges hands at the moment of acquisition (usually the cost of the crafts lessons and supplies is included in the tour package, which is never itemized for tourists). The cultural appropriation at work in such scenarios is more apparent, as tourists acquire not only the objects that aesthetically and functionally index indigenous culture and lifestyle, but also the traditional knowledge of how to make such products. Thus, the experience of production itself becomes an object of consumption—something sold, bought, and integrated as a part of an enlarged self. In fact, the process itself is arguably the most desirable part of the event, and the final products become mementos of cultural consumption—a souvenir of the experience of collecting clay by the river, using strands of hair as brushes, and employing native methods to produce an object to commemorate the experience of non-alienated labor. However, this experience can be only achieved by consuming another culture, a culture

[22] Mary Douglas and Baron Isherwood, *The World of Goods: Towards an Anthropology of Consumption* (New York: Routledge, 1996), 51.

which, at least in the tourists' fantasies, reinforces the value of that kind of labor.

Such semiotic exchanges also contextualize the production of culture by the community as a mass-scale enterprise for export, which, one could argue, makes performing culture a form of alienated labor.[23] The community members commodify their cultural knowledge, traditional lifestyles, and personal time when they dispense "the indigenous experience" for export. Thus the traditional elements of culture become "current" again, but as performative props in the supply-and-demand schema of the desirable "ethnographic present." Because both tourists and community members create objects that are not appropriate for use or barter, cultural production-for-export assumes the trajectory of alienated labor.

Performing Alterity (as Commodity)

While the socio-historical space in which indigenous culture is performed and consumed differs based on the nature of the tour group, performativity is present in *all* encounters. The performativity of culture is hardly new, and is not localized to the Amazon basin. Otovalo in the highlands was the first site of marketed culture in the development of Ecuadorian tourism. As Mary Crain describes tourism in the highlands:

> [Haciendas] were converted into "hosterias," country inns, slated for "ethnic and historical tourism." Modern conveniences, such as central heating and indoor plumbing, were installed in old homes and rooms refurbished to receive a foreign clientele. Quito-based travel agencies promoted packaged tours to sites in which guests were provided with a feel for pre-existing colonial relationship, with Indians serving sumptuous feasts in extensive formal gardens.[24]

---

[23] Although I use Marxist terminology in my analysis, I want to divest the terms I use of the orthodox Marxist connotations that associate alienated labor with a lack of agency. I argue that the Quichua communities involved with ecotourism have both agency and intentionality in such projects. I use "alienated labor" because its engages with the Western experience of production and labor, and informs Western fantasies of alterity in which the exchange mode somehow magically avoids engaging with the very forces of global capitalism that brought tourists to their destination(s) in the first place.

[24] Mary Crain, "Negotiating Identities in Quito's Cultural Borderlands: Native Women's Performances for the Ecuadorian Tourist Market." *Cross-Cultural*

Alterity-as-commodity can be manifested along several different axes. In fact, colonialism itself has been discursively, insistently, and explicitly other-ized as a product of our own wayward past. This past is not too distant from us in terms of the passage of time, but its location on the other side of historical paradigmatic rupture renders it virtually mythological. Thus a recreation of a colonial encounter is exotic in and of itself. The verisimilitude and "authenticity" of such hyperreal recreations make them that much more marketable. In a sense, such historical mimesis results in the production of a postcolonial present that is the "fantasy version" of the colonial past. Is, then, tourism a symptom of cultural repetition, a compulsion of postcolonial "today" still enchanted by the fantasies of a colonial "yesterday"? Do Otovaleno women, waiting on tourist tables in colonial costumes, enable fantasies of precapitalist, yet class-based, relationships with the cultural "Other"? Do Quichua children, gifting the tourists with necklaces in exchange for candy, act out the even older colonial trope of the colonizer and the colonized?

In a sense, any journey to a foreign land becomes part of the historically-mediated narrative of the Western Traveler. Such journeys have been ritualized as "quests" that entail the Western subject's search for authenticity, which is inexorably intertwined with the Western trope of "finding oneself." Of course, ethnographically, the self that is found through such encounters is one located in the history of colonialism that, in its current incarnation, makes a capitalist object out of its own mythology. Here, the fantasy offered for purchase and consumption through a retrocolonial encounter is, ultimately, a fantasy of the Western ideology of the past. The non-Western alterity constructed for tourists is designed to fulfill lingering colonial fantasies that reaffirm Western social ideology and the enduring legacy of the white man's burden.

One fundamental aspect of ecotourism in Ecuador is the fact that it has been assimilated to the processes and structures of capitalism, and thus shapes encounters and relationships predicated on capitalist exchange. Simultaneously, tourism is positioned at the intersection of long-standing Western traditions such as leisure travel, consuming foreign cultures and complex cultural myths and narratives of self. Western tourists produce their selves (as adventurers, as virtuous tourists, and as beneficiaries of esoteric experiences) through capitalist exchanges with indigenous communities. This project is enabled by local cultural brokers who

---

Consumption: Global Markets Local Realities, ed. David Howes (New York: Routledge, 1996), 125.

micromanage interactions between tourists and the "toured" to ensure that no disruptive interventions endanger the twinned processes of semiotic production and capitalist exchange.

One of the dominant aspects of tourism today is that it reproduces colonial structures of inequality, both microcosmically through interpersonal interactions framed by the tours' mimesis of "first contact," and macrocosmically by linking "satellites" with the "metropoles" of the global economy. Thus, globetrotting shopaholics, in their reincarnation as tourists, not only consume, but in a sense epitomize the historical processes of consumption as they take place between the West, and the rest.

CHAPTER NINE

BUYING INTO "HOME": EXPATRIATE WOMEN'S LANDSCAPES OF CONSUMPTION IN BUDAPEST

BRIGETTE ELYSE THOMPSON

In order to attempt to understand and critique the processes through which spaces are created and lived, one must consider culture, spatial politics, agency, geography, meaning, and nature, among other factors.[1] From everyday practices and engagements at home, to municipal construction projects that disrupt city rhythms for long periods of time, places are being written and rewritten constantly.[2] With its myriad of possible meanings, interpretations, and revisions, place is both a site for identity negotiation and the resolution of forces that can shape an individual's sense of belonging.[3] One way to create an attachment to place is through social relations and organizations.[4] For female expatriate populations, however, social organizations not only provide a venue to display capital, but also reinforce the existence of a transnational consumer landscape—one that transcends borders and creates identities

---

[1] John A. Agnew and James S. Duncan, eds., *The Power of Place: Bringing Together Geographical and Sociological Imaginations,* (Boston: Unwin Hyman, 1989).
[2] Arjun Appadurai, *Modernity at Large* (London: University of Minnesota Press, 1996).
[3] Dolores Hayden, *The Power of Place: Urban Landscapes as Public History* (Cambridge, MA: MIT Press, 1995), 18; Sarah Ahmed, "Home and Away: Narratives of Migration and Estrangement," *International Journal of Cultural Studies* 2.3 (1999), 341.
[4] Michael Dear and Jennifer Wolch, *The Power of Geography: How Territory Shapes Social Life* (Boston: Unwin Hyman, 1989), 4.

not based on "who you are," but on "what you buy."[5] Thus for expat women, consumption provides a framework for the negotiation of "belonging"—a way to feel at home in another part of the world without the inconvenience of true introspective cultural negotiation.

Using the ethnographic methodologies of participant observation and semi-structured interviewing, this chapter will explore the identity negotiations of expatriate women engaged with gendered social organizations in Budapest in 2007. After arriving in Budapest, expatriate women usually begin the work of carving out a sense of belonging while meeting their needs, and those of their families. From patronizing a particular salon, enrolling any children in an international school, joining an English-speaking yoga class, and learning where to purchase specific food items, expatriate women make strategic consumptive choices. In this transnational cosmopolitan space, consumption-based discourses frame interactions with Budapest, and serve to construct expatriate subjectivities. These subjectivities, in turn, shape the experiences of expat women in the urban milieu of Budapest. As this chapter will elucidate, consumption practices chosen by these transnational, elite women produce and reproduce imaginative, material, and social attachments which, despite spatial barriers involving movement and communication, are integral to expatriate women's perception of identity (meaning), place (belonging), and space (geography).

Social Organizations: Vehicles for Consuming Local Space

I sit around a large round table with seven other women, politely conversing with Claire.[6] From England, she was in her early thirties the first time we met. After graduating from an English university, she married a French banker. In Budapest, Claire stays home with their young children during the day. Each time we speak, she reminds me that she cares for her children and her home herself, without the help of a nanny or housekeeper. We discuss the appealing packages that many companies offer to employees to encourage them work abroad. Claire's husband received a relocation package when he worked in Cameroon, but not when they moved to Hungary. Although she is usually very upbeat, today she bemoans life in Hungary, "I have a Master's in law…the legal system here

[5] Daniel Miller, *Capitalism: An Ethnographic Approach* (Washington DC: Berg, 1997), 6.

[6] All names used in this study are pseudonyms.

is so corrupt, just like the medical system…they're all so corrupt. It's like Cameroon all over." Inquiring about her thoughts on living in Cameroon, I listen as she recounts the fear that paralyzed her family as she, while pregnant, caught malaria and had to be evacuated from the country. Meanwhile, sunlight streams through the large windows as servers whisk away my empty teacup onto a shiny silver tray, scarcely allowing it to touch my saucer after I swallow the last sip of milky black tea. At precisely eleven o'clock in the morning, the chair of IWCA (International Women's Club Association) addresses the hotel meeting room, which is full of members, vendors, and guests.

This monthly meeting of the IWCA is being held in an elegant five-star hotel on the Pest side of the Danube.[7] Around seventy five women, ranging in age from their twenties to eighties, gather to socialize, watch a spring fashion show, and enjoy a table of constantly replenished beverages and pastries. Another facet of the meeting is to encourage the women to browse the information tables promoting various goods and services, including plastic surgery, relocation services, Italian ties and cufflinks, used books, homemade bread loaves, and portioned bags of cookies tied with ribbons. This meeting is also a forum for IWCA to promote its social and charity events, including the selling of tickets for the charity ball that will take place in several days.

Expatriate women in Budapest also have another social organization: the North American Women's Association (NAWA). With about eighty members, compared to IWCA's 230 members, this smaller club is open to North American women as well as the spouses of North American men.[8] Sharon, the chair of NAWA, describes a typical member as one who is "here with a partner, doesn't need to work, is supported by someone else, and is able to meet during the day. We get women at the beginning of their career, the end, and everywhere in between." As Claire and others would often remind me, part-time employment in general is not very common and, if available, often inaccessible to non-Hungarians. For these reasons, expatriate women are often conceptualized as "trailing spouses." Some expatriate women, like Claire, translate the lack of desire, language skills, or necessity to work into a new focus on the home, the traditional center of the reproductive and familial sphere. In addition, many women

[7] The Danube River bisects Budapest into two cities, Buda on the left and Pest on the right.

[8] According to its website, NAWA is a non-profit, volunteer-run, association open to women from North American countries (Canada, Mexico and USA) or to women whose husbands have North American citizenship.
Last accessed July 2008: http://www.nawabudapest.com/index.php?title=1

also become highly involved in what Yeoh and Khoo call the third sphere. This sphere encompasses community involvement and charity work.[9]

NAWA and IWCA thrive in Budapest, partially because they are involved in multiple spheres. In addition to providing community service opportunities and social networks, they also serve to validate common aspects of expatriate women's lifestyles. During our interview at a popular expatriate coffee house in Buda one spring afternoon, Sharon described the purpose of her organization in the community in the following way:

> Mostly we're there to support each other and do charity work. We don't pretend to be just a charity organization, because we have to make it attractive to join, too. Sometimes women have small kids, or no kids. This is the only way to make friends, to meet ladies, and to share common interests. We're proud of our charity work, but we don't mind being a social club.[10]

Sharon's emphasis on marketing, charity work, and the social value of NAWA speaks to the various dynamics of group membership. Within these organizations, expatriate women can meet others, participate in mediated consumption, and access specific resources designed to assist them in constructing a sense of belonging as they actively exert claims of connection within a self-created community.[11]

The dominance of common reference points (the home, husbands, children, and, of course, shopping) serves to remind women of what they

---

[9] Brenda S. A. Yeoh and Luisa-May Khoo, "Home, Work, and Community: Skilled International Migration and Expatriate Women in Singapore," *International Migration* 36.2 (1998), 159.

[10] Sharon and I met at MOM park. Completed in 2001, the slogan of MOM park is "a new lifestyle." According to their website: "MOM Park Shopping Centre has more than 90 shops, cafes and restaurants, a multiplex cinema and an underground parking facility for 1540 vehicles […] MOM Park has introduced a new life style in the heart of Buda; the name is now identical with quality shopping. MOM Park Shopping Centre […] has become one of the most popular shopping malls and meeting-places. The key elements contributing to the unparalleled success story are the high quality tenants, the enduring elegance and aesthetic proportions of the shopping environment, the harmony of the built environment, and, last but not least, the well-chosen marketing and communications." Last accessed July 2008: http://www.mompark.com/shopping-centre.php?ln=en

[11] Fran Tonkiss, "The Ethics of Indifference: Community and Solitude in the City," *International Journal of Cultural Studies* 6.3 (2003); Katie Walsh, "British Expatriate Belongings: Mobile Homes and Transnational Homing," *Home Cultures* 3.2 (2006), 134.

have in common. These clubs often assist women in locating doctors, dentists, schools, hairdressers, and other service providers. Thus they also function as a means of translating the familiar, without the overwhelming anonymity of the urban landscape.[12] The club meetings can also create a sense of being "back home." At one meeting, I overheard two members, both with young babies, introduce themselves to each other for the first time. After exchanging names and past histories, one woman asked the other, "I have to ask you. How on earth do you get formula here?" By sharing a common need (the consumption of baby formula), these women were able to make "nowhere" into the "somewhere." Thus by actively "doing" consumption, these women "circulate, and embody, thresholds of belonging." For them, this is part of overcoming the unfamiliarity of Hungary.[13]

Disparate Consumptive Geographies

Overwhelmingly Anglo and mostly English-speaking, often with a minimal knowledge of Hungarian and how to access a network of English-speaking service providers, members of NAWA and IWCA are, generally, distinguishable from the more permanent local elites in Budapest. However, this subset of expatriate women is part of a transnational elite in their own right. Membership in both social organizations is relatively expensive by Hungarian standards.[14] Goods and services promoted through the organizations are mostly luxury items (often promoted with a "wellness" spin) such as lingerie, high-end salons, and plastic surgery. Most members have free time, money to spend, and are looking for women who share their tastes. With this in mind, service providers often target potential expatriates before they arrive in Hungary through advertising on relocation websites and electronic newsletters. Additionally, it is easy for new expatriates to tap into the existing networks through preview trips to Budapest, visits to international schools, or contact with NAWA or IWCA before relocation.

---

[12] Ahmed, 331.

[13] Anne-Marie Fortier, "Re-Membering Places and the Performance of Belonging(s)," *Theory, Culture & Society* 16.2 (1999), 42; Robert David Sack, *Place, Modernity, and the Consumer's World: A Relational Framework for Geographical Analysis* (Baltimore: Johns Hopkins University Press, 1992), 20.

[14] Current membership rates range from 10,000–15,000 HUF annually ($62–$94 US). Last accessed July 2008: www.iwc.org.hu/index-filer/Joinus.htm; www.nawabudapest.com

Individuals offered jobs abroad are usually offered packages that include a significantly higher salary than in their country of origin, a relocation allowance, moving services, assistance with housing, and educational stipends to fund children's school fees.[15] Some corporations offer preview trips for employees and spouses to highlight the appeal of the expatriate lifestyle, accentuating the benefits of "foreign" living, and familiarizing potential expatriates with comfortable spaces that validate their status as a group of transnational elites. These financial perks of expatriation are usually restricted to those working for large transnational corporations from outside central and eastern Europe, and target workers who are perceived as "giving up" the opportunity to work in a more prestigious location such as London, Tokyo, or Dubai.

Budapest has many well established resources for expatriates, as well as a constant stream of new service providers trying to gain a share of the market. Accordingly, educational, recreational, and social events tend to be gathered in the parts of the city that appeal to expatriate women. The landscape of expatriate consumption in Budapest reflects the geographical asymmetry and self-isolation that often characterize urban elite spaces: services and goods catering to expatriate desires are clustered in high rent, luxurious parts of town that are often inaccessible by public transportation.[16] Popular expat neighborhoods (the II and XII Districts) are primarily on the Buda side, and provide access to international schools, parks, and a wide range of services. Of eleven international schools (not including international kindergartens), all of them are located in Buda, with a total of seven located in the XII and II Districts.[17] The North American Women's Association meets in Buda's District II once a month, and various social evenings, book clubs, and dinners are also held this side of town. MOM Park (a large, newly built mall with several cafes) is located in District XII, while Mammut Shopping Center is in District II.[18]

---

[15] International school fees present a significant expense for many expatriate families. The annual fee for grades 11–12 in the American International School of Budapest is $18,840: http://www.aisb.hu/DOCS/2/admin_schoolfee.html
Fees at the British International School of Budapest range from $16,442 to $22,046: http://www.bisb.hu/index.php?page=60&l=1 Last accessed July 2008.

[16] Manuel Castells, *The Castells Reader on Cities and Social Theory,* ed. Ida Susser (Malden, MA: Blackwell, 2002).

[17] Krisztina Palhegyi, "Hungary Culture and Relocation Resources." Last accessed July 2008: http://www.filolog.com/crossscultureRelocation.html

[18] Mammut's two buildings opened in 1998 and 2001, respectively. According to their website: "The shopping centre has become the perfect location for shopping, entertainment and for taking care of daily errands, and it's all in under one roof. Today, the Mammut name symbolises quality. It represents a community space

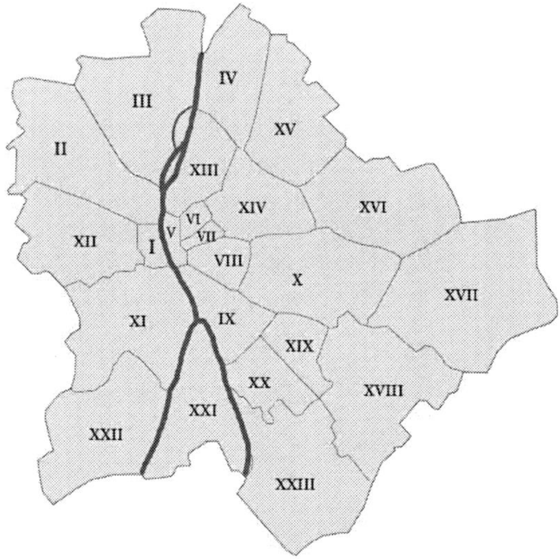

Figure 9.1: Map of Budapest's Districts [19]

According to Manuel Castells, elites produce an exclusive urban culture by self-segregating and retreating into privileged, spatially-fragmented spaces.[20] In the case of Budapest, much of Buda itself (particularly Districts II and XII) can be considered spatially- fragmented from the downtown area, and the suburbs that characterize Pest. Dotted with embassies, grand homes with sprawling yards, and upscale shopping and dining options, Districts II and XII serve as the home base for most of the women involved in the IWCA and NAWA.

Castells also suggests that access to such secluded locations reminds expats of their membership in an elite global, cosmopolitan lifestyle.

where the balance between shopping and entertainment, and between work and play is realised; and where families, friends and business partners can come together to share new experiences." Last accessed July 2008: http://www.mammut.hu/main.php?pg=altalanos_bemutatkozas

[19] This file is licensed under Creative Commons Attribution 2.5 by its creator, Wikipedia user Devil_m25. Last accessed July 2008. Copy of license available at: http://creativecommons.org/licenses/by/3.0/us/ Original image location: http://commons.wikimedia.org/wiki/Image:Hungary_budapest_districts_.jpg

[20] Castells (2002).

These sleek, urban, generic spaces insulate them against the multifaceted reality of city life, provide a sense of home, and shape a collective identity. At the cocktail and dinner event for International Women's day that I attended (Figure 9.2), a few vendors were present, selling makeup and Hungarian folk arts. However, both tables were largely ignored in favor of an international buffet, a seemingly endless rainbow of cocktails, cigarettes on the balcony, karaoke (in English), and raffle prizes. In some ways, a hint of escapism seemed to fuel this event in which women joined together socially to celebrate in a generic space, all the while identifying as "expatriate women" who happen to be in Budapest at this time. In this liminal space—tasting foods from many different cultures, speaking English indiscriminately, smoking Marlboro Reds, and singing 1980's American pop songs off-key at loud volumes—it was easy to forget I was in Hungary at all.

Figure 9.2: Sleek, Urban Space Chosen for IWCA Dinner Party [21]
Photograph property of author. Used with permission.

[21] This particular space was on the top floor of a four-star hotel located along a major shopping corridor in Pest, District VI. Admission to this women-only event was 5000 HUF (around $35 US). Tickets were pre-sold at NAWA and IWCA events and at the hotel itself, where I purchased mine. Publicity was solely through expatriate networks, and the dominant language of the event was English.

Shifting Relevancies of Buda and Pest

Clearly, the sociospheres of expatriate women do not develop in a vacuum; they are constantly informed by the dominant discourses about how to be an expatriate in Budapest.[22] Micro-networks of communication among expatriates, both formalized through organizational discourse and informally conveyed through websites and word-of-mouth, work to project discourses of consumption onto the urban landscape in precise ways. Through participation in these social networks, women are constantly reminded that service providers care about expatriate needs and wants, that they have choices of where and what to consume, and most importantly, that certain service providers are their *best* choices. By locating themselves within, or nearby, a popular multi-purpose shopping and recreation center (such as MOM or Mammut) and/or by advertising at IWCA or NAWA meetings and through English language media, service providers take steps to remind expatriate women that they are there to ease the transition into life in Budapest.

Figure 9.3: Interior, Mammut Shopping Center
Photograph property of author. Used with permission.

[22] The concept of the "sociosphere" comes from Ulf Hannerz, *Transnational Connections: Culture, People, Places* (New York: Routledge, 1996).

Websites also help create and promote binary distinctions about transnational elite space in Budapest. One online source directed to expatriates, the "Hungary Culture and Relocation Resources" website, tells readers to avoid "not so great" areas. On this website, District XIII is characterized as "a bit seedier, more working class." District VII is painted as "crowded, dark, and polluted; some side streets can even be dangerous." Their description of District VIII conjures up visions of "overweight women wearing spandex and thigh-high boots asking you if you'd like to have a good time." Alternatively, popular expatriate districts are praised. The website claims that by living in Obuda, in District III, one can "be somebody."[23] Moreover,

> Families love District 2, as many houses are private and even have yards and parks around. There is a definite minimum of riff-raff and low-life bard [sic] here. District 2 is home to Rózsadomb (means Rose Hill), with many gorgeous, high-rent places; not just trendy, but prestigious. District 12 is, therefore, a pretty nice and expensive neighborhood. With one hill after another, you've got winding roads, large houses and beautiful hiking trails. Clean air, a couple of bus lines—what more could you ask for?[24]

This is just one example of how such effusive, strongly-worded discourse of binary distinctions (bright/dark, dirty/clean, nobody/somebody) characterizes elite geographies. The prestige of these large, well-located houses is meant to motivate the expatriate even in the planning stages of relocation, compelling them to embrace this sense of "enforced luxury" as soon as they step onto Hungarian soil.

Usually with exemplary access to all parts of the city (including financial resources, ownership of a car, and possession of leisure time), expat women's tastes influence urban economics, not to mention urban tastes, smells, and appearances. When arranging interviews, one informant cheerfully invited me to her house in District XII, only to email me later saying that she was not aware of the fact that I did not have a car. She suggested meeting at either MOM Park or Budagyongye Shopping Center. Several women expressed surprise that I had never before been to MOM Park. As a female, twenty-two year old single student with no children who was living in Budapest for a year, I had clearly personalized my urban landscape in ways that did not necessarily overlap with their own.

---

[23] Hungary Culture and Relocation Resources. Last accessed September, 2008: http://www.filolog.com/crossscultureRelocation.html

[24] Ibid.

According to the women with whom I spoke, consumptive practices influenced how they perceive "home." Meeting for coffee at a café at MOM Park, for example, was a popular way for expatriate women to experience Budapest. The servers at the café speak English. There are no homeless people outside asking for money. The space is largely child-friendly, clean, and well-lit. It is sleek and modern, and, by all means, a comfortable place in which to experience Budapest. A visit to such a café helps transform the once unfamiliar local "public context" into a relevant and meaningful "private context," a safe, home-like place in which meanings are jointly created and shared.[25]

"We don't feel it's our job to filter out who you should support, just to disseminate information…and maybe offer a recommendation," the chair of NAWA explained to me over an afternoon coffee at a MOM Park café. However, despite the chair's explanation, these clubs clearly communicate aesthetic endorsements that, in turn, mediate (and facilitate) members' consumption practices. Sharon Zukin suggests that these practices make the organization a "didactic prism" through which cultural values are communicated and appreciated.[26] Club suggestions, when adopted, take some of the personal negotiations out of relating to local space and promote a stylish brand of "good" expatriate cosmopolitanism. During my fieldwork, the IWCA and NAWA promoted the following consumer practices, among others: Thai massage, villa rentals in Croatia, and regional Hungarian wine tastings designed specifically for expatriate audiences. These particular examples highlight the strong class distinctions present at many expatriate functions: they advocate the consumption of packaged cosmopolitanism, or what is often thought of as simply *living well*.

In evaluating such potentially disorienting cosmopolitan options, expatriate women may think of themselves as "both in place and in no place." The postmodern nature of these experiences can be overwhelming. The binaries of global/local, near/far, and home/away all converge in activities promoted by the IWCA and NAWA. However, because we all seek to understand ourselves through our own experiences, expatriate women, like everyone else, are also "reflexive agents" who cannot exist outside of space.[27] Thus these directed consumptive practices create a sense of belonging, or "being-at-home," both within expatriate circles, and in Budapest itself.

---

[25] Sack, 20.
[26] Sharon Zukin, *Landscapes of Power: From Detroit to Disney World* (Berkeley: University of California Press, 1991), 202.
[27] Sack, 84.

Resistance and Critique

For women involved in such social expatriate organizations, disapproval of consumer recommendations is not only an assertion of one's confidence in her own cosmopolitan self, but, in some circles, outright mutiny. Karin, a Swiss woman, was one such "traitor." She shared some of her personal consumption strategies with me as we sat over cappuccino in the lobby of the five-star hotel her husband manages:

> I don't want to go where the expats go, not at all. I prefer a mix of locals, it's not a price issue, it's just that I like to figure things out for myself. I have my own dentist who is special to our family. I don't want to tell everyone about her; I try to keep it low profile. If I recommend her to you maybe she doesn't have space for you. Maybe she doesn't have space for us anymore, or she gets arrogant… I don't want this to happen.

By assuring me (in a class-conscious way) that she could afford Western-style health services, Karin voices her elite cosmopolitan identity as a *somebody* inherently distancing herself from those whom she would consider *nobodies*. She clearly articulates that she has a choice of service providers, and considers her ability to make independent choices through her own tools (e.g., her husband's hotel, which provides her with local information) as an important step towards creating a home in Budapest. However, within minutes of stressing her preference for patronizing local merchants, Karin characterized popular local institutions as dirty, old fashioned, and overrated:

> Karin: I like tennis, jogging, swimming…and other nice things too, like beauty salons.
>
> Brigette: Does Budapest offer what you need in this regard?
>
> Karin: Budapest has nothing to offer. There's all this talk about Gellert, the mineral spas, etc., but I don't want to take my shoes off there. I mean, if you go to a hairdresser here it's like a time warp, back 50 years. Interesting, yeah, but…..

Although these two sentiments seem contradictory, in reality they reveal Karin's ability to blend her cosmopolitan mindset and with the desire to experience something local. Unlike many other expat women, she is comfortable navigating in and out of popular expatriate space in order to create "her own" Budapest—a sense of belonging and home that is independent of fashion, trends, and club dictates.

During our conversation at a café at MOM Park, Anna, originally from New York, explains "when we were driving around with the real estate agent looking at houses, we passed MOM Park. 'You'll probably do your shopping here at the Match [a grocery store],' he said, but I don't. After we moved in, I found a Kaiser [another grocery store]...which I like much better." The agent's attempts to acclimate Anna to her future neighborhood reveal one way in which expatriate spaces of consumption are imagined by those outside elite expat circles. Like Karin, Anna discussed her departure from expatriate consumption very early in our conversation, suggesting that her agency is much more important than the recommendations of strangers. Admittedly, Anna's cosmopolitan orientation (as a former New Yorker) further provided a base upon which she built her personal identity as an expatriate woman in Budapest.

As illustrated by this chapter, expat women in Budapest not only position themselves in relation to dominant discourses concerning expatriation, but also connect with a transnational consumerist culture that, despite attempts at resistance, ultimately shapes identity (meaning), place (belonging), and space (geography). The choice of what to buy, and where to buy it, is thus a telling strategy that expat women use to create a gendered sense of "home" in a foreign country. Taken together, these seemingly juxtaposed forces help carve out both individual and group landscapes of consumption among elite expatriate women in Budapest.

CHAPTER TEN

THE FILIPINO MALL EXPERIENCE: HOW MODERN MALLS TRANSFORMED A LOCAL SHOPPING CULTURE

AMPARO PAMELA H. FABE

Over the past twenty years, the Filipino shopping experience has been changed dramatically by the Shoemart (SM) Group's "malling phenomenon." The first SM Mall, SM City North EDSA, was opened in 1986. Although it was not the first mall in the Philippines, it became a leader in terms of foot traffic and revenues. Undaunted by an economic crisis caused by high fuel prices and political problems, on May 20, 2006, Shoemart opened "The Mall of Asia." Despite criticism from economists, The Mall Of Asia has prospered, becoming a tourist destination that not only showcases Filipino products, but also its modern prowess: the first "Olympic size" Ice Skating Rink; the first IMAX Theatre in the Philippines, which holds the distinction of having one of the largest movie screens in the world (eight stories high); the first mall overlooking the famous Manila Bay sunset; and the first mall equipped with golf carts, jeeps, and trolleys to help customers navigate its retail geography.

This chapter will discuss the malling phenomenon in the Philippines and how it has transformed the consumption culture of a nation. Prior to the establishment of SM Malls nationwide, Filipinos had to travel to a multitude of locations to buy goods and services. Trips to three different shopping districts to buy groceries, clothes and shoes were not uncommon. A simple series of shopping transactions could take several days as one had to visit a number of small, distant shops. Malls now allow Filipino consumers to engage in all types of transactions in one location, and have transformed shopping into a quick affair with far less physical effort. Malls have also provided Filipinos with a new recreational geography, encouraged the consumption of "new" technological products such as PDAs and computers, and have made previously-inaccessible leisure facilities, such as gyms and bowling allies, part of mainstream, middle-class life.

The Sociology of Filipino Consumption

Filipinos perceive consumption as an activity with a symbolic value. As Baudrillard has conveyed, attaching symbolic value to consumption is not a passive activity, but an active system of sign-value production.[1] In this system, choices, self-image, and desire imbue products, and the activity of consumption, with meaning. In the Philippines, for example, the meaning of goods and symbols (which collectively drive consumption) are constituted using both local and global ideologies. Filipinos consume for four main reasons. The first is, of course, necessity. The second is the belief that purchases fulfill some sort of familial duty. In other words, consumption (i.e., the purchase of gifts) can facilitate the expression of love towards one's family members, friends, relatives and colleagues. Filipinos also shop as a way of assessing consumer prices and product variety (i.e., "window shopping"). Most Filipinos purchase goods (especially costly electronic ones) only after having comparison shopped and consulted with "experts." The fourth and final reason why Filipinos shop is out of compulsion. Like many global shopaholics, compulsively-consuming Filipinos usually realize that the acquired object, product, or service loses its glitter once it has been purchased. The malling phenomenon, which has increased accessibility to new products, has undoubtedly exacerbated this condition, especially among middle and upper-class individuals with disposable income.[2]

As Kaj Ilmonen, the late Finnish sociologist explains,

> Although commodities are non-human actors, they shape our social life. They mediate everyday activities…and they bond us to other people. They capacitate our actions, and it is often hard to tell the limit between the object and the action using that object. Commodities and human action form a network where humans act and objects react. Meanings associated

---

[1] Jean Baudrillard, "The Implosion of Meaning in the Media," in *In the Shadow of the Silent Majorities or, The End of the Social and Other Essays* (New York: Semiotext(e), 1983), 95–110; Jean Baudrillard, "Rituals of Transparency." *The Ecstasy of Communication* (New York: Semiotext(e), 1988), 29–44.

[2] Grant McCracken, *Culture and Consumption: New Approaches to the Symbolic Character of Consumer Goods and Activities* (Bloomington, IN: Indiana University Press, 1988); Elaine Scarry, *Resisting Representation* (New York: Oxford University Press, 1994).

with objects turn them from raw material of action into social relationships.[3]

Consumption is increasingly shaping the identity of urban Filipinos in their teens and twenties, and, as Ilmonen predicts, is also impacting their social relationships. Filipino university students spend an average of thirty percent of their monthly allowance or income on high-tech products such as computers, personal digital aids (PDA), cellular phones and compact disk players, most of which are purchased at malls. About ninety percent of the students surveyed at the University of the Philippines have personal computers; five percent own PDAs; ninety percent have compact disk (CD) and/or MP3 players; and nearly twelve percent own portable CD players.[4] By providing young Filipinos with access to technological objects over which they can obsess, compete, and converse, malls are increasingly serving as the foundation of a new, modern network of social relations—one which, for the first time, is emphasizing consumption as the basis of self-worth and identity.

In the Philippines, designer brands play a particularly important role in the consumption of commodities because they not only convey one's identity to the outside world, but also help bridge the gap between the local and the global. Young Filipinos tend to be more loyal to foreign brands, routinely preferring Nokia cellular phones, Nike sportswear, Speedo swimwear, and Tag Heuer watches to domestic products. Moreover, the socialization of consumption in peer groups has compelled many young Filipino consumers to demand attractive packaging and product recognizability. The media is undoubtedly playing a major role in this new consumer-based youth identity: more than eighty eight percent of survey respondents believe that they are influenced by advertising, while only two percent maintain that advertisements are "a waste of time."[5]

Shopping in Manila before the SM Mall Invasion

Before the advent of SM shopping malls, Filipinos living in the capital city of Manila had to travel to five different venues in order to seek entertainment and purchase needs and wants: Quiapo, Rustan's Department Store, Araneta Center, Greenhills Shopping Center and

[3] Kaj Ilmonen (1944–2007) unfinished manuscript; European Sociology Association. Last accessed August 2008: www.europeansociology.org

[4] Amparo Pamela Fabe, "Shopping Preferences of Filipino University Students: An Examination." Seminar Paper, University of the Philippines, 2008, 4.

[5] Ibid., 2.

Malate. Quiapo, a central business district selling wholesale and retail products, located near Chinatown (Binondo District) and the Port of Manila, was a popular destination for fashion accessories, cameras, and jewelry. For luxury goods, shoppers sought Rustan's Department Store in Makati. One of the first department stores in the Philippines, Rustan's continues to provide foreign products to local consumers with disposable income. According to Anthony Huang, Executive Vice President of Store Specialists, Inc., and Rustan's Marketing Corporation, Rustan's prides itself on giving the Filipino consumer "choice." Rustan's negotiates with foreign vendors so they can offer the local and expatriate community the latest global products. Filipinos who shop at Rustan's are "pleasantly surprised at how the Philippine market is in fact more sophisticated then they anticipated…[Rustan's wants to] bring the best to the world, to the local consumer...[Our] goal is to make customers feel that they are entering a store here in the Philippines that is no different from entering the same store anywhere else in the world."[6]

Consumers flocked to Araneta Center in the Cubao area to have their shoes and watches repaired and to buy books and school supplies. According to the Center's website,

> The Araneta Center offers a one-stop shopping, dining and entertainment experience. The Araneta Center also houses the Ali Mall, the first multi-level commercial mall in the country, the New Frontier Cinema, which is the largest theater in the country with over thirty-five hundred seats, and the Fiesta Carnival, which was the Philippines' first all-year indoor amusement center.[7]

The Araneta Coliseum, which is part of the complex, has, over the past few decades, also served as a venue for the consumption of entertainment: it has hosted international basketball tournaments such as the World Basketball Championships, the Southeast Asian Games Basketball Championships, and the Asian Youth Basketball Championships. Some of its other memorable events include the "Thrilla in Manila" which was the 1975 Ali-Frazier World Heavyweight Championship Fight, the Philippine Basketball Association Games, and annually, the Bb. Pilipinas Beauty Pageant.[8]

---

[6] Interview with Anthony T. Huang, February 26, 2007. *World Investment News.* Last accessed July 2008: http://www.winne.com/dninterview.php?intervid=2011

[7] Rent the Big Dome—Araneta Coliseum. Last accessed July 2008: http://www.aranetacoliseum.com/2006/corporate.php

[8] Ibid.

Before the SM invasion, Filipinos also frequented the Greenhills Shopping Center at the Ortigas Commercial Center with the hope of finding a wide range of goods at affordable prices. With its "1,400 mini-stores and more than 2,000 merchants, the sixteen hectare Greenhills Shopping Center, located in San Juan, Metro Manila, has always been a favorite destination for bargain-hunting shoppers looking for an assortment of retail items." Despite the prevalence of malls, Greenhills offered, and continues to offer, consumers a diversity of choices: "With its shops and *tiangge* (bazaar) stalls offering jewelry, food, textiles, computers and cellular phones, the Greenhills Shopping Center brings in the whole market spectrum with its variety of product choices... Approximately 80,000 people troop to Greenhills daily during weekdays and 90,000 on weekends, with the numbers reaching 130,000 during the Christmas season."[9] For their entertainment needs, Filipinos frequented Malate, located in the heart of Manila. Famous for its variety of restaurants and jazz bars, Malate was, in addition to the few amusement parks in the area, one of the only venues that provided live entertainment. Today it is a favorite hangout of young professionals, many of whom reject the conformism of mall culture.

The Advent of the SM Malls

Consumer behavior in Manila changed permanently with the advent of the SM Malls. Henry Sy, the founder of SM Mall chain, opened his first mall in 1983: SM City North EDSA. Despite a political crisis, interest rates as high as forty five percent, and the fact that the mall was in the middle of nowhere, it was an instant success. It generated huge revenues, which allowed Sy to expand to thirty malls nationwide.[10]

The SM Malls have revolutionized Filipino consumption by making all sorts of merchandise available in one large air conditioned venue. Consumers can now shop as a family since the supermarket, department store, and entertainment center are all located in a single place. Instead of spending the whole day traveling from shop to shop, Filipinos can complete their consumption in a few hours, thereby increasing their leisure time, which, incidentally, can also be spent at the mall. Unlike local markets, SM Malls accept credit cards, bank cards and other special point-

---

[9] Alub D. Vitug, "Revitalizing the Greenhills Shopping Center." *Business World*, March 3, 2003. Last accessed July 2008:
http://www.bworldonline.com/OnlineExclusives/property/inside.php?id=009

[10] Wilson Lee Flores, "Why Henry Sy Believes that the Philippines is not Hopeless," *The Philippine Star*, June 5, 2006.

of-sale cards, all of which facilitate the shopping needs of consumers (as well as the accumulation of debt, which is a new phenomenon in developing nations such as the Philippines). The notion of "spending money at the mall" is reinforced by the numerous banks and financial institutions that are housed in SM complexes. The malls routinely rent space to insurance companies and foreign exchange bureaus which attract local shoppers as well as expat clientele who are unfamiliar with the area, or uncomfortable negotiating the streets of Manila.

The SM Malls also protect Filipinos from the incivility of the streets by providing a secure shopping environment protected by uniformed and civilian security guards. Theft, personal assault, and robbery (which were, in the past, occasional possibilities while shopping in Manila) have almost been completely eliminated. The malls provide ample, safe parking, which reduces the hassle involved with shopping in the city. More importantly, the malls serve as a gathering place for the observance of historical and cultural events such as plays, classical concerts and musical programs. Recently, 20,149 SM employees, affiliates, tenants and agencies (representing all thirty SM malls nationwide), simultaneously waved the national flag as a way to celebrate Philippine Independence Day. Clearly, SM malls have functioned, and continue to function, as venues for the expression of patriotism, national pride and consumption.

Understandably, tourists have also been attracted to Filipino malls. The Mall of Asia with its has 700 shops, restaurants, entertainment venues and numerous amenities (the first Mall overlooking the famous Manila Bay sunset and the first mall equipped with golf cars, jeeps, trams and trolleys to help customers navigate the space) is the largest SM Mall. "Inspired by Manila Bay, the mall evokes the ocean's fluid forms through its ellipses and curving spaces in a predominantly white palette with highlights in aquamarine and blue. It boasts 4.2 million square feet of retail space, and was built at a cost of $130 million, or roughly PhP 6.5 billion…The Entertainment Mall [houses] the Philippines' first IMAX Theater; a Director's Screening Room with thirty La-Z-Boy chairs; seven more movie theaters; an Olympic-size ice-skating rink; and a future science museum/aquarium."[11] Moreover, with its wide variety of foreign shops, the Mall of Asia is at the forefront of "bringing the global home"—defining the "must have" items of the Filipinos youth culture, and dictating how "sophisticated" post-moderns keep themselves fit (through gyms) and

[11] Mall of Asia. Last accessed July 2008:
http://www.smprime.com.ph/Supermalls.php?MallsID=14

entertained (through movies, bowling allies, music halls and planetariums).

While the Mall of Asia and the other SM malls have not driven local Manila shops and merchants out of business yet, it is very possible that as the malling phenomenon grows in the Philippines, the country will begin to suffer from many of the same socio-cultural ailments that have plagued the West: conformity, a loss of identity, a meaningless obsession with designer brands, domination by a self-obsessed youth culture, and an overwhelming urge to consume even when there is nothing left to consume. The SM Malls are already cashing in on the ailment: they have begun to encourage customer loyalty through a rewards card which allows shoppers the opportunity to earn and redeem points at SM supermarkets and all of their partner stores. Thus, while the all-pervading presence of the SM Malls has simplified consumption practices in the Philippines, and has transformed the shopping experience from an individual into a collective activity, the jury is still out on whether or not Filipinos will control their consumption habits, or if they will allow shopping to control them.

CHAPTER ELEVEN

PASSING TIME AT WEST EDMONTON MALL

PETER CLANDFIELD

Shopping malls privatize public space, perpetuate suburban sprawl, provoke unsustainable forms of consumption, and promote the displacement of authentic things by simulacra.[1] Yet, to see malls exclusively in terms of these prominent features and effects is to risk buying into the same kind of superficial perception that malls themselves promote. English cultural theorist Joe Moran critiques these "hyperbolic emphases of postmodern theory," along with the "tendency to focus on the cutting-edge contemporaneity of flagship architecture [and] high-end consumerism." Instead, Moran advocates paying closer attention to "the mundane, repetitive spaces in which we live our daily lives."[2] As Australian theorist Meaghan Morris conveys, shopping malls are the ultimate mundane spaces of our quotidian world:

> A shopping center is a "place" combining an extreme project of general "planning" competence (efforts at total unification, total management) with an intense degree of aberrance and diversity in local performance. It is also a "place" consecrated to timelessness and stasis (no clocks, perfect weather…) yet lived and celebrated, lived and loathed, in intimately historic terms: for some, as ruptural event (catastrophic or Edenic) in the social experience of a community, for others, as the enduring scene (as the cinema once was, and the home still may be) of all the changes, fluctuations, and repetitions of the passing of everyday life.[3]

---

[1] For a trenchant if hyperbolic prosecution of such charges, see English psychogeographer Iain Sinclair's description of the Bluewater Mall in Essex, in *London Orbital: A Walk around the M25* (London: Granta, 2002), 467–473.

[2] Joe Moran, *Reading the Everyday* (London: Routledge, 2005), 128.

[3] Meaghan Morris, "Things to Do with Shopping Centers." *The Cultural Studies Reader*, ed. Simon During (London: Routledge, 1993), 306.

Though recently surpassed in retail area by at least two malls in China and the Mall of Asia in the Philippines, West Edmonton Mall (WEM) still bills itself as "the world's largest entertainment and shopping center."[4] Between 1986 and 1989, it was the central mundane space of my quotidian world, when I worked for what was then known as "Fantasyland Parks and Attractions," the administrative division responsible for the entertainment-oriented features that inflated both the mall's size and its claims to uniqueness. While WEM was undoubtedly meant to be a dazzlingly efficient, consumer machine, in actuality, it has been a vast, untidy microcity whose perpetually unfinished, liminal condition leaves it open to multiple readings and diverse uses, most notably by mall employees. WEM serves partly as a monument to the conformism that malls breed, yet its specific history also suggests how the place of malls in the consumer landscape has changed over the past thirty years.

Phases and Passages

WEM grew in three main Phases. Phase I was launched in September 1981 as a large but relatively orthodox two-story retail complex. Phase II opened in August 1983, and greatly expanded the retail space by adding an NHL-size skating rink and an indoor amusement park, known as "Fantasyland." Phase III, completed in stages between September 1985 and October 1986, further extended both the mall's retail capacity and, even more dramatically, its emphasis on "Attractions," most prominent among which were the vast indoor "World Waterpark" and an expanded Fantasyland, complete with the world's largest indoor rollercoaster, The Mindbender, whose fourteen-story enclosed structure can be seen across the city. Fantasyland Hotel opened in October 1986 featuring various themed rooms, including Polynesian, African, Roman, Arabian, and Hollywood suites. Other notable features of Phase III included Deep Sea Adventure, an artificial lake with real submarines; Bourbon Street, a corridor of restaurants modeled loosely on the New Orleans nightlife district; Pebble Beach Golf, a mini-golf course; and extensive displays of

[4] See "About" at *westedmall.com*. Last accessed July 2008: www.westedmall.com/about/default.asp On the "Great Malls of China," see David Barbosa, "New Land of Shoppers: China Builds Malls on Gigantic Scale," *New York Times*, May 25, 2005. Last accessed July 2008: http://theseoultimes.com/ST/?url=/ST/db/read.php?idx=1962 Also see *Shopping Mall and Shopping Center Studies*, Eastern Connecticut State University. Last accessed July 2008: http://www.easternct.edu/depts/amerst/Malls.htm

captive wildlife, including an aquarium, an oversized saltwater fish tank occupied by four performing dolphins, and, in 1986–1987, half-grown big cats, including lions, tigers, and jaguars.[5] Even more ostentatious than the mall itself were the promotional claims of its developers, Triple Five Corporation. As Triple Five spokesman and co-owner Nader Ghermezian stated in 1985: "This project comprises every major tourist attraction in the world. It is the largest, most comprehensive tourist attraction ever built in the *universe*. Now people in this area never need go to New York or Paris or Miami…we have put it all under one roof. So now you don't even have to worry if it's raining."[6]

Coming into being when and where it did, the WEM project was undoubtedly audacious: Edmonton was not short of indoor retail or entertainment space in the early 1980s, and was experiencing a downturn in the economic prosperity that the postwar discovery of oil had brought to the region. It was through entrepreneurial vision and aggression that the Ghermezian family was able to develop something so vast from what city planners had originally envisioned as an ordinary, regional, suburban shopping center.[7] Yet, like much else about the mall, its developers' promotional rhetoric itself recycles material from other times and places. Nader Ghermezian's description of WEM uncannily echoes a passage from an 1852 *Illustrated Guide to Paris* that Walter Benjamin quotes in his *Arcades Project*: "Lining both sides of these corridors, which get their light from above, are the most elegant shops, so that the arcade is a city, a world in miniature…in which customers will find everything they need."[8]

The most prestigious—or prestige-seeking—retail zone of WEM's third phase is a second-story wing called "Europa Boulevard," which houses high-end clothing stores and bears a definite, if non-specific, visual

---

[5] The dolphins, all now deceased, may have been WEM's worst-treated employees, and the fact that they were named after members of the Triple Five Corporation office staff was more sinister than charming.

[6] Quoted in Rob Shields, "Social Spatialization and the Built Environment: The West Edmonton Mall," *Environment and Planning D: Society and Space* 7 (1989): 150.

[7] On the Ghermezians' entrepreneurship, see Kenneth J. Fairbairn, "West Edmonton Mall: Entrepreneurial Innovation and Consumer Response," *The Canadian Geographer* 35.3 (1991): 261–268. On their negotiations with planners and politicians, see P. J. Smith, "Coping with Mega-Mall Development: An Urban Planning Perspective on West Edmonton Mall," *The Canadian Geographer* 35.3 (1991): 295–305; and Barry Maitland, *The New Architecture of the Retail Mall* (London: Architecture Design and Technology Press, 1990), 232.

[8] Walter Benjamin, *The Arcades Project*, trans. Howard Eiland and Kevin McLaughlin (Cambridge, MA: Harvard University Press, 1999), 31.

resemblance to the arcades of nineteenth-century Paris. Europa Boulevard is WEM's most obvious attempt at recreating the mall as historical simulacrum. Canadian geographer R. W. Butler comments on WEM's marketing of "the image of 'elsewhereness,'" and suggests that "To a tourist…the whole mall is Fantasyland."[9] Another Canadian geographer, Rob Shields, argues that WEM's reproduction of world-renowned tourist attractions "represents an allegorical rejection of the geographic world of distant centers in which Edmonton is on the periphery."[10] Yet, part of the project of making WEM into a world in miniature entailed transforming it into a tourist destination for world citizens.

In *The Arcades Project*, Benjamin identifies nineteenth-century world exhibitions as key sites in the development of consumerism: "Within these *divertissements*, to which the individual abandons himself in the framework of the entertainment industry, he remains always an element of a compact mass. This mass delights in amusement parks—with their roller coasters, their 'twisters,' their 'caterpillars'—in an attitude that is pure reaction. It is thus led to that state of subjection which propaganda, industrial as well as political, relies on."[11] This passage points to WEM's combination of shopping and mass entertainment as mutually reinforcing spectacles. By 1986 WEM had three multiplex cinemas with nineteen screens in total, all showing mainstream Hollywood movies, many of which featured product-placements for the same goods abundantly available in the surrounding mall. Postmodern media theorist Anne Friedberg argues that "both the multiplex cinema and the shopping mall…sell the pleasures of imaginary mobility as psychic transformation" and that "the shopping mall propagates a form of subjectivity that is directly analogous to the subjectivity produced by cinematic spectatorship."[12]

However, the idea of a mass of people in a "state of subjection" to displays of consumer goods needs qualifying. According to Benjamin, "with the destabilizing of the market economy, we begin to recognize the monuments of the bourgeoisie as ruins even before they have crumbled."[13] The fact that the market economy has not actually collapsed in the seventy-plus years since Benjamin wrote this statement suggests that the destabilizing and crumbling of capitalism (which drives the built retail

---

[9] R. W. Butler, "West Edmonton Mall as a Tourist Attraction," *The Canadian Geographer* 35.3 (1991): 291.

[10] Shields, 153.

[11] Benjamin, 18.

[12] Anne Friedberg, *Window Shopping: Cinema and the Postmodern* (Berkeley: University of California Press, 1993), xi, 120.

[13] Benjamin, 13.

setting) is more like a semi-permanent condition than a finite process. One of WEM's academic explorers, literary scholar and game theorist Robert R. Wilson, has suggested that such a "sense of 'eternal nowness'...is further heightened...by the almost-overpowering impression the mall gives of an artificial paradise, a pleasure dome in which time has not merely stopped but has never begun." However, Wilson also notes that "WEM changes all the time," implying that if anything, the mall imposes a sense of timeless, yet perpetual, flux.[14] Thus, the mall's abounding novelties suggest its transience. In this context, WEM's employment of the term *phase* is particularly revealing: asserting the exciting newness of each spatial extension of the mall, while registering the structure's problematic relationship to time.

While WEM did attract numerous and diverse "guests" (as mall employees, à la Disney, were expected to call all visitors), its magic quickly began to wear out, just like the mass-produced consumer items it sold in its stores. Three riders of Fantasyland's roller-coaster died in a June 14, 1986 accident caused by a combination of manufacturing defects and poor maintenance.[15] WEM's financing, like its back hallways, was mysterious, complicated, and untidy. The entrepreneurship of the Ghermezians included a notable willingness to solicit assistance from the public sector, and in the mid-1990s, through a scheme that may have involved clandestine help from Alberta's provincial government, the mall's owners staved off possible bankruptcy.[16] Around the same time, Disney forced WEM to drop the name "Fantasyland"; the amusement park was renamed Galaxyland.[17]

WEM's operation as a conventional shopping center was not particularly smooth. Several major tenants left the mall for "Power Centers" (Big Box or "category-killer" stores grouped around large parking areas), whose proliferation WEM may have hastened, since one of Canada's first such centers, Mayfield Common, arose in the early 1990s

---

[14] Robert R. Wilson, "Playing and Being Played: Experiencing West Edmonton Mall." *Pop Can: Popular Culture in Canada*, eds. Lynne Van Luven and Priscilla L. Walton (Scarborough, Canada: Prentice Hall, 1999), 86, 89 n. 2.

[15] Susan Chung, "Coaster Victims' Kin Want New Law," *Edmonton Journal*, June 15, 1991, B1.

[16] Brian Hutchinson, "Trouble in Big Mall Country," *Canadian Business* 67.9 (September 1994): 68.

[17] The mall hotel retains the name "Fantasyland," since it does not infringe upon Disney's amusement-park branding rights. James Carlisle, "Canada's Biggest Mall Versus the World's Toughest Mouse," *Financial Post*, June 25, 1996, 14.

on the site of an older mall rendered obsolete by WEM's arrival.[18] In the late 1990s, the western end of Phase III, the newest part of the mall, was remodeled and retroactively designated "Phase IV," though the internal alterations brought little change to the building's external size. Over the last decade, Phases III and IV have undergone further serial mini-renovations, and in the late 1990s, mall management trumpeted an increased emphasis on entertainment over traditional retail sales.[19] Yet, WEM's most recently apparent trend is retail-oriented, and foregrounds international fashion chains such as Zara and H&M. WEM's publicity machine also makes a virtue of the ever-changing nature of the retail roster: the mall's website prominently lists various tenants that are "coming soon." This marketing of businesses as though they were movies corroborates Friedberg's assessment of the shopping mall as the "logical extension" of the movie theater.[20] The Mindbender has operated without serious incident since its post-accident modification and re-opening in the summer of 1987, but its enclosure, once iconic in itself, now sports large signs for featured mall retailers, suggesting that WEM is not so much an "entertainment mall" as a structure that, at least in its current form, highlights the central cultural roles of brand-driven shopping and contemporary marketing.

WEM's history suggests how malls themselves are subject to fashion cycles which are analogous to those of the goods they sell. The mall, unlike a slick Hollywood movie, cannot disguise its gaps and transitions, since renovations, and the labor that goes into them, are always to some extent visible and audible. As Benjamin remarks in *The Arcades Project*, "Fashions are a collective medicament for the ravages of oblivion."[21] This seems especially true for malls, which must evolve, as WEM has, or die, as has, for example, another Edmonton mall built in the early 1980s—Heritage—which is currently being redeveloped as housing.[22] Postmodern

---

[18] Gina Teel, "Category-Killers vs. All-Day Dawdlers," *Alberta Report* 20.37 (August 1993): 18.

[19] See Peter Verburg, "The West Edmonton Mall_Uh, Rocks," *Canadian Business* 70.13 (October 1997): 92. In 2002, the Ghermezians announced plans for a further expansion of WEM to include retail space, offices, and apartments, but these changes have yet to materialize. Tim Cook, "West Edmonton Mall Mega-Expansion Draws Ire of Residents," *The Canadian Press*, November 17, 2002.

[20] Friedberg, 120.

[21] Benjamin, 80.

[22] For more information on mall makeovers and life-cycles, see David J. Smiley, ed., *Sprawl and Public Space: Redressing the Mall* (Washington, DC: National

consumer culture itself might be described as a period of increasingly short-lived periods, where the new must be manufactured through a rapid recycling, renovation, and recombination of the old.

Theorists in Fantasyland

Thanks partly to its unfinished quality, WEM has functioned as a theoretical laboratory testing the potential of malls, and perhaps even, in the words of Rob Shields, as "a palimpsest…of past practices and…future possibilities."[23] While objective figures for the number of out-of-town and international visitors to WEM have been notoriously hard to determine, WEM has definitely been a popular destination for scholars of postmodernity and consumer culture.[24] Such tourist-theorists, however, tend to take its ostentatious features at face value, often neglecting to examine the quotidian. Theater scholar Tracy C. Davis, for example, has critiqued WEM's arcades, exhibitions, and carnivalesque artificial atmosphere, without fully dissecting the mall's relationship to the "drab," or mundane, external/internal world: "West Edmonton Mall has no windows so there are no reminders of the dreary suburbs beyond, but if one accidentally turns back the curtains in the fantasy rooms of the hotel, the illusion of Rome, Polynesia, or Hollywood is quickly shattered by an endless vista of drab suburbia."[25]

Other theorists have been particularly quick to make assumptions about the regimented nature of WEM without engaging in serious reflection on the meaning of such day-to-day activities. Friedberg states that "Like the theme park, the mall is 'imagineered' with maintenance and management techniques… concealing the security guards and bouncers who control its entrances."[26] Similarly, Shields describes WEM, and malls generally, as marked by "control, [and] new forms of discipline, and surveillance."[27] Architectural scholar Margaret Crawford, in her 1992

Endowment for the Arts, 2002); and Paco Underhill, *Call of the Mall* (New York: Simon & Schuster, 2004), 202–203.

[23] Shields, 152.

[24] Janice Williamson, "I-less and Gaga in the West Edmonton Mall: Towards a Pedestrian Feminist Reading." *The Anatomy of Gender: Women's Struggle for the Body*, eds. Dawn H. Currie and Valerie Raoul (Ottawa: Carleton University Press, 1992), 112 n. 1; Wilson, 89 n. 2.

[25] Tracy C. Davis, "Theatrical Antecedents of the Mall that Ate Downtown," *Journal of Popular Culture* 24.4 (Spring 1991): 10–11.

[26] Friedberg, 113.

[27] Shields, 160.

essay "The World in a Shopping Mall," characterizes WEM in strongly dystopian terms, interpreting the prominent central security office as an "electronic Panopticon survey[ing] every corner of the mall." While some commentators, such as Shields, admit that malls offer possibilities for resistant, tactical use, their accounts of such use remain largely theoretical. Shields warns against "reifying [WEM] as solely…an unmediated expression of capital" and adds that "there are many strategies by which people impose their own agendas," yet cites no instances of such strategies in operation.[28] With some exceptions, theoretical reflections on malls have neglected a whole category of "mundane" mall users: mall workers.

My Mall Phases

My first major mall hangout was the 1970s-built HUB (Housing Union Building) on the University of Alberta campus, a three-block elevated arcade with apartments overlooking a central, shop-lined pedestrian street. While completing high school and then a somewhat aimless BA, I spent considerable time and money first in HUB's video arcade, and later in its record store and pub.[29] While my everyday experience of HUB may have propelled me toward WEM, my conscious motivation seemed simple at the time: after seventeen years as a student, I needed a change, and Fantasyland was the first place that offered me a full-time job. I began employment as a "cast member" (the term was yet another example of how WEM borrowed from Disney) in June 1986, soon before the rollercoaster accident I recall a food-court conversation where a fellow cast-member pointed out that the accident was particularly horrific because roller coasters are founded on the carefully-controlled illusion of danger. The accident, however, had relatively little immediate effect on

---

[28] Margaret Crawford, "The World in a Shopping Mall." *Variations on a Theme Park: The New American City and the End of Public Space*, ed. Michael Sorkin (New York: Hill and Wang, 1992), 27, 156. The security office is now located in a side corridor.

[29] Developed by the University of Alberta Students' Union, HUB encountered financial problems and came under the control of the University not long after its opening. Its original atmosphere of modernist utopianism has been adulterated by renovations, and some of the original independent businesses and public spaces have given way to chain stores, but it remains a distinctive space with diverse users. University of Alberta Alumni Association, "Twenty-five years of life at the HUB" (1997). Last accessed July 2008:
http://www.ualberta.ca/ALUMNI/history/buildings/97authub.htm

day-to-day park operations, whose routine challenges it may even have normalized as mundane.

My job in its early phases entailed carrying cash, and escorting cashiers, back and forth between the Fantasyland amusement park's offices and its various cash desks. The cash itself was at first protected minimally by a secret pocket in my uniform, a "Miami Vice" white linen blazer. I and my fellow "cash pick-up" clerks soon abandoned the blazers when they became permanently ink-stained. Despite these less-than-rigorous security arrangements, and the often-crowded and chaotic state of the amusement park and its environs, I ran into no serious trouble, and the job was excellent exercise in several ways. Walking around Fantasyland and the mall for hours daily, I underwent a semi-accidental makeover, losing thirty pounds and gaining comfort in dealing with people and responsibility. I also acquired several pairs of acid-washed jeans, illustrating how any large mall has a built-in, trend-ready customer base in its employees.[30]

Janice Williamson's feminist reading of WEM conveys how my experiences as a relatively well-paid male cash clerk differed from those of low-waged female workers, who were "the repressed subjects [who] disappeared in WEM's theatre, [and] reminded us of the fantasy behind 'Fantasyland.'"[31] I enjoyed the ability to move around the park, and the mall, while my predominantly female colleagues remained in cramped ticket booths, clad in ill-fitting uniforms, forced to listen to the same music on the surrounding rides day after day as they performed endless repetitions of the same transactions. Their boredom meant that they often welcomed my change-bringing visits, and my chief contribution to the alleviation of this boredom was to smuggle soft drinks to the cashiers I particularly liked. While my immediate motives were more personal than political, technically such practices could be classified as examples of

[30] Exact figures on employee numbers are, like other WEM statistics, uncertain, but it seems reasonable to estimate cautiously that at any given moment the mall has employed at least ten thousand people, albeit many of them part-time.

[31] Williamson, 112. Another striking view of female mall workers as commodities comes from *Silvermeadow* (2000), by British/Australian mall architect and crime novelist Barry Maitland, in which a London-area mega-mall becomes the scene, and partial inspiration, for complicated crimes. These include the murder of a young mall employee whose fate, an investigating psychologist suggests, may be linked to the fact that she "'wore [a] uniform and a big happy smile, like she was an accessory, part of the whole fun process, like the wrapping paper and the music and the finger-licking food.'" Maitland, *Silvermeadow* (London: Orion, 2000), 196.

tactical subversion of the strategic plans of authority. Certainly, they were made possible by the gaps in supervision created by the often haphazard operation of the mall attractions.

This haphazardness extended notably to the handling of incoming revenue. Cash registers broke down regularly and had to await attention from the only technician in the city who knew their quirks: a man who was often happily stoned when summoned outside weekday business hours, but still able to fix the machines quickly. More impaired was the computer system that was tasked with monitoring all cash registers, but whose glitches sometimes left accounting staff unable to reconcile receipts with revenue. These deficiencies helped provoke and facilitate a notably elegant, if inherently small-scale, form of employee retaliation. Frustrated by ambiguous guidelines, complicated promotion procedures, and quotidian indignities (such as pocketless uniforms, which were based on the assumption they would steal), cashiers could "accidentally" charge adults children's rates. Cashiers were thus able to clandestinely redistribute the employer's resources, engaging in a subtle form of subversion which was beneath the disciplinary radar.

Most of my co-workers were honest, but a few exploited Fantasyland's systemic gaps in more self-interested ways. The most dramatic instance involved an affable and popular employee of the Waterpark cash office, whose creative accounting practices could easily have gone undetected longer than they did had he not felt compelled to consume the funds he appropriated in a manner that became conspicuous. Managerial suspicions were activated when, in the span of a few months, he upgraded his car from a generic North American sedan to a late-model Honda Prelude, and then a brand-new 1987 Acura Legend. Although the employee was fired, he was treated leniently by the legal system, and the case did not lead to a drastic tightening of discipline. WEM continued to suffer from managerial loopholes, since control strategies were instituted by ordinary human beings susceptible not only to the pressures of multi-tasking, but also to the same everyday temptations and provocations that the mall presented to its "guests."

Fantasyland's treatment of its employees did have its progressive social aspects. If WEM's world-encompassing self-promotion was hard to take seriously from the inside, one consolation was that there was a degree of genuine multiculturalism amongst the mall employees. "Cast members" came not only from all parts of Edmonton, Alberta, and Canada, but also from the increasingly diverse population of recent immigrants. I worked with first- and second-generation settlers from many regions of the world including East Asia, South Asia, South America, Africa, the Caribbean, and the former Soviet Union. The Ghermezians, who were of Iranian-Jewish heritage, had themselves immigrated to Canada in the 1960s. Arguably, their most valuable achievement was facilitating everyday interactions, and a degree of mutual understanding, among a wide range of Canadians. Semi-accidentally, they created a genuine multicultural microcosm within WEM's artificial environment.

As my WEM career continued, I gained increased responsibility, more because of rapid managerial turnover than personal merit. By the Spring of 1989, I was "Admissions Manager." Although this position sounds vaguely imposing, as if conferring actual power to control who entered Fantasyland or the Waterpark, it was an expanded version of my original job of counting cash, marshalling staff, coping with temperamental equipment, and trying to keep guests happy on the frequent occasions when problems arose. Now my duties extended from Fantasyland near the mall's eastern end, to the mini-golf course near its western end. I roamed more widely than ever, and encountered exciting new challenges. These ranged from designing new signage, despite having no particular qualification for the task, to placating Deep Sea Adventure submarine passengers stranded by the vessels' extremely regular habit of going off the rails (a team of divers was employed largely for the purpose of pushing errant subs back on course). The far-flung nature of my duties meant, however, that I could always remove myself from the scene of a contretemps to search for a new adventure. Because they were usually occupied with their own concerns, my immediate superiors were generally non-authoritarian. The most visible member of the Ghermezian family was its patriarch, Jacob, who traveled the corridors on a scooter, glowering. The rumor was that he carried a cane in order to administer corporal correction to employees his would-be panoptic gaze judged delinquent, but I never saw this happen.

At least in the late 1980s, WEM's panoptic quality was almost as much a simulation as were the mall's versions of the world's best attractions. The prominent central security office that drew the attention of theorists like Crawford served not so much to oversee and regulate activities in the mall, as to promote the illusion that the mall's space was under tight control. Given the chronic understaffing of the mall's actual security forces, my tie, ID badge, and the two-way radio I usually carried for cross-mall communications cast me occasionally as a security-guard impersonator, drafted to help deal with sporadic disturbances. On one occasion, I attempted ineffectually to restrain a young woman who bit me on the forearm (not, to my relief, breaking the skin) and fled with her friends into the parking lot, quite possibly to re-enter the mall via another door. Even though Robert R. Wilson has suggested that "Within [WEM's] perpetual ambience of carnival, there is no room for truly carnivalesque behavior," my everyday experiences at WEM suggest that behind the mall's simulated carnival atmosphere, there is indeed room for unofficial uses.[32]

While the carnivalesque is not inherently subversive, it also cannot be considered a simple safety-valve by which dominant social forces channel popular energies that otherwise might present a challenge. To the untrained gaze, WEM appears to be a seamless machine, channeling its visitors into the pursuit of consumption. However, the hastily-built and labyrinthine back corridors (or bowels) of the mall can afford considerable space for the illicit activities of unruly bodies. Regularly, while navigating these corridors on my way to deal with routine annoyances such as the Waterpark's malfunctioning laundry machines, I smelled marijuana, heard suggestive laughter around the bend, or came across couples (including fellow cast members) adjusting their clothing with exaggerated nonchalance. One evening in 1989, as "duty manager" for the attractions I was led by an indignant Waterpark guest to the artificial beach, where assorted people were gathered around a sizable specimen of what was presumably human excrement. Nobody knew where it had come from, but it nevertheless represented a particularly clever disruption of the simulated carnival atmosphere of the mall. Meanwhile, carnivalesque energies of my own were asserting themselves: more than once I took unscheduled breaks from my managerial duties in order to recover from a night in one of the mall's pubs. Such incidents made me realize that it was time for me to leave WEM.

Back to School

I did not think of WEM in terms of the carnivalesque until after my return to academia. Yet, the interest in cultural studies and theory that I developed as a graduate student was the direct by-product of my desire to figure out how I could have had such life-altering experiences in such an artificial place. Moreover, my choice of graduate program was in part a consumer decision, influenced by the efficient marketing and self-promotion of the well-established Eastern-Canadian university I attended. Furthermore, at my current institution (Nipissing University), a markedly mall-like megabuilding that sprawls across an escarpment in Northern Ontario, students see themselves partly as customers, for the

[32] Wilson, 83.

understandable reason that many work customer-service jobs just to pay tuition. The university is currently planning a new Learning Commons, which will offer students what amounts to one-stop shopping for academic services. This project's open, inviting floor plan resembles Anne Friedberg's description of the Paris *Bibliothèque Nationale* where Benjamin did much of his research on arcades: "The relation between the reading room and the library stack, which offers the reader a clear view of the articles in stock, [is] a spatial model for the department store, where the consumer also has a clear view of the commodities on display."[33] Contemporary university buildings, which increasingly feature coffee-shops and other consumer amenities, may thus have come full circle.

The apparent convergence of academia and consumer culture supports the claims of some theorists that shopping is becoming not just a common cultural activity, but a pervasive cultural climate grounded in conformity, discipline, and (self) deception. Sze Tsung Leong concludes a 2001 essay on the proliferating influences of consumerism with the prediction that "in the end, there will be little else for us to do but shop."[34] In 1992, Margaret Crawford drew a similar conclusion, asserting that "the world of the shopping mall…has become the world."[35] Yet in a 2002 essay, Crawford distances herself from such claims, and looks at possible new roles for malls. As she contends, if shopping is ubiquitous, then it becomes important to differentiate among specific shopping places and practices within the macrocosm of consumption.[36]

My recent impressions of WEM are contradictory. The most daunting is that WEM's 1980s excesses foreshadowed the frantic state of contemporary Alberta, which is booming under global demand for its oil resources, whose rapid consumption the provincial government promotes eagerly. WEM presently enjoys near-ideal market conditions, with an abundant local supply of affluent consumers. However, since these conditions are linked to the exploitation of a finite resource, WEM's current boom may be its final phase of success. Crawford remarks that "experts [are] now estimating the average mall life at less than 10 years,"

---

[33] Friedberg, 79.

[34] Sze Tsung Leong, "…And Then There Was Shopping." *Cultural Studies: An Anthology*, ed. Michael Ryan (Malden, MA: Blackwell, 2008), 702.

[35] Crawford, "The World in a Shopping Mall," 30.

[36] Margaret Crawford, "Suburban Life and Public Space." *Sprawl and Public Space: Redressing the Mall*, ed. David J. Smiley (Washington, DC: National Endowment for the Arts, 2002), 29.

and thus today's WEM could be seen as a live museum of a culture of recreational consumption that is headed for extinction.[37]

Yet, Crawford's observation also points to the possibility that WEM's more prosaic features will secure its future. WEM, like many other Canadian malls, is adjacent to a transit center, where many routes converge. More accessible than Power Centers, in the long run it may be altogether more sustainable than such automobile-centered sites, which are clearer examples of wasteful design and social regimentation masquerading as consumer choice. Moreover, Phase I, the oldest and most traditionally-designed part of WEM, is also the least altered over the years. Quotidian forms of shopping dominate both here and elsewhere in the mall, notably in a wing which has been renovated around a supermarket catering to Edmonton's growing Asian communities. Thus, as developments elsewhere continue to challenge its cutting-edge status, WEM may be reclaimed by local residents as a center for mundanely diverse consumer purposes.

[37] Ibid.

CHAPTER TWELVE

SHOPPING, DROPPING, NEVER STOPPING: ONE SHOPPING MEMOIR

MICHAEL ANGELO TATA

> Fashion prescribes the ritual according to which the commodity fetish demands to be worshipped...It couples the living body to the inorganic world. To the living, it defends the rights of the corpse. The fetishism which thus succumbs to the sex appeal of the inorganic is its vital nerve.
>
> —Walter Benjamin, *The Arcades Project* (trans. 2002)

> Shopping all day on Rodeo Drive.
> Out all night just to stay alive.
> People working hard making dreams come true.
> Palm trees line every avenue.
> Everyone is someone
> Everyone is someone
> ...In LA.
>
> —Felix Da Housecat, *Everyone Is Someone in LA* (2004)

Since every essay on the subject of *flânerie* should de rigueur begin with an invocation of the disembodied spirit of Walter Benjamin, as it floats benevolently above textual attempts to grasp the lurid mysteries of cultural itinerancy, I too begin this piece of commodity *rêverie* under the spell of the one individual who truly comprehended what the awesome power of rootless spectatorship could unleash for a society seriously committed to its perceptual illusions—its daguerreotypes, its panoramas, its *actualités*. Unlike other philosophers of modernity for whom mass production and consumption mark the end of human civilization or at minimum its fatal corrosion, Benjamin inherently grasps the overwhelming pleasure of visually shopping the city for ideas, spectacles and phantasms. Less Puritanical than Theodor Adorno, less pedantic than

Martin Heidegger, and more playful than even Hannah Arendt at her most light-hearted moments, for inhabitants of the postmodern nulliverse Benjamin translates as a philosopher deeply in love with the present.

Wanderer lost in the ocular excesses of a world on the brink of breaking culturally with an authentic, aura-ringed past increasingly accessible only via the products of various nostalgia industries—greeting cards, movies, package tours—Benjamin takes ephemerality as his central problem. Comprehending the space of the arcade and department store as phantasmagoric, polymorphous and synaesthetic, he makes possible philosophic analysis and physical enjoyment of the charmed space of the retail "high" and the retinal "rush." To whom else can I turn for inspiration as I begin my own journey through the charged environment of the Southern California shopping mall? Specifically, I choose the Los Angeles Mecca the Beverly Center (for junkies, there is always a substance of choice). Thank you Walter, for whom, as conveyed in the essay "Unpacking My Library," ownership marks the most intimate relationship that can exist between a human being and an inanimate object.[1] It is with you in mind that I clutch an imaginary bag stuffed with pleasure and ride an escalator to the stars. Off we go, traveling beyond the arcade or department store to an even more dazzling entity: the shopping mall. Mixing theory with autobiography, I too will be so bold as to alternate between the two poles of philosophy and sensuality, the only true method for thinking through the fleeting phenomenological now whose disappearance produces history.

Beverly Frills

When seeking designer couture in the global epicenter of overindulgence (Beverly Hills, California), three options immediately present themselves to the experienced label whore: Rodeo Drive, Sunset Plaza and the Beverly Center.[2] Other regional shopping centers, like the Westside Pavilion, Century City, or the Grove contain mediocre stores that simply do not count from the standpoint of high fashion or radical chic.[3]

---

1 Walter Benjamin, *Illuminations,* trans. Harry Zohn (New York: Harcourt Brace Jovanovich, 1968).

2 I have previously theorized on the psychology of the label whore. Please see Michael Angelo Tata, "Confessions of a D&G Label Whore," *to the quick* 3 (Winter 2000): 29–39.

3 Anne Friedberg discusses the Westside Pavilion in her essay "*Les Flâneurs du Mal(l)*: Cinema and the Postmodern Condition." *Publications of the Modern Language Association of America,* 106.3 (May 1991): 419–431. Also see Anne

Most often captured by popular cinema, the acquisitional dementia of Los Angeles finds itself immortalized in films as varied as *Troop Beverly Hills* (1987) or *Clueless* (1995), cinematic testaments to the garish and unsavory conspicuous consumption which marks Los Angeles as vulgar and important. Here, and only here, do the Valley girl, mall rat and fashion brat find themselves apotheosized—as when, in *Troop Beverly Hills*, Shelly Long introduces badges for excellence in gemology and the selection of divorce attorneys to the gaggle of Wilderness Girls under her tutelage, or when, in *Clueless*, Alicia Silverstone carefully selects the day's attire with a computer programmed to avoid wardrobe malfunctions that would surely spell social death.

Rodeo Drive, Sunset Plaza and the Beverly Center all promise instant gratification and ostentation, as well as the chance to promenade and strut for an audience of fashion victims and *poseurs*, all of whom are dying to lord their fashion savvy over a host of chic failures while demanding justification for their sumptuary choices (such is the fragility of the fashion ego). Modeled partially on the famous Spanish Steps of Rome's high-end shopping district *Il Corso*, Rodeo Drive is the favorite haunt of the vestimentary elite. For example, it would not be uncommon to see a South American soccer star trying on destroyed alligator jeans while Wonder Woman (Lynda Carter) rifles casually through various witch boots inches away, or to encounter children named after various world capitals hunting for Gucci sunglasses which will presumably replace last season's trash ("Paris—do you like these? Try them on!"). For, sadly, true stars only shop at boutiques, never at malls—even LaToya Jackson refuses to set foot in one, as she confessed during the 2004 episode of *VH1 All Access* which coincided with the release of her 2005 "comeback" album *Startin' Over*.[4] Like Rodeo Drive, Sunset Plaza—the newest addition to LA's shopping scene, having barely come into its own in 2006—offers a mix of high-end boutiques (Just Cavalli, D&G, and Nicole Miller) and restaurants (Clafoutis, Mel's Diner), where to be seen is everything. With so many tempting options, how is one to choose?

Ultimately, the selection lies between a street and a container, between an open and a closed system, entities delineated most compellingly by systems theory, which seeks to differentiate organizational schemas in

---

Friedberg, *Window Shopping: Cinema and the Postmodern* (Berkeley: University of California Press, 1993).

[4] *VH1 All Access: LaToya Jackson* first aired in 2004. Her album *Startin' Over*, which was produced by the record label JA-TAIL, launched her new sound in 2005.

terms of input, output, permeability and autonomy.[5] In practice, only degrees of "openness" or "closedness" matter, since "open" and "closed" modify purely idealized situations (as Steven Hawking has demonstrated, even a black hole displays entropy). As with any open system which allows elements to enter or escape, many variables influence output and outcome. One variable influencing all aspects of life in Los Angeles is traffic flow. Unfortunately for Sunset Plaza, parking is abysmal, and the traffic a total horror, thereby ruining its chances of offering Rodeo Drive or the Beverly Center any true competition. Hence, its status as a "dead mall" (at present, Sunset Millennium Plaza, the center's anchor, is virtually vacant, with the notable exception of a gelato shop and a gym). In addition, both Sunset Plaza and Rodeo Drive present potential climactic dangers to *flâneurs* and shoppers alike. For example, what will be the fate of one's Miu Miu loafers or Chanel facial bronzer if it rains? Moreover, as open spaces, they permit exit from the shopping circuit more readily (one might dash out of the Versace store and into a Jaguar, never to be seen again), while also making it inevitable that some unwanted vagrant or shopping bag psycho might intersect the path of an underwear model or debutante.

As Anne Friedberg notes in her essay *"Les Flâneurs du Mal(l):* Cinema and the Postmodern Condition," no such perils are presented by the controlled environment of the shopping mall, where regulation guarantees a predictable and repeatable experience for the shopper: "Like the theme park, the mall is 'imagineered' with maintenance and management techniques, concealing the delivery bays and support systems, the security guards and bouncers who control its entrances. It defers urban realities, blocks urban blights—the homeless, beggars, crime, traffic, even weather."[6] True—a homeless schizo could wander past Neiman Marcus, interrupting a socialite's day with impertinent questions about finances or religion, or worse yet, Lindsay Lohan could run somebody down in her Mercedes while fleeing real and imagined stalkerazzi.[7] Or, Winona Ryder might knock a manny down as she flees

[5] Klaus Krippendorf, *Dictionary of Cybernetics.* Last accessed June 2008: pespmc1.vub.ac.be/ASC/Kripp.html

[6] Friedberg, 424.

[7] First, paparazzo Galo Cesar Ramirez rammed into the famous Mercedes on May 31, 2005; then, on October 5, 2005, she crashed it into a van in Beverly Hills, supposedly after leaving either a boutique (Sky Showbiz) or the Ivy (CBS News), depending on the source. Whether one blames the media machine or Lohan's failed "care of self" (bulimia, booze, drugs, as *Vanity Fair* suggests in its February 2006 issue), the point is to run when you see her coming! See Evgenia Peretz,

BHPD with a klepto's cache of Michael Kors. Life is clearly much safer at the Beverly Center, where possible dangers include scalding an upper lip on an overheated double mocha, or losing a precious garment to someone more nimble. As documented by the film *Crash* (2005), LA thrives on fear, always seeking new ways to manage it through the erection of racial and sexual barricades. Here, indoors is safe, and safe is good. Stars or no stars, the Beverly Center wins—this despite the fact that even the most regulated mall can only ideally be closed, its revolving doors beckoning everybody to pop in for a quick session of shopping, histrionics, and showing off.

Collisions

First and foremost, malls are for looking, for aiming Benjamin's "ambulatory gaze" at social spectacles, at mannequins done up in ideal poses and ensembles, and at racks of fabric that might indeed change one's life permanently. "Buy Me, I'll Change Your Life," as the Barbra Kruger slogan goes. Even she doesn't realize how on the money she is; however professional shoppers, such as those frequenting the Beverly Center, get it intuitively. Following Benjamin's historicist logic, the arcade gives way to the department store, which then gives way to the mall, as *flâneurs* become shoppers and prostitutes become *midinettes*.[8] Though most of my trips to the Bev involve some semi-firm primary goal, such as "Get to D&G to see if Deana has any more of those belts left," as well as an itinerary (first, Macy's; then, Bloomie's; then, the Coffee Bean, etc.), there is, as with any goal-directed behavior, room for chance intrusions to impinge upon the day's labor, as when one Sunday afternoon at the

---

"Lindsay Lohan: Confessions of a Teenage Movie Queen," *Vanity Fair* (February 2006), 120–127; "Lindsay Lohan in Car Crash," Sky Showbiz. Last accessed June 2008: www.sky.com/showbiz/article/0,,50001-1197896,00.html
"No Charge in Lohan Crash," CBS News. Last accessed June 2008: www.cbsnews.com/stories

[8] As Friedberg elucidates, the operant gendered duo for Baudelaire (and Benjamin) is *flâneur*/prostitute, never *flâneur/flâneuse*. One such pairing can be found in Thomas De Quincey's dyad De Quincey/Anne of Oxford Street in his *Confessions of an English Opium Eater* (New York: Penguin, 2003). Ultimately, there is no "Woman of the Crowd" to complement Edgar Allan Poe's "Man of the Crowd." See "The Man of the Crowd" in *Complete Stories and Poems of Edgar Allan Poe* (New York: Doubleday, 1966), 215–222. For the ontic emergence of the special class of women known as *les midinettes*, see Marcel Proust's *The Captive* in *Remembrance of Things Past* (New York: Vintage Books, 1982).

Macy's Men's Shop, Deacon (Sean Kanan) from the CBS soap opera *The Bold and the Beautiful* materialized in full panic mode. Convinced everybody was looking at him (which they were not), he dragged his shockingly ample, junk-filled trunk around the store, manically grabbing at clothing he was too terrified even to try on, lest he be ripped limb from limb like Sebastian from Tennessee Williams' *Suddenly Last Summer*. After his sales associate, a Hong Kong expatriate, stuffed everything into a bag, he flew out the door before anybody could molest him for an autograph, which nobody had any interest in doing anyway (in Hollywood, soap star status is slightly above waiter, and below hustler).

In 2005, the Beverly Center commissioned Santa Monica advertising agency Dentsu to launch a prestigious and multifaceted advertising blitz titled "amiordinary.com" with the objective "to reinforce Beverly Center's positioning as the place for distinctive specialty stores that allows one to express his/her own personal style."[9] For this campaign, diverse marketing components were used, ranging from traditional media (billboards and a microsite), to guerilla venues (sidewalk clings, coffee sleeves, gym towels, and other "wild postings")—all following the "key insight" that "our target takes shopping seriously and enjoys finding unique items that express their unique style. They don't want to look like everyone else." At "amiordinary.com," the managing powers of the Beverly Center provide some insight into the clientele they court—a more diverse and oddball crowd than either Sunset Plaza or Rodeo Drive, or at least a group positing as such. "I walk around the house naked." "I wear underwear to bed." "I lick my fingers." "I tickle adults." Offering a variety of strange quotes indicative of lifestyles and attitudes revealed via personal eccentricity, the Beverly Center website caters to an audience obsessed with selfhood—especially those shoppers bent on erecting a unique self among a sea of clones and copycats, LA's greatest threats. The Beverly Center thus directs its online and print advertising (primarily billboards) to LA's throngs of burgeoning fashion plates—individuals obsessed with translating their respective differences into sartorial displays that can be read, emulated, interpreted.

As elucidated in books such as Ted Polhemus' *Street Style* or *Style Surfing* and Dick Hebdige's *Subculture: The Meaning of Style*, the idea of resolving philosophical or cultural concerns at surface level is precisely

[9] My source for all Dentsu references is a collection of Dentsu marketing notes from the amiordinary.com campaign. These were generously provided to the author by Brianna Mandell. Used with permission.

the crux of any metaphysics of personal style.[10] For the "citizen of the world," style negotiates and facilitates a racial, sexual and economic discussion to which all are invited to respond. Capitalizing upon the insight that fashion involves so much more than fabric, the Beverly Center searches for shoppers claiming a life "less ordinary." The merchandise it offers for sale can undertake acts of *legerdemain* and prestidigitation, as one is made over in the image of whichever social type one desires to become.[11] The "amiordinary" site entices one to take the "ordinariness" test: a series of ten questions slightly less cheeky than a Cosmo quiz, yet troublesome enough to differentiate the Beverly Center from a Westside Pavilion. Allowing web visitors to check off boxes indicating everything from underwear preferences to sexual tastes, the site's test culminates in the assignment of a number/label to participants. According to the sociologist at the other end of the computer, I am a "4: on the verge of extraordinary"—perhaps in the same way that Wayne Koestenbaum in *Cleavage* is "on the verge" of Elizabeth Taylor, or in *Jackie Under My Skin*, on the edge of Jacqueline Kennedy Onassis.[12]

Friends visiting from New York City cannot understand why I should find any joy at all in entering and squandering the day away at the Beverly Center, a place they find most loathsome, when I could be strolling Melrose with the punk girls from the Jezebels or Maxi Tit, or rummaging through discarded Oscar gowns at local thrift shops with Blondie Baby. Occasionally, charged situations emerge when East meets West, like the day I dragged rising Queens DJ phenom Lady 180 down La Cienega Boulevard to my favorite mall. This day, we had only one task: to buy my

---

[10] See Ted Polhemus, *Street Style: From Sidewalk to Catwalk* (London: Thames & Hudson, 1994) as well as his *Style Surfing: What to Wear in the 3rd Millennium* (London: Thames & Hudson, 1996). Also see Dick Hebdige, *Subculture: The Meaning of Style* (London: Routledge, 1988).

[11] As the translators' foreword of Benjamin's *Arcades Project* clarifies, the central danger of the dandy's or *flâneur*'s gaze is that it reduces the social tableau to a series of anticipated types. Mall *flânerie* articulates the same problem, although with the distinction that one does not merely behold the type, but makes every attempt at embodying and repeating it. Yet, strangely enough, there is creativity and ingenuity in this process, hence the fashion system's central paradox. For more information on Benjamin, please see his *The Arcades Project,* trans. Howard Eiland and Kevin McLaughlin (Cambridge: Belknap Press, 2002) and Susan Buck-Morss, *The Dialectics of Seeing: Walter Benjamin and The Arcades Project* (Cambridge, MA: MIT Press, 1991).

[12] For more on Koestenbaum's celebrity-edginess, see his *Cleavage: Essays on Sex, Stars, and Aesthetics* (New York: Ballantine Books, 2000), particularly the chapter on "The Elizabeth Taylor Puzzle," 107–125.

husband a shirt at Macy's for his upcoming birthday extravaganza. As the two of us stepped onto the Epcot-like escalator carrying shoppers into a magical city where dreams assume the form of currency, we found ourselves squarely in the visual field of an Ashton Kutcher wannabe who refused to stop gawking at my shoes, bright green Diesel flip-flops. Lady 180 had not yet been schooled in the visual dynamics of the Beverly Hills set, unaware that its initiates only stare when experiencing envy; the pleasures of the grotesque are not common among LA's genteel (it is for this reason that comedians like Kathy Griffin cannot extricate themselves from the D-List quagmire).[13] Unsure if he stared at me because he found me sexually piquant, or perhaps deemed some dimension of my appearance fascinating (like my big toe), Lady 180 assumed the worst of this paraphiliac and went Fresh Meadows on his glutes.

"You got glaucoma? What the hell you looking at?" she obstreperously lobbed his way, terrifying him to the core and forcing him to pick up the pace and walk the rest of the way, rather than wait for the *trottoir roulant* to carry him the full distance to the parking garage. As his slightly-askew trucker hat grew further and further away from us, I explained to her that he probably thought my shoes were cute, but could not bring himself to tell me, lest his metrosexuality collapse to homosexuality and the Sunset crowd force him to ease on down to Santa Monica Boulevard. Later that day, another incident occurred; this time, as we were in line for iced Americanos at the Coffee Bean. Finding herself queued up behind two Valley girls with large, colorful flowers in their hair evocative of *Sex and the City*, Lady 180 could hardly restrain herself. "Who the hell do those freaks think they are? Sarah Jessica Parker? Get real—even on her that shit looks bad." Offended, yet shaken by her foreign accent and confrontational pose, they grabbed their libations posthaste and split. From an evolutionary standpoint, neither they nor their friend on the *escalier* had any defense against her immediacy. If she only knew that later in the week I would hook her up with someone whose sole ambition was to become an action hero, she might have saved some of her disdain for future use. Mercifully, by then she was so tired of attacking the superficial that even his desires seemed logical.

---

[13] Kathy Griffin, *My Life on the D-List*, Bravo TV, 2005–2007, and *Allegedly*, Anchor Bay, 2004.

Authentic Inauthenticity

As the tension between the metrosexuality and homosexuality of my Ashton Kutcher aspirant illustrates, the mall is precisely the spot where it is safest for budding gays to engage their sexuality via a proliferation of fledgling queer looks and poses. Long before I found my extraordinariness converted into a number by the Beverly Center's advertising machine, I discovered that the local mall was the best place to experiment with my appearance—far superior to the Bristol Ten Pin or St. Anthony's Church, local Connecticut spots reinforcing a masculinity more suited to boys named Rocco or T-Bone. Over the years, my sexuality would lead me from one mall to another, much as other homosexual men are led from club to club or bathhouse to bathhouse.[14] When I was a child, our local department store became associated with sexuality through a scandal: as reported by an indubitable source (a three-foot tall Estelle Getty look-alike named Sister Florence), several local men were arrested in the men's room of Hartford G. Fox (now a Filene's) for public lewdness. Although I could not imagine what that meant, I gleaned from her tone that these heathens had publicly done something that was better off happening nowhere.

Years later, in his video for the 1998 single *Outside*, George Michael would make their offences seem silly and innocent, but back then, my emergent sexuality connected homosexuality with the peddling of wares, all via the water closet. To think, my grandmother and mother took me to lunch for chicken croquettes at G. Fox! Why these men had to resort to a bathroom to find love I could not understand, but what I did absorb was that shopping edifices and homosexuals were a marriage made in heaven. As I grew up, my preferred spot to spend whatever money I had earned as a teller at Bristol Savings Bank was the Westfarms Mall. Poised at the intersection of the affluent communities of West Hartford and Farmington, Connecticut, just as the Beverly Center straddles the division between West Hollywood and Beverly Hills, it offered me a glimpse at what life might be like for strange borderline creatures such as myself. There,

---

[14] Piers Paolo Pasolini's poems about the Caracalla Baths provide one such testament to the importance of the "safe space" to burgeoning homos. When the "safe space" is violated, as in the Mathew Shepard case, or as in the film *Cruising* (1980), or when it is compromised from within, as with the murder of Angel Melendez, a particular vulnerability is experienced. See Pasolini's *Roman Poems*, trans. Lawrence Ferlinghetti and Francesca Valente (San Francisco: City Lights Books, 1986). James St. James' *Disco Bloodbath: A Fabulous but True Story of Murder in Clubland* (New York: Simon & Schuster, 1999) still remains the final word on the Melendez murder.

accompanied by my first non-familial shopping partners and stylists, my zaftig girlfriend Bubbles and anorexic best friend Alice ("Beepsy," as her intimates referred to her, based on the fact that she was so starved that she could barely speak), I wandered blissfully from store to store in a relentless pursuit of garments which would allow me to express my individuality in a publicly recognizable mode. As a budding creature of fashion, I was born among ACA JOE T-shirts, Generra floral button-downs resembling wallpaper from a rest home, and acid-washed Guess jeans.

One store in particular fixated me and marked the course of my future fashion sense: the acid house and punk emporium Le Château. Turned onto it by Tracy, an eccentric "first-chair" flutist who played Mozart perfectly while sporting ripped-up blazers and large sweaters with the New York City skyline knitted into the fabric, Tracy rocked. Following her advice, I dragged my Mother, the best shopping partner and fag hag ever, along to the second floor of the Westfarms Mall, where, across from J.C. Penney's, loomed a store dedicated entirely to the project of clothing the lunatic fringe. From that moment on, it was a ritual to cart Mom along to Le Château, where she would entertain the genderbenders working the register and floor with tales of her life as a divorcée, while I combed the aisles endlessly searching for chartreuse mock turtlenecks, knee-high combat boots, and utterly demolished jeans.

When Mom was not with me, Bubbles was (the two despised one another). No amount of persuasion could convince Beepsy to grace this den of iniquity with her presence. She preferred to wear an XL Disney T-shirt bearing the physique of Minnie Mouse with bright red pumps, no skirt or pants necessary; besides which, she was too skinny to fit into the clothing Le Château offered. Even my father's mistress got with the program and began buying my birthday and Christmas presents there. Through these travels, two men in particular arrested my gaze. Overtly and self-proclaimedly gay, they amazed me. One of them, Paul Z, trotted around the mall with half-shirts reading quips and aphorisms like "Gay Men Make Me Hard" or "I'm Not Gay, But My Boyfriend Is," while Michael, a Le Château manager, regaled me with stories of his weekends driving to and from New York City with a car full of queens ("A queen? What's that?"). Michael always wore black palazzo pants, a look I could never emulate, being short and Italian, but one which impressed me in and of its bravado. There were no metros in the 80s. Michael could be nothing other than gay; ditto for Paul Z. Consequently, they could afford to make whatever statements they wanted, not being forced to hide behind a protective screen. No matter what Oscar Wilde says, there are advantages to obviousness.

As centers of experimentation, malls like Westfarms or the Beverly Center facilitate a wide array of nascent performances, as I discovered in the earliest stages of my fashion metamorphosis. Within their food courts, elevators and dressing rooms, people of all backgrounds try out personae to which they find themselves attracted, most likely because the local mean girls have lodged an irrepressible image in their heads, or a magazine image has them hell-bent on reinvention. A safe haven for improvisation and carnivalesque inversion, the mall offers itself as transmogrification chamber to all interested parties, who flock there in search of a trial audience whose responses will determine if leg warmers are still cool and whether one should tie a sequined bandana in one's blonde-highlighted faux-hawk, or use it to dry the dishes. With the entire mall's population as a focus group, it becomes safe to adopt novel ways of communicating, locomoting and informing, as surfacing subcultures make their presence vividly known. So much more than avatars of a crass commercialism marking the end of modernism, the mall, and its partner in crime, the department store, make the production of selves entertaining and exciting.

Even today, as my tween-age nieces drag me along to a store like Hot Topic, I can vicariously feel the utter exhilaration of finding that one pair of pants which makes a human being of any age position her- or himself at the apex of universal bliss. So many writers and theorists ignore this gleeful dimension of the mall experience, focusing instead on topics as uninteresting as the perverse bodily images used to lure young women into a dysmorphic future of Pilates and purging, or as banal as the insidiousness of the commodity as it co-opts consciousness and lures the mind into a sleep worthy of the best Vicodin dose.[15] Only Walter Benjamin seems to grasp the wanderer's delirium, as he loses himself in the intricate surfaces confronting his senses. Nobody else could think of making it his life's work to generate and collate fragments as scintillating and intoxicating as those filling the thousand pages of *The Arcades*

---

[15] For Naomi Wolf's consummate and influential critique of the beauty-industrial complex, see her *The Beauty Myth: How Images of Beauty Are Used Against Women* (New York: Harper Collins, 1991). For an excoriating critique of the automaton's mania for consumption, consult "The Culture Industry: Enlightenment as Mass Deception" in Theodor Adorno and Max Horkheimer, *Dialectic of Enlightenment*, trans. Edmund Jephcott (Palo Alto, CA: Stanford University Press, 2002).

Project, a work to which all shopping-writing and writing-shopping owe their deepest gratitude.

Most importantly, the fugue state so dear to Benjamin and mallrats like myself speaks to the inauthentic manifestations of selfhood, which Martin Heidegger opposes to the healthier ways the "I" uses the "They" to embrace finitude and achieve authentic selfhood in the midst of ontological oblivion.[16] For Heidegger, the linguistic practice of "idle talk" (*gerede*) constitutes one of the more critical ways in which *Da-sein* ("being there") gets lost on the way to authenticity: along with curiosity, ambiguity, and falling prey (*verfallen*), idle talk represents one of the self's traps. Instead of using the "They" to support an "I," *Da-sein* fails to see a reason why it should extricate itself from the pleasure afforded by immersion in the world, and opts instead to linger, gripped by gossip, and tranquilized by illusions of otherworldliness and infinitude. For this reason, Avital Ronell in *Crack Wars: Literature, Addiction, Mania* identifies *Da-sein* as primordial addict—and even Sartre, for whom authenticity is everything, finds his world perforated by acute nothingness when he attempts to relinquish cigarettes, making it possible that even the most *pour-soi pour soi* experiences face the enticement of material domination.[17]

Adrift in the world's idleness, ambiguously wandering from possibility to possibility, *Da-sein* actualizes nothing short of its own descent into a deluded pseudo-existence. As illustrated by Ronell, the world possesses an intrinsic allure which produces the effect of inebriation in the human subject traversing the arc of its own subjectivity. The postmodern perspective on this "lostness" would be to savor each precious moment, something mall aficionados without a doubt comprehend. Phenomenologically, they offer an education to existentialism proper, proving that even a mass-produced self can be a wonder. For what every mallrat knows deep inside his or her heart, yet would never readily admit, is that the veritable inauthenticity of shopping produces an excitement that

---

[16] Heidegger is infinitely kinder to the inauthentic state than Jean-Paul Sartre, for whom *mauvaise foi* and the life of the *en soi,* are forever revolting. Martin Heidegger, *Being and Time,* trans. Joan Stambaugh (Albany, NY: SUNY Press, 1996), 35–38.

[17] In *Crack Wars: Literature, Addiction, Mania* (Urbana: University of Illinois Press, 2004) Avital Ronell discusses the primordial addictivity coded into human consciousness, a tropism she identifies with Heidegger's notion of *verfallen*. Sartre discusses his own nicotine addiction in *Being and Nothingness: A Phenomenal Essay on Ontology,* trans. Hazel E. Barnes (New York: Washington Square Press, 1984), Part 4, Chapter 2, II "'Doing' and 'Having': Possession," 760.

projects and propels the shopper ever forward into a future brimming with fantastic luncheons, impossible *fêtes*, and hallucinated photo-ops. How wonderful, to mistake a garment for a catapult, to dive with the fearlessness of an amnesiac into a new identity without ever bothering to notice the loss of a previous one! This pleasure Lady 180 could not comprehend, because from the perspective of a native New Yorker, Los Angeles embodies sheer superficiality, plasticity and vacuousness; hence, its value to postmodern theory, with its noble attempt to comprehend the work of selfhood in an era of virtuality, frustrated anamnesis and oblivion. In fact, my only intention in dragging her along to a place I knew she would most surely detest was not to throw my own character into question—after all, what must she think of me, if this horrible mall has come to mark my life with such significance?—but rather to introduce her to the subtle joys of brash, unadulterated inauthenticity of the kind that no true city could ever tolerate.

Only a collection of suburbs loosely organized into a great Peloponnesus, and suffering under the delusion that somehow its elements came together into a coherent urban structure, could produce such a stilted, unreal worldview. Whether the human subject at stake is a confused metrosexual casting furtive glances at presumably another metrosexual in order to score a fashion tip before other members of his clan, or a young girl so infatuated with the magic of *Sex and the City* that she holds her hair gently in place with tendrils of a fluorescent red anemone, the paradigm remains the same: experimentation excites, innervates, and incites. Like 180, Heidegger found himself unable to see the happiness of the authentically inauthentic as productive of a "positive" determination of *Da-sein*, rather than the unfortunate tributary of a current flowing in the wrong direction—important in its own right, yet pathetic. If only Martin had made it to Beverly Hills, and I had been the one to take him shopping.

Thus it is the authentic inauthenticity, or AI, of the shopping experience which constitutes the crux of my obsession with upscale malls and the never-ending process of securing ever more designer labels within their rarefied, regulated membranes. Malls foster AI, which circulates in the atmosphere along with cooled air and the smell of baking Cinnabons. As shocking as my words may sound, inauthenticity actually finds itself in crisis in the first decade of the twenty-first century due in no small part to the "War on Terror": a protracted conflict with a dubious foe. When Madonna Ritchie begins to probe the depths of consciousness and starts speaking in an odd language vaguely reminiscent of the philosophy of mind, there is no doubt that trouble is on the way (even Edie Sedgwick's spirituality was more advanced).[18] It is Hollywood's greatest scandal that it finds itself in love with depth, a cruel shag buddy who continues to recede into a past so distant that it can never be reached by human effort. There is at least something refreshing about those who admit their vapidity, like local celebrity Bobby Trendy or (gasp) Anna Nicole Smith. But what of those bizarre celebrities, wannabes and nobodies who find themselves lusting after a depth that exists nowhere save within their own desire for social mobility and individual panache? As with Bobby, the late Anna, and other real fakes comfortable with their depthlessness, the good, old-fashioned postmodern pleasures of conspicuous consumption, semantic shallowness and schizophrenic *flânerie* are what I crave, and are what draw me time and time again to haul ass to the Beverly Center and overdose on designer denim, rhinestone-encrusted junk accessories and sunglasses fit for endless $25 chicken Caesars salads at the Ivy.

[18] Madonna's philosophical bent begins with her album *Ray of Light* (Warner Brothers, 1998) and continues in kabbalistic strength with *Music* (Warner Brothers, 2000) and *American Life* (Warner Brothers, 2003). Mercifully, *Confessions on a Dance Floor* (Warner Brothers, 2005) and *Hard Candy* (Warner Brothers, 2008) offer some respite from the hilarious new spirituality that has somehow rubbed off on Madonna in (where else?)...LA. The escape is only partial, however. As the VH1 documentary *I'm Going to Tell You a Secret* (2005) manifests in unflattering detail, Madonna has lost touch with the marvelous superficiality that garnered her early fame. Convinced that she can actually sing, play the guitar, write poetry and nurture the indigent, she has forgotten what draws fans to her in the first place: her wonderful nothingness.

PART III:

GLOBAL PRODUCTS AND STYLES OF CONSUMPTION

CHAPTER THIRTEEN

THE *TOKUNBO*: A SOCIOLOGICAL EXAMINATION OF THE IMPORTED SECOND-HAND AUTOMOBILE MARKET IN NIGERIA

AYOKUNLE OLUMUYIWA OMOBOWALE

Depending on the cost, taste and financial ability, consumers develop preferences for products to satisfy their needs. Vehicles are products which attract consumption from a wide spectrum of consumers, irrespective of class and socio-cultural differences. However, ownership or non-ownership of cars, as well as the type or brand of cars bought, may depend on socio-economic factors. Motor vehicles have been a medium of land transportation ever since their debut in the early twentieth century. They have been transformed through technological breakthroughs, as well as in response to consumers' demands and expectations. They have become necessities in developed countries, and luxuries in developing nations.[1] As new vehicles are produced and purchased, older models enter a ready second-hand market, where they are either resold, or salvaged for their usable parts.[2] Soderman and Carter describe the salvage yard as "a space where the souls of objects are saved"—a place where used automobiles and/or auto-parts acquire new value and the renewed potential to attract consumers.[3]

---

[1] N. Myers and J. Kent, "New Consumers: The Influence of Affluence on the Environment." *Proceedings of National Academy of Sciences of the United States of America* 100.8 (2003): 4963–4968; A. Greenspan and D. Cohen, "Motor Vehicle Stocks, Scrappage, and Sales." *The Review of Economics and Statistics* 81.3 (1999): 369–383; J. Eberly, "Adjustment of Consumers' Durables Stocks: Evidence from Automobile Purchases." *The Journal of Political Economy* 102.3 (1994): 403–436; J. Lehmann, "France, Japan, Europe, and Industrial Competition: The Automotive Case." *International Affairs* 68.1 (1992): 37–53.

[2] Greenspan and Cohen, 369–383.

[3] B. Soderman and R. Carter, "The Auto Salvage: A Space of Second Chances." *Space and Culture* 11.1 (2008): 22.

In Nigeria, imported Japanese vehicles have strong resale value because new models (popularly called "tear-rubber") are not affordable for the average consumer.[4] Consequently, imported second-hand vehicles have attracted significant patronage within the past twenty years, and have acquired their own identity and niche market. They have been re-christened as *tokunbo* (from across the sea), with many buyers treating them as if they were tear-rubber, even when they know they are not. Unlike second-hand vehicles from Nigeria, *tokunbo* have a higher resale value due to their generally better condition. Among the Yoruba of Southwestern Nigeria, an imported second-hand car would not be considered *aloku* (used). Only vehicles used in Nigeria would be perceived as *aloku.* This is because used vehicles imported from the Americas, Europe, or Asia have a certain *caché* that can never be ascribed to *aloku.* Like the children born to migrant Yoruba parents living abroad (who were the first to be called *tokunbo*), imported second-hand vehicles have a degree of implied social value because they come from a "wealthy" foreign land.

This chapter, which is based on empirical sociological data collected in the city of Lagos, where there is an abundance of imported second-hand vehicles, will examine the socio-economic role of *tokunbo* in Nigeria.[5] Using rational choice theory as its theoretical framework, this study posits that Nigerians choose *tokunbo* because they satisfy their goal of vehicle ownership, as well as their desire to acquire status symbols which will rank them above the "lower classes."[6] This phenomenon, in turn, strengthens the *tokunbo* market in Nigeria, making it a profitable addition to the local economy for both buyers and sellers.

---

[4] Tear-rubber means that the polythene covering on the seats are still in place. The car is therefore brand new, and should be driven home in celebration with family and friends. It should also be noted that this is a status symbol, even among members of the middle class. An individual who is able to afford a tear-rubber is seen as successful, comfortable and rich, irrespective of the fact that s/he might have taken out a loan to purchase it.

[5] Twenty oral interviews were conducted with willing users and sellers of *tokunbo.* Ten of the interviewees were sellers, while the remaining ten were users. Five of the respondents were female (all were users), while fifteen were males (ten sellers and five users). The data generated were subjected to content analysis.

[6] The rational choice theory views individuals as actors with goals and/or intentionalities, who subject their actions to rational thought processes in order to realize a "preferred action." For more information, please see G. Ritzer, *Sociological Theory* (New York: McGraw Hill, 1996) and G. Ritzer and D. Goodman, *Sociological Theory* (New York: McGraw Hill, 2003).

Preference for *Tokunbo* Vehicles

While it is difficult, if not totally impossible, to obtain secondary data on the volume of second-hand vehicles imported to Nigeria, close observation shows their preponderance in auto shops and on Nigerian roads. *Tokunbo* are imported through official routes via ports, but they are also smuggled in through illegal bush paths. Sighting convoys of smuggled vehicles being driven recklessly at top speed in order to escape law enforcement agents is a common sight in many Nigerian cities and border communities. Indeed, the second-hand vehicles keep coming into the market irrespective of official control due to the availability of a ready market. One such consumer provides insight into why these imported second-hand vehicles are preferred:

> People buy *tokunbo* vehicles because of the price, which is relatively less compared with new ones. Besides, people can hardly afford new vehicles because of the deplorable socio-economic conditions in the country today. Nonetheless, it is important to note that once you buy a *tokunbo* vehicle, you begin to spend money on it for its maintenance. *Tokunbo* vehicles are quite expensive to maintain.[7]

Likewise another respondent stated:

> People go for *tokunbo* vehicles because they are cheaper…It is not that people prefer *tokunbo*, but it is what they can afford. A fairly used car can be bought for N 450,000 ($3,750 US) [compared to] N 2.5 million ($16,600 US) for a new one. Too many demands are on the little income one earns. There is more liability with *tokunbo* vehicles. It is part of the liabilities one buys.[8]

The opinions of the above users are also echoed in the response given by the seller below:

> Customers go for *tokunbo* vehicles due to financial constraints… Everybody would like a new thing. But financial constraints will limit what can buy.[9]

---

[7] Oral Interview, Male User, February 4, 2008.

[8] Oral Interview, Male User, February 1, 2008. Responses from other interviewees also affirm that many users purchase *tokunbo* vehicles due to Nigeria's deplorable socio-economic conditions, which make brand new vehicles unaffordable.

[9] Oral Interview, Male Seller, February 1, 2008.

This qualitative data illustrates that many buyers opt for second-hand vehicles due to financial constraints. Ordinarily, brand new vehicles are preferred, but since the cost of new automobiles is rather prohibitive, Nigerians choose a more economical option to satisfy their goal of car ownership. Despite consumers' skepticism about the durability of second-hand cars, the *tokunbo* remains an option. Nevertheless, users of imported second-hand vehicles readily admit that maintenance is expensive. They often begin spending large amounts of money on repairs shortly after purchase. In the words of one respondent:

> Unlike a brand new car, once you purchase a *tokunbo* vehicle, you start spending on it almost immediately. In fact you may have to take it to a mechanic to assess it before you can use it. Many *tokunbo* cars are refurbished...I will say the cost and maintenance is somewhat more expensive because one starts to spend on it [as soon as] you buy it.[10]

In addition to satisfying their goal of car ownership, *tokunbo* cars also elevate class status. In this context, car brand also matters. Japanese brands are preferred because they are perceived to be more durable and "prestigious" than other Asian cars, even ones that are brand new. As one interviewee conveys:

> The brand of the car matters. A *tokunbo* Toyota is still better appreciated than a brand new KIA or Hyundai. I may drive a 1995 Toyota Camry and another person uses a 2008 model...What matters more is that I use Toyota Camry.[11]

Another respondent, a seller, states:

> I would rather buy a new vehicle depending on the type provided if it is [a] Honda, Toyota or Nissan...because they are easier to maintain and the spare parts are readily available and cheap. Otherwise, I will go for a *tokunbo* of any of the same brands... I would not say that *tokunbo* vehicles are better than new ones. But definitely the likes of Honda, Toyota and Nissan have better and more durable engines than KIA and other Korean and Asian brands.[12]

---

[10] Oral Interview, Female User, February 4, 2008.
[11] Oral Interview, Female User, January 28, 2008.
[12] Oral Interview, Male Seller, February 21, 2008.

As another user claims:

> The new [Asian] cars that are coming to the market are not the brands we used to…I would rather go for the *tokunbo* brands that have proved worthy over the years. There was a friend who bought a brand new Hyundai and the vehicle engine suddenly exploded six months later. To repair it, he had to import some of the parts from Dubai through the help of a relation. In fact there were many…parts...brought but [they] were incompatible with the car. Yes there are service centers [for Korean vehicles] in some locations round the country, but the services there may be more expensive than the roadside mechanics that we are used to. I would rather buy a new car if I had the means, but it has to be Toyota, because of its fuel efficiency and because it is a common brand that we are used to. The spare parts are also readily available. A new vehicle is better than *tokunbo*. But I will not go for a KIA or Hyundai. I am…more concerned about the efficiency and durability of any car I buy, even if it is a *tokunbo*.[13]

The preference for Japanese brands was confirmed by a seller who claimed: "The brand customers buy most are *tokunbo* Toyota, Nissan and Mitsubishi because they believe that they are durable in terms of maintenance and fuel efficiency. Although the new KIA vehicles are less preferred, I believe they are good too, though this is my opinion."[14] Another seller added: "The brands of *tokunbo* vehicles they buy are Toyota, Nissan and Honda because they are easy to maintain and their spare parts are cheap."[15]

Nigerians thus prefer Japanese *tokunbo* even over brand new Korean cars for a number of reasons: durability, efficiency, gas mileage, affordability, availability of spare parts and the accessibility of semi-skilled automobile mechanics who specialize in Japanese *tokunbo*. These factors have also collectively contributed to the symbolic value of Japanese cars, which have been used in Nigeria for four decades. Thus, in this case, part of the prestige of Hondas, Toyotas and Mitsubishis derives from the fact that they are reliable—an old standby in an uncertain new world. Hence, a buyer who has struggled to save money to buy a vehicle would rather purchase a Japanese *tokunbo* instead of a new Korean model because the latter usually requires specialized service centers to maintain. Under this configuration, attention is diverted away from the fact that new Korean vehicles are "new," and is redirected towards the notion that

[13] Oral Interview, Male User, January 28, 2008.

[14] Oral Interview, Male Seller, February 1, 2008.

[15] Oral Interview, Male Seller, February 21, 2008.

"good" cars, whether old *or* new, come from Japan. Hence, Nigerians are much more likely to make the rational choice of Japanese *tokunbo*.

The Growing Market for New Vehicles

Even though Nigerians continue to prefer Japanese brands, over the past couple of years, a small segment of the population has begun purchasing new cars from South Korea and China. This burgeoning shift is the result of the sudden availability of bank financing for new vehicles.[16] Until recently, only the government and the super-rich could afford brand new vehicles. However, bank loans have now made new cars more accessible, especially for the middle class, and there is an indication that Nigeria may be reverting to the good old days (of the 1960s and 1970s) when people could afford new vehicles. This certainly stands to have a major impact on the *tokunbo* automobile market. Nevertheless, as one interviewee reflected:

> The growing market for new vehicles is good but the fact still remains how many people can afford new cars? It is certain that if someone cannot earn enough money for a new car, he will go and buy a *tokunbo* car for the same purpose that the new car will serve.[17]

According to a male *tokunbo* seller:

> I do not think the emerging market for new vehicles will be a threat to the sale of *tokunbo* vehicles because there is higher patronage for *tokunbo* vehicles [compared to new cars]. Except for the government and other corporate bodies who can go for new vehicles, most other people still go for *tokunbo* vehicles because they are cheaper.[18]

Another respondent stated:

> It is good that new vehicles are beginning to come on Nigerian roads once again. I still feel however that the market and products are meant for the rich who can spend huge sums of money for brand new vehicles. Others simply opt for *tokunbo* vehicles, which they can afford.[19]

---

[16] D. Ochefu, "Auto Loans Boost Banks' Risk Assets," *Sunday Punch*, April 6, 2008, 40.
[17] Oral Interview, Male User, January 29, 2008.
[18] Oral Interview, Male Seller, February 21, 2008.
[19] Oral Interview, Male User, January 29, 2008.

Although new vehicles are valued, their costs still remain prohibitive for a large segment of the population. Thus, according to the interviewees, despite the growing enthusiasm for new cars, they are not seen as a possible threat to the *tokunbo* vehicle market. It is safe to say that, at least for the foreseeable future, *tokunbo* vehicles will remain the preserve of Nigerians who cannot afford new vehicles.

The *Tokunbo* Automobile Market in Nigeria: A Discussion

As human beings consume, they satisfy various personal requirements, which may include survival needs or those directed at self-esteem and self-actualization (i.e., wants).[20] In the twenty-first century, the consumption of goods has become increasingly directed at the satisfaction of socially-constructed values or expectations, usually in response to group or class pressures. According to Brekke and Howarth, "prevailing consumption patterns and class identifications establish the vantage point through which individuals evaluate their personal well-being. As such, the consumption bundle necessary to achieve the 'good life' is a moving target that depends on one's social environment."[21] In most social environments, "consumption bundles" take the form of symbolic goods, or status symbols, that are accompanied by culture-bound, socially-constructed interpretive meanings which have the potential to change over time. Automobiles clearly fall into the category of a contemporary consumption bundle. When one consumes a car, s/he not only buys the vehicle itself, but also the image, or lifestyle, projected by the car. While it is true that vehicles are primarily a means of transportation, they also reflect their drivers' socio-economic standing, and thus serve as overt, and interpretable, status symbols.

Even five decades after independence from British colonial rule (they introduced cars in the first half of the twentieth century, and withdrew from the country in 1960), automobile ownership in Nigeria still remains a status symbol. Nevertheless, within the past twenty years, vehicle markets in Nigeria have reached phenomenal dimensions, especially in terms of the

---

[20] H. Baumgartner, "Towards a Personology of the Consumer." *The Journal of Consumer Research* 29.2 (2002): 286–292; M. Csikszentmihalyi, "The Cost and Benefits of Consuming." *The Journal of Consumer Research* 27.2 (2000): 267–272; R. Belk, "Possession and the Extended Self." *The Journal of Consumer Research* 15.2 (1988): 139–168.

[21] K. Brekke and R. Howarth, "The Social Contingency of Wants." *Land Economics* 76.4 (2002): 494.

importation of second-hand vehicles. Since their introduction as a transportation option, *tokunbo* have become popular alternatives to mass transit, Nigerian second-hand vehicles, and even some brand new foreign imports. One reason behind this is the positive public perception of Japanese cars in terms of reliability, efficiency and durability. Another is the deplorable socio-economic conditions of the country which make it financially impossible for most to own new (especially Japanese) cars. The Structural Adjustment Program (SAP), which was a World Bank-administered socio-economic policy adopted by Nigeria in 1986, perpetuated the poverty of Nigerians by encouraging the privatization of social services. No longer able to rely on government support for their basic needs, Nigerians had to redistribute their economic resources, and unfortunately for most, cars became luxuries, not necessities. If a buyer did manage to save enough money to purchase a car, chances were it was only enough for a *tokunbo*.

While this socio-economic analysis certainly explains the preponderance of second-hand vehicles in Nigeria, it is also crucial to note that the socially-constructed meaning attached to *tokunbo* is just as important in its success as a second-hand product. Ordinarily, in Nigeria, the use of second-hand products (*aloku*) is stigmatized for its association with the working class. Such products are commonly displayed in markets and along the roadside in Lagos on Mondays, Wednesdays, and Fridays; those who cannot afford to purchase new items patronize second-hand dealers. A middle-class professional would very rarely be seen buying used merchandise. However, this is not the case with *tokunbo*. Since these second-hand vehicles have been shipped from abroad, and are thus imbued with a certain level of sophistication, they constitute a category of previously-owned goods that are desired by all levels of Nigerian society. In this case, what should be considered "*aloku*" has been recast as "*tokunbo*."

The substitution of *tokunbo* for *aloku* has had a tremendous impact on Nigerian society. For one, it has had the net result of democratizing car ownership. No longer the domain of the extreme wealthy, vehicles can now be seen throughout the country, especially in large cities. Because the acquisition of an automobile was a dream for many Nigerians even until quite recently, when a *tokunbo* vehicle is purchased, it is celebrated as if it were new. Even though bank loans are increasingly making it possible for a Nigerian to purchase a new car, many still opt for a used Japanese import since consumer confidence, especially in new Korean models, remains weak. Moreover, despite the global pressure to consume the "latest and greatest" products on the market, Nigerian car buyers and sellers remain comfortable with *tokunbo* because both groups (and thus by extension the local economy) benefit from the secondary resale market. Thus, at least for the foreseeable future, new cars do not pose a serious threat to *tokunbo*, which, because of its *caché* as a status symbol, has become an indelible part of the Nigerian social fabric.

CHAPTER FOURTEEN

IDENTITY FOR SALE: THE BILLION DOLLAR AFRICAN AMERICAN HAIR TRADE

ELIZABETH JOHNSON

There is an identity struggle that takes place in the African American female community on a daily basis: choosing to value and love one's blackness as a form of resistance against white supremacy. While many examples illustrating this phenomenon exist, one of the best is Spike Lee's 1988 film *School Daze*. In the film, Lee forces African American women to face their skin color and hair issues and be honest about how they view their blackness through a scene which focuses on African American female college students arguing over what constitutes good or bad hair. In this scene, which is set at Madame Re-Re's, a fictitious hair salon, the women argue over the issue of altering their hair from its natural state, which to some, suggests being ashamed of their blackness. Throughout the movie, female characters with "good" (i.e., straight) hair repeatedly express their superiority over women with "bad" (i.e., kinky) hair, thus reinforcing the idea that black women should have "good hair" at any cost.

In contemporary culture, many African American women feel compelled to straighten or "relax" their hair (i.e., transform it into "good hair") in order to access the power and wealth enjoyed by European American women. Relaxing is a chemical process which permanently alters the natural structure of hair. As new hair emerges, relaxer must be reapplied to the roots in a time-consuming and painful process.[1] Today, roughly sixty to sixty five percent of African American women straighten their hair with chemical-based relaxers.[2] Many African American women begin relaxing their hair in their teens, and continue to do so well into their

---

[1] For further discussion on relaxers see Mary J. Tenerelli, "Ethnic Hair Fare." *Global Cosmetic Industry* 168.6 (2001): 32–33.

[2] Dale H. Johnson, ed. *Hair and Hair Care* (Cosmetic Science and Technology Series) (New York: Marcel Dekker, Inc., 1997).

sixties. Thus, it is not surprising that African American women spend millions of dollars each year on hair products.[3] In 2004, the sale of relaxers alone totaled $41.3 million.[4]

African American women are not just purchasing relaxers, however. In 2007, $1.8 billion was spent on black hair care products (including relaxer kits, conditioners, styling aids, hair color, shampoos, after-shampoo conditioners, and moisturizers).[5] Although African Americans only comprise twelve percent of the US population, their purchasing power is over $650 billion, which explains why the hair care industry is vying for a substantial portion of this market segment.[6] African Americans outspend European Americans three to one on the beauty-product dollar.[7] But why do African American women place so much emphasis on chemically-altered hair? Why are African American women spending so much money on getting their hair chemically relaxed and sitting through a painful, burning process? The choice of African American women to chemically relax their hair is not a new phenomenon, and is one that rests in the politics of identity.

As recipients of messages that urge them to reject their blackness, African American women face an identity crisis, specifically with respect to who they are and who they would like to become.[8] Their crisis is accentuated by that fact that identity functions on two levels: it is self-constructed from *within* (i.e., it is a project that we do ourselves), and is defined from *without*, or imposed on us by our physical appearance and/or behavior. The identities of those who exercise power or effective control in a society are valued; the identities of those without power are denigrated, ignored, and devalued.

---

[3] In 2001, ethnic hair care product sales at drug stores alone were over $100 million. Molly Prior, "Ethnic Makers Expand Lines, Taking Cue from Professional Brands," Drug Store News 24.14 (2002): 45–46.

[4] Nanci McArdie, "Ethnic Hair Care: Room for Growth." *Happi Household and Personal Products Industry*. Last accessed July 2008: http://www.happi.com/articles/2005/04/ethnic-hair-care-room-for-growth.

[5] Dionne Walker, "Black Hair Gives Rise to Natural Products: African-American Entrepreneurs Respond to Push for Alternatives to Straightened Tresses," *The Atlanta Journal Constitution*, March 9, 2008. Last accessed July 2008: www.ajc.com/metro/content/business/stories/2008/03/09

[6] Joia Shillingford, "Hair-care Firms Wise Up to Ethnic Pound." *BBC News*. Last accessed July 2008: http://news.bbc.co.uk/go/pr/fr/-/2/hi/business/4417725.stm

[7] Victoria Wurdinger, *The Multicultural Client: Cuts, Styles, and Chemical Services* (Albany, NY: Milady Publishing Co., 1996), 110.

[8] Ayana Byrd and Lori L. Tharps, *Hair Story: Untangling the Roots of Black Hair in America* (New York: St. Martin's Press, 2001), 134–135.

This chapter will investigate the choices involved when African American women decide to purchase newly-textured hair/hair products, and how the purchase of altered hair, which is fueled by marketing messages that promote dominant beauty standards, impacts their identity. *Essence* magazine (1985, 1990, 1995, 2000, and 2005) will be subjected to a content analysis which will be used to examine how hair products are sold to the African American community. *Essence* was chosen because the publication has a monthly circulation of over one million copies and a readership of eight million (ninety one percent of whom are women, with an average age of thirty seven), and is geared towards middle-class and professional African Americans (i.e., the demographic segment who, because of income, most likely to purchase upscale hair products).[9]

Numerous hair care manufacturers have chosen to advertise their products in *Essence* because it is the world's leading fashion and hair magazine for women of color. Throughout the years, *Essence* has addressed social issues, fashion, hairstyles, money management, health, and relationship issues. Thus, it is a commercial magazine and an important way to reach the African American community.[10] Because of this fact, *Essence* is a very powerful tool of persuasion, and an effective method of disseminating hair identity messages to the African American adult female population. In addition to selling goods to African Americans, this medium also sells an identity based on dominant standards of white beauty (e.g., products are usually sold using black models with straightened hair and European features). As the advertisements in *Essence* demonstrate, the desire to emulate white norms can be directly correlated to the chemically-straightened hairstyle choices of African American women.

Essence: A Content Analysis

1985 was a pivotal year for African Americans for two reasons. Firstly, Vanessa Williams had recently become the first African American Miss America (after Williams resigned from the position, her runner-up,

---

[9] *Essence: Our Company* (2008). Last accessed July 2008: http://www.essence. com/essence/ourcompany/ In 1994, the median age of the readership for Essence was 35.6 years old. Nancy I. Maxwell, "Social Differences in Women's Use of Personal Care Products: A Study of Magazine Advertisements, 1950–1994," *Silent Spring Institute*, November 1, 2000. Last accessed July 2008: http://library. silentspring.org/publications/pdfs/magazinestudy.pdf

[10] Patricia Reid-Merritt, *Sister Power: How Phenomenal Black Women are Rising at the Top* (New York: John Wiley & Sons, Inc., 1996), 106.

Suzette Charles, also an African American woman, assumed the crown). Secondly, 1985 marked the juncture when white-owned companies began to absorb many black-owned hair care companies.[11] Competition would become intensely fierce by 2000, as more and more white-owned hair care manufacturers bought out smaller black-owned hair care manufacturers, and gained a stronger place in the ethnic hair care market. Since, in the 1980s, African American women were not accustomed to having culturally-specific marketing directed towards them, it was a surprise to see white manufacturers attempting to cater to their hair care needs (albeit out of the not-so-altruistic motive of retail competition).[12]

The ultimate goal of this content analysis is to look at the hair care manufactures that chose to advertise in sixty issues of *Essence* published between 1985 and 2005. The advertisements examined all featured at least one hair care product and at least one adult African American female model. If the advertisement had more than one African American female model, the ad was only counted once, unless two different hairstyles were represented in the ad (e.g., straight hair and a curl). In ads where two or more hairstyles were represented, each hairstyle was counted separately, which, in some cases, led to over-representation of certain hairstyles.

(Whites) Selling Black Identity

Since the 1980s, manufacturers have increasingly been advertising in black magazines such as *Essence* order to encourage African Americans to purchase hair straightening products which will "give African Americans a more European American look."[13] By normalizing whiteness through the models' hairstyles (i.e., straightened hair through the use of chemicals), these ads have encouraged African American women to assimilate into white beauty standards. As illustrated in Figure 14.1, there has been a dramatic decline in the number of advertisements placed by black hair companies in *Essence*. In 1985, fifty nine percent of the hair care ads were placed by black-owned companies; in 1990, forty percent; in 1995, thirty percent; in 2000, seven percent; and in 2005, only eight percent of the hair ads were placed by black-owned companies. On the other hand, there has been a dramatic increase in the number of ads placed by white-owned

[11] Cliff Hocker and Sakina P. Spruell, "Bad Hair Day," *Black Enterprise* 31.4 (2000): 144.

[12] Kimberly Palmer, "Ethnic Hair-Care Ads Show New Faces," *The Miami Herald*, Sept. 1, 2003, sec. G, 13.

[13] Marilyn Hunter, *Shopping for Identity: The Marketing of Ethnicity* (New York: Schocken Books, 2000), 31–32.

companies, which corroborates the fact that most large black hair care firms are white-owned.

Figure 14.1: Advertisements 1985-2005

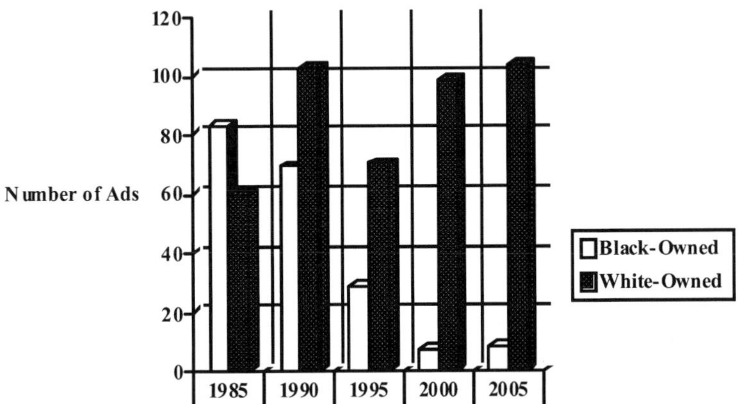

	1985	1990	1995	2000	2005
Black-Owned	83	69	29	7	8
White-Owned	59	102	70	98	103

Division of Companies

Figure 14.2 evaluates the hairstyles of the advertising models. Consistently, both black and white-owned companies' models overwhelmingly had straight hair. Repeatedly, models whose hair and facial features were close to a European aesthetic were utilized, thus marginalizing anything associated with blackness. Although African American male and child models were excluded from the study, it must be noted that both groups also engage in the identity politics of straight "white" hair. In fact, there are chemical relaxers geared exclusively towards African American female children, and some alter their hair textures as early as five years of age. Only a small number of advertisements utilized braids, Afros, natural hairstyles, and curls (which were popular in the 1980s), which, to *Essence* readers, only reinforces the importance of having chemically-straightened hair (or at least a straight wig).[14] Alternatives were not provided, which explains why, during this time period (1985–2005), many African American women sought (and as a result made popular) magazines that featured Afros, braids, (dread)locks and twists such as *Beat*, *Braidsworld*, *Honey*, *Hype Hair*, *Sophisticate's Black Hairstyles and Care Guide Magazine*, and *Streaks*.[15]

Figure 14. 2: Total Ads - Hair Sales

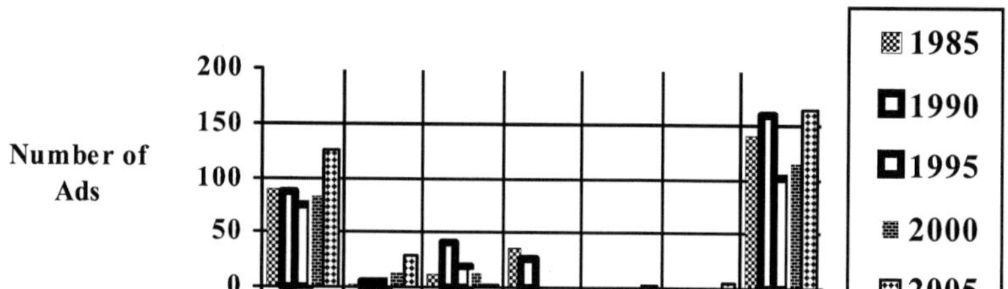

	Straight	Natural	Wig	Curl	Braids	Afros	Totals
1985	89	2	12	36	0	0	139
1990	87	6	40	27	0	0	160
1995	75	5	20	0	1	0	101
2000	84	15	15	0	2	0	116
2005	126	28	2	0	2	5	163

Styles

The power of hair care manufacturers to determine styles and promote styles that are costly to achieve and maintain has to be included in any explanation of advertising, as do the gender-specific codes that many young women strive to follow in their pursuit of dominant standards of

[14] Dionne Walker, "Black Hair Gives Rise to Natural Products: African-American Entrepreneurs Respond to Push for Alternatives to Straightened Tresses," *The Atlanta Journal Constitution*, March 9, 2008. Last accessed July 2008: http://www.ajc.com/metro/content/business/stories/2008/03/09/
Maxine Leed Craig, *Ain't I a Beauty Queen: Black Women, Beauty, and the Politics of Race* (Oxford, UK: Oxford University Press, 2002), 24. All of the wig companies were white-owned, even those that utilized the names of African American celebrities (i.e. Beverly Johnson, Naomi Sims, Star Jones, Dianne Carroll, and Michael Weeks).

[15] Adémola Mandella, Preston Phillips, and Anasuya Isaacs, *Authentic Hair: Photos, Poems and Prose Celebrating the Beauty and Versatility of Natural Hair* (New York: Cosmic Nubian Enterprises, 2002).

beauty. Understanding how powerful forces manipulate people through hairstyles is only one side of the power relationship. The need and/or desire not to be labeled as rebellious, deviant, or radical, serves the main motivator for hair conformity.[16] As bell hooks has illustrated, "practically speaking, a lot of black women learned to prefer straightened hair…because it took less time…Certainly, going out to work in a white world that has always been threatened by black people who appear to be decolonized has had a major impact on what black females choose to do with our hair."[17]

The most profound finding of this content analysis was the overwhelming number of ads for straight hairstyles. In these ads, African American identity was clearly linked to chemically-straightened hair, which, in a positive feedback loop, was reinforced by the large number of straight-haired models in *Essence*. As Lanita Jacobs-Huey notes, identity is intimately connected with hairstyling choices, whether chemically processed or not. For African American women, especially, "it is hard to ignore the racial and societal implications that go along with their choice."[18] As Noliwe Rooks observes, it is through the semiotics of advertisements that one may discern "culturally acceptable fashions and hairstyles that promise not only the means of achieving beauty, but a particularized bodily relation to the dominant culture," which, in *Essence*, plays a major role in identity formation.[19]

Another finding was that over the years, advertisements have become more technical and detail-oriented, most likely in response to the criticism that black hair was becoming increasingly artificial and unattainable. In 2005 Avlon Industries, a white-owned company, noted on all their advertisements that their models did not wear hairpieces or weaves, thus conveying to the reader that the hairstyles used in the advertisements were not constructed from the models' own hair. Another tactic was the repeated use buzz words (e.g. natural, improved, organic, and advanced formula) to sell products. Celebrity endorsements have also helped reinforce the legitimacy of the advertisements' claims. Stars have included Beyonce (singer and actress), Tamyra Gray (from "American

---

[16] Alf Hiltebeitel and Barbara D. Miller, eds., *Hair: Its Power and Meaning in Asian Cultures* (Albany, NY: SUNY Press, 1998), 284–286.

[17] bell hooks, *Sisters of the Yam: Black Women and Self-Recovery* (Boston: South End Press, 1993), 85–86.

[18] Edward North-Hager, "Hair-Raising Thoughts on Cultural Coifs," *USC News*, June 16, 2006. Last accessed July 2008: www.usc.edu/usnews/stories/12525.html

[19] Noliwe Rooks, *Hair Raising: Beauty, Culture, and African American Women* (New Brunswick, NJ: Rutgers University Press, 1996), 11.

Idol"), Kelly Rowlands (singer in the musical group Destiny's Child), Laila Ali (daughter of boxing star Mohammed Ali), Mary J. Blige (singer), Roshumba (supermodel in the late 1980s-early 1990s), Anita Baker (singer), Sheila Johnson (supermodel in the 1980s), Mpule Kwelagobe (Miss Universe 1999), Jayne Kennedy (actress, model, and 1980s NFL analyst), Nia Long (actress), and many others. The ultimate goal of using these celebrities is not only to the increase sales of white-owned companies, but also to add credibility to the products that are being sold in terms of both efficacy and their ability to transform identities.

Laila Ali, who modeled for white-owned Soft Sheen-Carson® Optimum Care™ Regular Relaxer and Soft Sheen-Carson® Optimum Care™ Shampoo and Conditioner, used her father's trademark boxer pose to link the products she was advertising to narratives of "strength and beauty," even though Mohammad Ali and the hair products being sold were not inherently connected. Here, the importance is Ali's image—in other words, what Ali's identity means to consumers.[20] The hair products are being substituted for the glamour and strength that Ali symbolized during his career, and, as a result, the products that Laila Ali is peddling can also be interpreted as a source of resistance against dominant cultural standards of beauty (i.e., in much the same way that Ali himself resisted white social norms during the 1960s and 1970s).

Another phenomenon exhibited during the years examined was the technique of "shared advertisements." As Kathy Myers explains, "shared advertisements [are when] the expense of an advertisement [is] shared by two or more interested companies," and thus both (or all) of them are featured in the same advertisement.[21] The shared advertisements featured in *Essence* were usually for hair care products sold at K-Mart or Sally's Beauty Supply, placed on sale for a certain time frame, or with special coupon offers only available at their stores. One example of a shared advertisement included African Pride® Hair Relaxer (with an African American female model with auburn hair on the packaging, sporting a shoulder-length flipped bob) and TCB Naturals® Relaxer (with an African American female model with black hair on the packaging, adorned in a shorter chin-length bob). Both of these women exhibited features that adhere to white society's cultural expectations of beauty—features that are

[20] Judith Williamson, "Decoding Advertisements." *Media Studies: A Reader*, eds. Paul Marris and Sue Thornham (Edinburgh: Edinburgh University Press, 1996), 490.

[21] Kathy Myers, "Understanding Advertisers." *Media Studies: A Reader*, eds. Paul Marris and Sue Thornham (Edinburgh: Edinburgh University Press, 1996), 481.

often difficult for African American women to obtain: cosmetic smiles, perfect skin, perfect auburn hair, and thin noses and lips.

One weakness of this content analysis is that its findings are correlational, qualitative, and open to multiple interpretations. For example, one might argue that white-owned hair manufacturers' increased use of advertising in *Essence* was simply the result of their larger advertising budgets, rather than a strategic plan to dominate, and whiten, the ethnic hair care market. It is also arguable that the use of African American celebrities to endorse hair care products is a simple marketing strategy, rather than a political tactic used to change the nature of black female identity. Another weakness of this content analysis is that it does not take into consideration the Internet explosion that occurred during the years studied. It is impossible to decipher the impact that the Internet has had on the purchase of hair care products: we cannot determine whether or not readers researched products before making a final decision to purchase hair care products, just as we cannot asses the extent to which African American identity has been shaped by the various forms of media (e.g., music, pictures, streaming video, etc.) available online.

The Effects of Advertising: Unattainable Beauty

Advertisements create mass consumer demand. This point is confirmed through research conducted on African American women aged eighteen to forty four, which found that seventy percent of respondents are "always looking for new [hair] products."[22] While advertisements for African American women's hair products function as visual and written texts on the control and normalization of hair, the reality is that African American female beauty standards have become so unattainable that only wig wearers can keep up with the socially-constructed demands of "good hair."[23] African American women do have the potential to resist these often white beauty norms, but many are trapped because they cannot interpret black female beauty through a black lens. Thus it is not surprising that black models and entertainers choose not to exercise the power of resistance. Instead, they willingly endorse products that promote dominant cultural beauty standards. The benchmark for young African American women has become mimicking models who themselves are

[22] "Ethnic Hair Care Focuses on Organic," *Drug Store News* 29.9 (2007): 75.

[23] Deborah. R. Grayson, "Is it Fake? Black Women's Hair as a Spectacle and Spectacular," *Camera Obscura—A Journal of Feminism and Film Theory* 36.9 (1995): 15.

mimicking the white look, which only lasts until the next application of chemical relaxers.

Even black manufacturers have become participants in this game by promising that their products will transform and "normalize" African American hair so that it will more closely resemble (white) social expectations of beautiful or "long straight hair."[24] Luster Products, (a black-owned business) placed five ads in *Essence* in 2000, and presumably, as a result, grossed $4.4 million in drug store sales of chemical relaxers (Luster was the only black-owned company that advertised in *Essence* in 2005 with eight ads).[25] As Veronica MacDonald explains, "The small players [African American manufacturers] view the market in a different light. Often they have to be much more creative and innovative to compete with multinationals...But some African American manufacturers feel betrayed by the consolidation in the industry."[26] Consequently, many have had to employ the same strategies as white companies in order to sell products.

According to industry research, more than twenty three percent of African American women now wear their hair in various natural hairstyles for a multitude of personal and political reasons.[27] However, as exhibited in Figure 14.2, advertisements featuring models with natural hair (e.g., non-extended braids and Afros) accounted for less than one percent of all advertisements. It is clear that African Americans, or at least companies that claim to be in touch with African American identity, continue to marginalize traditionally black hairstyles, and like in the film *School Daze*, still associate straight hair with "good/desirable" hair, lumping everything else into the ambiguous category of "undesirable" hair.[28]

When an African American woman applies a chemical relaxer every six weeks or so, she is, essentially, making a readjustment to her race.

---

[24] Ibid.

[25] This does not include sales from grocery stores, mass merchandisers, or beauty supply stores.

[26] Veronica MacDonald, "Ethnic Hair Care: Acquisitions are Changing the Market, But When it Comes to Product Development, Moisturization Remains the Mantra," *Household & Personal Products Industry* 39.4 (2002): 60.

[27] "Coloring Hottest Thing in Ethnic Hair Care," *Chain Drug Review* 23.7 (2001): 21.

[28] Kathy Peiss, "On Beauty and the History of Business." *Beauty and Business: Commerce, Gender, and Culture in Modern America*, ed. Philip Scranton (New York: Routledge, 2001), 9; Susannah Walker, "Black is Profitable: The Commodification of the Afro, 1960–1975." *Beauty and Business: Commerce, Gender, and Culture in Modern America*, ed. Philip Scranton (New York: Routledge, 2001), 255.

Relaxed straightened hair is not a fashion choice; it is a socially-constructed disciplinary tool that burns African American women physically, psychologically, and financially. Repeatedly, hair advertisements convey a symbolic message that any African American woman can achieve "normal" status by purchasing these products. Without such hair products, black women are deceptively told that they will never be able to approach the assumed physical beauty of white women, or the benefits they have accrued by virtue of their social status.[29]

Feminists encourage white women not to be bound by sexist images of women who are ultra thin with dyed-blond hair and blue eyes.[30] Likewise, there cannot be freedom for African American women until they learn that marketers are actively targeting blacks to turn a profit, and are not necessarily keeping their best interests in mind. Our consciousness about hairstyling choices should penetrate deeper than their advertising power. We must conduct further research in order to understand fully why generations of black women have subjected themselves to burning chemicals, caustic fumes, the possibility of hair loss, the possibly of scalp damage, and the possibility of hair color alteration all in the name of "beauty." While emulating white society is clearly one answer, it is not the only answer. What makes these advertisements work are the years of internalized oppression and racism which have shaped African American identity into its present form: vulnerable and looking for external validation from white society.

While *Essence* is not the only mass media tool used by manufacturers to sell hair care products to black American consumers, it is arguably the most powerful source of popular print media in the United States today. Because of its ability to reach a large consumer base of African American women, the goals and aims of *Essence* must be reassessed, and reformulated, to counteract the damage that has been done to the black female psyche. Culturally insensitive advertisements that falsely depict a homogenized look must be eliminated, as they perpetuate the dynamics of enslavement and white superiority. However, the key to black women's liberation will be the search for our own definitions of beauty and an acceptance of our own cultural voice, free from the controlling identities of mainstream society. When we as African American women no longer feel less than beautiful because our hair does not match white magazine models, then we will have made a step towards equality. When we as

[29] Glenn Jordan and Chris Weedon, *Cultural Politics: Class, Gender, Race, and the Postmodern World* (Cambridge, MA: Basil Blackwell Inc., 1995), 26.
[30] bell hooks, *Feminism is for Everybody: Passionate Politics* (Boston: South End Press, 2000), 34.

African American women no longer struggle with the bondage of dominant hair aesthetics, or are driven to spend our last dollar to "fix" ourselves, then we have truly straightened a kink in historical thinking.

CHAPTER FIFTEEN

EXPANDING SEAMS: EXPERIENCES OF AUSTRALIAN MATERNITY SHOPPING

MEREDITH NASH

Middle-class Melbourne women have become part of a distinctly contemporary and increasingly global market catering to the consumption of high-fashion clothing during pregnancy, following a long period when pregnant Australian women had been nothing less than inadequately provisioned.[1] Australian retailers, including major department store chains, have largely been unwilling to invest in maternity clothing, perceiving it as "anti-fashion" and unprofitable. To illustrate, one woman shopping for maternity clothing sixteen years ago in Melbourne noted:

> I remember walking into Myer desperate to find something to wear. The clothes were absolutely horrible. The first dress I saw was this horrendous blue and green smock with teaspoons all over it. At that moment, I just thought, "My life is over. I'll just be serving my whole life. I am a teaspoon."[2]

It is only recently that *maternity wear*, long regarded *outside* the boundaries of women's wear, has come to be known legitimately as maternity *fashion*. The production of boutique Australian maternity wear has arisen in tandem with the increasing visibility of pregnant bodies,

---

[1] Melbourne is a bustling metropolis located on the south-eastern edge of Australia on Port Philip Bay. Melbourne has a diverse population of approximately 3.7 million people in a metropolitan area in which almost fifty seven percent of residents were born overseas; City of Melbourne, "Melbourne—A Snapshot." Last accessed July 2008: www.melbourne.vic.gov.au/info.cfm?top=91&pg=862

[2] Myer is a national chain of department stores found in major Australian cities.

particularly those of celebrities, who have provided a cultural/visual narrative for dressing (and consuming) during pregnancy.[3]

With the increasing array of maternity clothing options available to pregnant women in Melbourne comes the added pressure for pregnant women to use maternity clothing to conform to normative feminine body ideals. By Australian middle-class cultural standards, there is no longer any reason for pregnant women to look "frumpy." Now, more than ever, pregnant bodies are constructed as legitimate sites of consumption and production. Thus, dressing the pregnant body is integral to the performance of successful femininity, and in particular, highlights the primacy of slenderness. Dressing in pregnancy has become a means of pregnant corporeal management, and the shape, sizing and retailing of Melbourne maternity boutique fashion are key components in the (self) perception of pregnant bodies.

This chapter contends that the ways in which pregnant Australian women choose, purchase and wear maternity clothing is a meaningful contribution to feminist research exploring the centrality of clothing to women's identities and body images. Utilizing narratives from a diverse group of pregnant Australian informants, this chapter demonstrates that dressing in pregnancy is a complex project of embodied negotiation that is influenced by the geography of Australian maternity retail spaces, as well as their semiotics. In-depth, semi-structured interviews with pregnant women focusing on body image, fashion, exercise, and eating were conducted over a two year period, as were in-depth, semi-structured interviews with maternity industry professionals.[4] Data analysis was performed using situational analysis, building upon Glaser and Strauss's theory in which the "situation" becomes the "ultimate unit of analysis."[5] Clarke's method for creating "situational maps" was also used to

[3] See Meredith Nash, "Yummy Mummies, Baby Bumps and Body Image: Shaping 'Postmodern' Pregnancy in Melbourne" (PhD Dissertation, University of Melbourne, forthcoming) and "Oh Baby, Baby: (Un)veiling Britney Spears' Pregnant Body," *Michigan Feminist Studies* 19 (Fall 2006–Spring 2007): 27–50. Also see Harriet Gross and Helen Pattison, *Sanctioning Pregnancy: A Psychological Perspective on the Paradoxes and Culture of Research* (London: Routledge, 2007).

[4] All informants have been given pseudonyms throughout this chapter.

[5] Barney Glaser and Anselm Strauss, *The Discovery of Grounded Theory: Strategies for Qualitative Research* (Chicago: Aldine, 1967).

understand how discourses of pregnancy entered the social worlds of informants.[6]

Fashion as Embodied Experience

Clothing is a "lived" daily experience in which garments are used to construct an image of "who we are" to the rest of the world. It is a "fleshy practice of the body" or an embodied experience.[7] This means that how we feel about our bodies on any given day dictates the clothing that we choose to wear. An overarching theme in the majority of feminist research surrounding women and their experiences of fashion is that of body size and/or body bigness.[8] Clothing provides a means for women to quantify the size of their body with a number; losing or gaining weight produces a different fit and a different emotional experience for the wearer.

Feminists have long argued that women's fashion is oppressive and that images from the fashion industry promote unachievable standards of feminine beauty, especially when it comes to thinness.[9] However, there is a growing body of feminist scholarship arguing for more nuanced readings of fashion as a potential source of women's liberation.[10] Contemporary

---

[6] Adele Clarke, *Situational Analysis: Grounded Theory after the Postmodern Turn* (Thousand Oaks, CA: Sage, 2005), 85.

[7] Joanne Entwistle and Elizabeth Wilson, *Body Dressing* (Oxford, UK: Berg, 2001), 4; Fred Davis, *Fashion, Culture and Identity* (Chicago: University of Chicago Press, 1992); Jane Gaines and Charlotte Herzog, *Fabrications: Costume and the Female Body* (London: The Hogarth Press, 1990); Juliet Ash and Elizabeth Wilson, *Chic Thrills: A Fashion Reader* (Berkeley: University of California Press, 1992).

[8] Rachel Colls, "Outsize/Outside: Bodily Bigness and the Emotional Experiences of British Women Shopping for Clothes." *Gender, Place and Culture* 13.5 (2006): 529–545.

[9] Catherine Egley Waggoner and D. Lynne O'Brien Hallstein, "Feminist Ideologies Meet Fashionable Bodies: Managing the Agency/Constraint Conundrum." *Text and Performance Quarterly* 21.1 (2001): 26–46.

[10] See Shari Benstock and Suzanne Ferriss, *On Fashion* (New Brunswick: Rutgers University Press, 1994); Diana Fuss, "Fashion and the Homospectatorial Look." *On Fashion*, eds. Shari Benstock and Suzanne Ferriss (New Brunswick: Rutgers University Press, 1994), 211–232; Jane Gaines, "Fabricating the Female Body." *Fabrications: Costume and the Female Body*, eds. Jane Gaines and Charlotte Herzog (New York: Routledge, 1990), 1–27; Cheryl Herr, "Terrorist Chic: Style and Domination in Contemporary Ireland." *On Fashion*, eds. Shari Benstock and Suzanne Ferriss (New Brunswick: Rutgers University Press, 1994), 236–266; Norma Claire Moruzzi, "Veiled Agents: Feminine Agency and Masquerade in *The*

feminists argue that fashion should no longer be viewed as a "seamless web of oppression" with women as its cultural dupes.[11] Yet, the bodies of overweight women are still read as not quite "fitting in"—literally and metaphorically—with the dictates of mainstream fashion. For example, Kathleen LeBesco suggests that "the fat woman is indeed the forgotten woman" across race, class and age boundaries in fashion because popular brand names do not want to be associated with the negative connotations of overweight bodies.[12] LeBesco contends that it was not until the 1990s that fat women were embraced as valued consumers. This "commodification of corpulence" has facilitated the explosion of the plus-sized clothing market in Australia and elsewhere.[13]

The historical invisibility of fat women in fashion highlights the Western cultural ambivalence towards women's bodily boundaries. In light of this ambivalence, how does fashion accommodate women who are neither conventionally fat nor thin, but have to contend with rapidly-changing bodies? How do pregnant women factor into mainstream Australian fashion? Moreover, how has the development of the Australian maternity fashion industry challenged the historical invisibility of pregnant bodies in public? Most importantly, how are pregnant Australian women experiencing this shift?

Battle of Algiers." Negotiating at the Margins: The Gendered Discourses of Power and Resistance, eds. Sue Fischer and Kathy Davis (New Brunswick: Rutgers University Press, 1993), 255–277; Leslie W. Rabine, "A Woman's Two Bodies: Fashion Magazines, Consumerism and Feminism." *On Fashion*, eds. Shari Benstock and Suzanne Ferriss (New Brunswick: Rutgers University Press, 1994), 59–75; Elizabeth Wilson, *Adorned in Dreams: Fashion and Modernity* (Berkeley: University of California Press, 1987); Iris Marion Young, "Women Recovering Our Clothes." *On Fashion*, eds. Shari Benstock and Suzanne Ferriss (New Brunswick, Rutgers University Press, 1990), 197–210.

[11] Wilson, *Adorned*, 53; Also see Susan Bordo, *Unbearable Weight: Feminism, Western Culture, and the Body* (Berkeley: University of California Press, 1993); Jennifer Craik, *The Face of Fashion: Cultural Studies in Fashion* (London: Routledge, 1994); Egley Waggoner and O'Brien Hallstein, "Feminist," 2001; Young, "Women Recovering," 1990.

[12] Kathleen LeBesco, "Revolution on a Rack: Fatness, Fashion and Commodification." *Revolting Bodies? The Struggle to Redefine Fat Identity* (Boston: University of Massachusetts Press, 2004), 66.

[13] Ibid., 66–67.

Dressing Pregnant Bodies

Until recently, relatively little attention has been paid to dressing (and sizing) pregnant bodies in the West.[14] Although maternity clothing is only worn for a relatively short period of time (approximately four to six months, and for up to one year postpartum) it, in fact, is central in the construction of identity during pregnancy. Given the growing body of international literature about the relationships women have with their clothes, it is surprising that there is a large gap in the literature when it comes to maternity wear. The few existing studies in this area focus mainly on British and North American women.[15]

There has been no sustained historical work looking at the production and consumption of maternity wear by Australian women. Robyn Longhurst, a feminist geographer, has produced the only qualitative study of maternity clothing in Oceania, focusing on women in New Zealand between 1992 and 1994.[16] Australian maternity fashion is superficially derivative of the UK, US, and Asia. Yet, as dress historian Margaret Maynard argues, middle-class Australian women have sometimes been "stubbornly resistant" to styles from overseas, mostly because Australian fashion has had a strained relationship with "European metropolitan style."[17]

---

[14] See Vikki Beale, "Fashioning the Pregnant Body: Wearing Pregnant Bodies" (PhD Dissertation, University of Sheffield, 2003); Nicky Gregson and Vikki Beale, "Wardrobe Matter: The Sorting, Displacement and Circulation of Women's Clothing," *Geoforum* 35.6 (2004): 689–700; Rebecca Bailey, "Clothes Encounters of the Gynecological Kind: Medical Mandates and Maternity Modes in the USA, 1850–1990." *Dress and Gender: Making and Meaning*, eds. Ruth Barnes and Joanne B. Eicher (New York: Berg, 1992), 248–265; Rebecca Bailey, "Fashions in Pregnancy: An Analysis of Selected Cultural Influences, 1850–1980" (PhD Dissertation, Michigan State University, 1981); Robyn Longhurst, "(Ad)dressing Pregnant Bodies in New Zealand: Clothing, Fashion, Subjectivities and Spatialities," *Gender Place and Culture* 12.4 (2005): 433–446; Robyn Longhurst, "Corporeographies of Pregnancy: Bikini Babes," *Environment and Planning D: Society and Space* 18 (2000): 453–472; Robyn Longhurst,"(Re)presenting Shopping Centres and Bodies: Questions of Pregnancy." *New Frontiers of Space, Bodies and Gender*, ed. Rosa Ainley (London: Routledge, 1998), 20–34.

[15] Bailey, "Clothes Encounters," 1992; Davidson, "Pregnant," 2001; Gregson and Beale, "Wardrobe," 2004.

[16] See Longhurst, "(Re)presenting," 1998; "(Ad)dressing", 2005; *Maternities*, London, Routledge, 2008.

[17] Margaret Maynard, *Out of Line: Australian Women and Style* (Sydney: UNSW Press, 2001), 4–5.

As Rebecca Bailey suggests, historically, the "shaping" of maternity clothing has been inextricably linked with how pregnant bodies have been perceived medically. In particular, Bailey contends that "pregnancy was a very telling marker of whether pregnant women were allowed to participate fully in society."[18] As non-pregnant women's clothing became more form-fitting between 1850 and 1880 due to the advent of the sewing machine in the US, the UK, and Australia, pregnant women were, conversely, encouraged to avoid figure-hugging garments altogether. The mass production of maternity wear originated in the US and was publicly sanctioned in 1911 in New York, when the Lane Bryant Company "was mobbed by excited pregnant women." Bryant's maternity tea dress, called "Number 5" after its position on an order form, was the "first dress designed and advertised, by word-of-mouth, as a maternity garment" in the world.[19] While there is no definitive history of Australian maternity clothing to date, the sale of maternity clothing in Australia closely followed the American model.

It was not until the late 1940s, after World War II, that the social mores of pregnancy started to change in the US, the UK, and Australia. By the late 1940s, most garments worn by non-pregnant women were available in maternity sizes—even sportswear—which previously did not exist given the restrictions on exercise.[20] In the 1960s, however, middle-class Australian pregnant women were depicted as demure and child-like in mainstream maternity advertisements, often posing by themselves, or with a girlfriend, in shapeless shifts made specifically to conceal a belly.[21] Moreover, maternity clothing was only available in very limited quantities in large department stores. In the 1970s, the increased use of Lycra, the stretchy fabric that allows clothing to fit like a second skin, encouraged the production of a number of figure-hugging maternity garments such as jeans and leggings.[22] For instance, in a 1971 issue of *Australian Women's Weekly*, pregnant women described as "trendy mums" are shown wearing

---

[18] Bailey, "Clothes Encounters," 251.

[19] Ibid., 255, 258.

[20] For instance, knee-length maternity shorts became popular around the same time that a pregnant Lauren Bacall appeared in *Life* magazine (1948) wearing "demure Bermudas." Bailey, "Clothes Encounters," 259.

[21] Women were rarely photographed with a male partner, presumably to avoid sexual associations.

[22] See the official Lycra website for the history of the product. Last accessed July 2008: http://www.lycra.com

a range of body-hugging maternity styles.[23] At least until the late 1980s, in the US pregnant women continued to be portrayed as relatively asexual: maternity wear mimicked baby clothes, often featuring pastel colors, animal prints, puffed sleeves and oversized bows.

The famous 1991 *Vanity Fair* cover photo of a pregnant Demi Moore revolutionized maternity wear by catalyzing the construction of middle-class pregnant women as a significant market with buying power.[24] In 1994, the maternity market began to boom in the US. Australia's smaller population limited the expansion of the maternity marketplace, and it was not until 1996 that the first boutique maternity clothing stores opened in Melbourne. This burgeoning maternity industry not only challenged the designs of conventional maternity wear, but also permanently changed the representation and performance of Australian pregnancy.

A Snapshot of Maternity Retail in Melbourne

One does not necessarily have to be pregnant in order to gain a sense of contemporary Australian pregnant body aesthetics. The current Australian maternity retail market insists on low-cut, tightly fitting tops, hipster jeans and sexy lingerie. Following a trend of one-word or short-phrase names, the majority of mainstream Melbourne maternity shops pay tribute to pregnancy with cheeky and often childish plays on words. For example, a selection of the most popular maternity labels include Ripe, Belly Button, Egg, Soon, Froü Froü, Pea in the Pod, Pumpkin Patch, Mother2B, Bump Babies, Fillyboo, One Plus One, Bloom, Precious Cargo, Mamalicious, Queen Bee, and Fertile Mind.

Melbourne maternity stores engage a variety of semiotic resources (for example, layout, color, and language) to create a meaningful text for maternity shopping. Through this symbolic packaging, pregnant women's needs are structured and codified in the geography of contemporary retail spaces. In particular, the vision of pregnancy embodied in Melbourne maternity spaces reflects the social perception of what pregnant women should be, and what they should wear. Pregnant women are offered hyper-feminized identities as contemporary maternity fashion is designed to enhance aspects of pregnancy that are symbolic of classical femininity such as enlarged breasts, wide hips, and a round belly.

---

[23] "Maternity Fashion Glamour for All Occasions." *Australian Women's Weekly* 5, May 1971, 3–4.

[24] Imogen Tyler, "Skin Tight: Celebrity, Pregnancy and Subjectivity." *Thinking Through the Skin*, eds. Sarah Ahmed and Jackie Stacey (London: Routledge, 2001), 69–84.

Melbourne maternity boutiques rely on unique visual images to attract customers. The visual impact of the retail interior often makes a lasting impression on the pregnant customer's perception of the shopping environment and its associated products. While maternity stores attempt to present unique images, they also have striking similarities. Pastel colors are frequently used, as is magenta, which emphasizes the "sexy", "fun" and "glamorous" clothing available for mothers-to-be (Figure 15.1). Phenomena of the last twelve years, Melbourne's maternity boutiques target specific demographics of pregnant shoppers, and often operate in affluent areas to capitalize on a valuable market.[25] Retail interiors thus make a "price statement" through visual messages, even if actual prices are not necessarily higher than other maternity stores.[26]

Figure 15.1: Example of a Popular Melbourne Maternity Boutique Storefront

Photograph property of author. Used with permission.

[25] To illustrate, a simple Google search of "funky maternity wear in Melbourne" resulted in 6,000 references to a variety of online and retail shops with "funky fashions" for pregnancy. In contrast, "trendy maternity clothing" resulted in only 1,900 references. This disparity illustrates the ways in which Melbourne maternity boutiques have positioned themselves within the Australian market. Whereas "funky" is about taking fashion risks, "trendy" is about following the crowd. Clearly, associating fashion-forward maternity wear with "funky" is important in establishing a following with women who were invested in fashion prior to becoming pregnant and who now do not want to look like everyone other pregnant woman in Melbourne.

[26] Frederick W. Langrehr, "Retail Shopping Mall Semiotics and Hedonic Consumption," *Advances in Consumer Research* 18 (1991): 428–433.

The semiotics used in these relatively upscale maternity boutiques are designed to encourage the middle-class pregnant Melbourne woman to see herself in each outfit, and purchase accordingly.[27] One boutique maternity store, Bump, even has the semiotics of retail stores written into its franchise policies:

> The POS [point-of-sale] counter with its clean, modern lines and branding is the focal point in the store. The...beech and chrome provides flexibility within the store and the softness of the beech gives a nurturing aspect. The black/white walls and ceiling give a clean palette to profile the merchandise. The floor is a choice of either polished concrete or lime-washed timber. Halogen lighting is used throughout with light boxes presenting images of the current season. It is recommended that…changing rooms are as spacious as possible. A comfortable sofa and small play area with toys is available if space allows. Branding externally needs to be of a high standard and approved by Head Office to ensure the brand maintains a high profile/quality image.[28]

With retail outlets throughout Melbourne, Bump has designated a specific design profile to maintain its appeal as a "high-status" store. The symbolic identity of the pregnant Bump customer is defined by the minimalist interiors of its retail boutiques, with soft lighting and branding replicating mainstream non-maternity fashion lines. Thus the "packaging" of a Bump shop encourages middle-class female consumers to commodify themselves during pregnancy.

As the structure and shape of maternity clothing has evolved, so too has the maternity shopping "experience." Maternity retailers have realized that focusing on the entire retail environment is essential in changing the negative image of maternity clothes. Part of the success of one prominent Melbourne maternity design duo has come from seeing the link between semiotic variables and a shopper's emotional experience in-store. For example, they noted it was their mission to re-brand the "daggy-ness" (i.e., dorkiness) associated with maternity clothing. This perception still existed among a number of pregnant informants who said they dreaded the thought of buying maternity clothes because they were "old-fashioned" and "dowdy."

---

[27] Ipsita Chatterjee, "Packaging of Identity and Identifiable Packages: A Study of Women-Commodity Negotiation through Product Packaging," *Gender, Place & Culture* 14.3 (2007): 294.

[28] Bump head designers. Tape recorded interview with author. Melbourne, Australia, May 15, 2006.

How do Melbourne maternity boutiques maintain a unique sense of place while establishing an identity in a widening market? The answer is reflected in the dramatic revising of Australian maternity spaces. For example, the designers of the most popular Melbourne maternity brand, Bump, noted that making maternity shopping more like the pre-pregnancy shopping experience was a key step towards helping pregnant women change their preconceptions about maternity clothing. This approach is integral to creating a space that is "readable" to all pregnant women. Part of the Bump high-end retailing strategy is displaying clothing according to a particular conceptual design; nothing is placed on a rack at random. In "low-end" shops like outlets and discount stores, clothing is often jumbled on racks without necessarily conforming to a particular visual aesthetic.

As Dianne Horgan argues, "high" and "low" status stores display different attitudes towards pregnant shoppers. According to Horgan, in "high status" maternity shops, "pregnancy is seen as feminine, delicate, luxurious, joyous, [and] personal...," whereas "lower status" stores, pregnancy is viewed as an unglamorous "job."[29] This language suggests that the shopper is in the store for a bargain, not an ego boost.

Store layout is so pivotal to a pregnant woman's shopping experience that even the design of the fitting room, and the positioning of mirrors, are manipulated to impact the shopper's body image. Whereas such details can be taken into consideration in a big budget, high profile "concept" store like Bump, outlet or designer discount warehouses usually cannot afford such design approaches. Laura's Preggi Belli discount outlet incident was far more negative than her Preggi Belli "concept" store experience near Melbourne's central business district. She remarked that the outlet mirrors were "fat mirrors," and that the dim lighting had her on the verge of tears.[30] Clearly, consumer goods can be experienced differently depending on their spatial settings. Laura discovered that the geography of the retail space affected her perception of her pregnant body in a way that the higher status store did not.

Suzanne liked shopping at Bump because not only were the clothes arranged nicely, but the fabrics themselves were also "nice and soft." Moreover, the clothes were "flattering" and mostly in solid colors. In lower status stores, the shopper is in the store for a bargain, not an "experience." Suzanne noted that in lower-priced stores, the prints were

---

[29] Dianne Horgan, "The Pregnant Woman's Place and Where to Find It," *Sex Roles* 9.3 (1983): 338.

[30] "Laura." Tape recorded interview with author. Melbourne, Australia, August 8, 2006.

"loud and tacky."[31] Lower status stores have no overarching aesthetic and exist as self-service alternatives for lower-income women. Unlike Suzanne, who chose to frequent upscale shops, Laura did not have the benefit of having a salesperson allay her fears that she looked fat and pregnant.

The Complexities of Dressing

Whether a pregnant woman chooses to purchase maternity clothing or not is intimately connected with her feelings about her growing body or "corporeal ambivalence," and is not necessarily a function of financial resources or style incompatibility. Wearing maternity clothing was important for many women because it signaled that a swollen belly was pregnant, and not fat. During her fifteenth week of pregnancy, Noel was surprised that most of her pre-pregnancy clothes still fit but that she still felt fat and not properly pregnant.[32] She said that her pregnancy would probably sink in when she went to buy maternity clothes because they were not her usual style. For Noel, the purchase of maternity clothes marked the point where normal ended (in terms of culturally-acceptable body sizes and her self-identity) and where ambiguity or bigness began. In her mind, there was a certain type of clothing associated with big bodies (pregnant or not), and these outfits were generally "very conformist and conventional, containing those bodies that threatened to break out."[33]

Clarissa was also particularly concerned with dressing her pregnant body, which she felt was "no longer her own." Maternity clothing only reinforced this feeling of being disassociated with her body, and she openly admitted that she agonized over what to wear. She remarked, "It's just been really hard for me…if you have a particular style that you're used to wearing, it's that whole thing of being outside of your comfort zone."[34] Clarissa felt dressing had become a chore and a challenge rather than a source of pleasure as it had been pre-pregnancy. Moreover, she acknowledged that her lack of enthusiasm for shopping was directly linked

---

[31] "Suzanne." Tape recorded interview with author. Melbourne, Australia, August 7, 2006.

[32] "Noel." Tape recorded interview with author. Melbourne, Australia, June 14, 2006.

[33] Alison Adam, "Big Girls' Blouses: Learning to Live with Polyester." *Through the Wardrobe: Women's Relationships with Their Clothes*, eds. Ali Guy, Eileen Green and Maura Banim (Oxford, UK: Berg, 2001), 50–51.

[34] "Clarissa." Tape recorded interview with author. Melbourne, Australia, September 6, 2006.

to the way she felt about her body. Maternity clothing was not like her normal clothing: the outfits felt like fat clothes, and they were temporary. Thus, her chief difficulty was "the mismatch between the required sartorial performance [in public] and her [personal] embodiment."[35]

In contrast, at ten weeks, Charlene did not yet have a belly, but she had already purchased some maternity clothing as a way to make the pregnancy feel real.[36] Charlene needed to purchase a few maternity pieces, whether she would wear them or not, as a means of forging a meaningful self-identity that encompassed her pregnancy and her mother-to-be status. Charlene's status was thus defined by wearing clothing similar to other pregnant women. This automatically conferred a visible group identity which provided her with a sense of purpose.[37]

Plus-Sized Pregnancy Fashion

In her discussion of "big women" and their shopping experiences, Alison Adam suggests that "largeness is not a suitable part of femininity for all that it conjures up about age, maturity and motherhood; largeness is outside or 'outsized'." As such, "big women" are not even within the boundaries of "normal" or "woman"; they are literally "outside of that boundary."[38] At fourteen weeks Diane, who was plus-sized before pregnancy, noted: "What bothers me about maternity clothes is that they're really expensive and really hard to get in larger sizes. Like fat people don't have children!"[39] Clearly, Diane was aware of the Western, and increasingly global, message that fat people are asexual and un-sexy and therefore not in need of maternity clothes. In order to avoid the trouble of trying to find clothing in her size, Diane, an extremely accomplished seamstress, made most of her clothing both before and after pregnancy. She was thus able to achieve a personal style, and resist the mainstream maternity market with its limited range of clothing for plus-sized pregnant women, by fashioning her own custom-made look.[40] In doing so, Diane was able to derive pleasure from pregnancy fashion in a way that was unavailable via the mainstream Melbourne maternity market.

---

[35] Gregson and Beale, "Wardrobe Matter," 696.

[36] "Charlene." Tape recorded interview with author. Melbourne, Australia, May 27, 2006.

[37] Joanne Entwistle, *The Fashioned Body* (Cambridge, UK: Polity, 2000), 117.

[38] Adam, 46.

[39] "Diane." Tape recorded interview with author. Melbourne, Australia, August 16, 2006.

[40] LeBesco, 66–67.

There are very few maternity shops that actually carry plus-size maternity wear in Melbourne. Overweight pregnant women must make do with "normal" maternity clothing shops that carry a limited range of larger sizes, typically stopping at an Australian size 16 or extra-large (in Australia, plus-sized refers to sizes above 14, and large/extra-large). This is distressing considering that the average Australian woman is getting larger, and definitely not smaller.[41] While Bump confirmed that they have always manufactured larger sizes, they also admitted that there is a stigma associated with plus-sized mothers-to-be: "Some stores don't want a 'Large' in their store. Different stores have a different clientele and the people who sell the clothes have a particular idea of how the clothes should look."[42] The designers at Bump revealed that the credibility of mainstream boutiques relied on their aesthetic appeal. The intentional exclusion of certain sizes and, as a result, certain groups of women from mainstream maternity boutiques, confirms that Australian maternity shopping spaces are imbued with a material habitus that is not necessarily based on class.[43]

The only online Australian store carrying plus-size maternity clothing had ten basic items ranging in price from $45–$120 AU. Moreover, a disproportionate number of the available garments were bland and constructed from polyester, the artificial fiber with which fatness has long been associated. With its ability to almost interminably hold its shape, polyester has been the easy care, no-iron-needed boon to the plus-size fashion system. The clothing assumes its wearer is easy care, bland, boring and happy to minimize the threat of her excessive flesh. As Alison Adam has conveyed, "Is it that manufacturers think that the bulges…[of] big women makes our clothes crush, crease and strain more"?[44] The polyesterization of big women's clothing is a means of camouflaging fatness and hiding excess flesh in shapeless shells that do not expose skin

---

[41] Obesity is defined as having a BMI over 30. See Mandy Biggs. "Overweight and Obesity in Australia," Parliamentary Library (October 5, 2006). Last accessed July 2008: www.aph.gov.au/library/INTGUIDE/sp/obesity.htm ; Australian Institute of Health and Welfare, "Australia's Health 2006," Cat. No. AUS 73 (June 21, 2006). Last accessed July 2008: www.aihw.gov.au/publications/index.cfm/title/10321

[42] Bump head designers. Tape recorded interview with author. Melbourne, Australia, May 15, 2006.

[43] See Pierre Bourdieu, *Distinction: A Social Critique of the Judgment of Taste* (London: Routledge, 1984); Peter Williams et al, "Consumption, Exclusion and Emotion: The Social Geographies of Shopping," *Social & Cultural Geography* 2.2 (2001): 203–220.

[44] Adam, 46–47.

or emphasize sexuality. This is also the case during pregnancy, perhaps the only time when fat women's "oversized" bodies are socially acceptable.[45] Whereas average-sized pregnant Australian women are increasingly encouraged to expose their pregnant bellies with tightly fitting tops and low-slung maternity jeans, overweight pregnant women are encouraged to cover up their bodies as much as possible.

Another popular maternity retailer, BabyBoo, confirmed that their company avoided an association with fatness in their sizing "system." Rather than labeling sizes from 00 to 18, clothing is sized from 00 to 5. This is a thinly veiled attempt at "vanity sizing." The purpose of standardized sizing has been to fit a huge range of body sizes into predetermined manufacturer's dimensions. "Vanity sizing," on the other hand, allows customers to believe they fit into more culturally appropriate sizes.[46] The actual dimensions of the garment may fit a woman sized 18, or XXL, however, the BabyBoo sizing tag tells the customer she is a waifish size 5. This strategy is employed because retailers believe that pregnant women are inclined to have a more positive body image if they trick themselves into thinking they are smaller than they actually are. Vanity sizing encourages pregnant women to psychologically disconnect from the changes taking place with their bodies by reframing the fact that they do not fit into "normal" clothes any longer. Plus-sized women can thus acquire a more positive image of themselves during pregnancy despite the fact that they were overweight pre-pregnancy.[47] For retailers, this translates into happier customers and increased sales.

This is not to say that women are unaware that they are purchasing a size 5 instead of a size 18. As Rachel Colls suggests, "What is interesting is that women know they are in some ways 'cheating the system' and their own embodied knowledge counters what they are told in a shopping context…It is the inconsistency of clothes sizing from shop to shop that provides women with an uncertainty as to how the consumption moment

---

[45] Rose Wiles, "'I'm Not Fat, I'm Pregnant': The Impact of Pregnancy on Fat Women's Body Image." *Women and Health: Feminist Perspectives*, eds. Sue Wilkinson and Celia Kitzinger (London: Taylor & Francis, 1994), 33–48.

[46] Marina Alexander, Lenda Jo Connell, and Ann Beth Presley, "Clothing Fit Preferences of Young Female Adult Consumers." *International Journal of Clothing Science and Technology* 17.1 (2005): 56.

[47] Alison Guy and Maura Banim, "Personal Collections: Women's Clothing Use and Identity," *Journal of Gender Studies* 93 (2000): 323.

will be experienced."[48] Thus, it seems inevitable that boosted body-confidence in one maternity retail shop will lead to disappointment as soon as the plus-sized pregnant woman sets foot in another maternity store using conventional sizing.

Through a feminist geographical analysis of Australian maternity retails spaces, this chapter has illustrated how pregnant women's involvement in consumption is a project of physical and emotional self-fashioning, and an experience that both accommodates and destabilizes normative modes of mainstream fashion performance. Although pregnant bodies have been embraced and fetishized as "objects" to be publicly displayed, the shape, sizing and cut of contemporary Australian maternity wear often reinforces the aesthetic of mainstream non-pregnant women's fashion. Moreover, the "packaging" of certain pregnancy boutiques not only promises to confer a particular identity (e.g., as "funky," "trendy," or "glamorous"), but also attempts to normalize the pregnant body into mainstream fashion. Contemporary attitudes toward pregnant bodies encourage women to use clothing as a means of disciplining a body shape that clearly refuses to conform.[49]

As an important locus of female self-identity in pregnancy, the consumption of maternity clothing can be both a source of power and pleasure as well as a vehicle for the objectification of middle-class Australian women.[50] A number of women reported that they liked wearing maternity clothing because their bodies were less likely to be read as "fat." This negotiation was context dependent and temporally distinct depending on how much space informants literally inhabited at any particular time. Media representations of maternity *fashion,* drawing largely on trends in celebrity culture, were also critical in the construction of an idealized fashionable "self." "High fashion" and up-market maternity boutiques in Melbourne were equated with wealth, idealized beauty and disciplined bodies. Thus, in this context, boutique maternity fashion was not simply an arbitrary mark of "distinction" for the informants, but rather a reflection of general, global trends concerning "publicly" pregnant bodies.

---

[48] Rachel Colls, "'Looking Alright, Feeling Alright': Emotions, Sizing and the Geographies of Women's Experiences of Clothing Consumption," *Social & Cultural Geography* 5.4 (2004): 588–589.

[49] Alexandra Warwick and Dani Cavallaro, *Fashioning the Frame: Boundaries, Dress and the Body* (Oxford, UK: Berg, 1998), 82.

[50] Wilson, *Adorned,* 1987; Young, "Women Recovering," 1990; Christine Delhaye, "The Development of Consumption Culture and the Individualization of Female Identity," *Journal of Consumer Culture* 6.1 (2006): 87–115.

CHAPTER SIXTEEN

HOME DEPOT'S WAREHOUSE RETAILING: GLOBALIZING LOADING DOCKS AND LOGISTICS

SARA STEVENS

The retail experience of shopping at a Home Depot store involves expansive parking lots, orange-vested employees, and extra-wide aisles holding everything from arrays of tiny screws to large sheets of plywood. As the second largest retailer in the United States, the chain's market saturation guarantees that most Americans are familiar with it, if not enamored of it. Anti-sprawl advocates cite Home Depot's stores as major offenders in wasteful urban planning. However, while its stores do contribute to suburban sprawl and retail blight, Home Depot's influence extends much further into the economic landscape than its orange-garbed real estate holdings suggest. Any serious study on how to move away from the energy-intensive consumer lifestyle must consider a wider angle of corporate practices and global material flows beyond what happens at the check-out. Home Depot's sourcing and distribution system is one place to begin. Studying the full path made by consumer products from raw materials to store shelf, including corporate retail expansion and methods of transportation and storage, will illustrate the expansive reach that large retailers have on consumer practices and the global economy.

The overland shipping industry—trucking, that is—is feeling the effects of the increased market share of big box stores. By requiring shorter travel times, tighter delivery windows, frequent progress updates, and efficiently-managed small deliveries, the carrier companies for large retailers have forced changes on the industry and ultimately on truckers. An investigation of the Port of Oakland recently showed how pressure on carrier companies comes from large retailers who control the greatest market share, and use their power to push down prices and wages for truck drivers.[1] Home Depot is one of the major agents causing the shift to independent contracting for truckers, and more broadly, causing industry-wide shifts for trucking, storage, and logistics. In order to fill its high shelves, Home Depot optimizes its logistics to satisfy its unusual system of product sourcing and distribution, simultaneously drawing in an increasingly global array of products as store expansion spreads beyond national borders.

Home Depot entered the US retail market with eight stores in 1979, applying discounting techniques to the home improvement industry, while operating as a warehouse retailer (meaning back-of-house storage is eliminated and front-of-house selling space is the primary storage space). Warehouse retailing grew out of the discounting trend in American retail in the late 1960s, which emphasized volume buying, large stores, and self-service. Early discount chains aimed to increase sales by reducing profit margins and relying on high sales volumes to make up for the lost margin. In short, they sought to sell more for less. Warehouse retailing sends goods directly from distribution centers to the selling floor, which combines storage capacity with display space, and reduces overhead costs. This method saves money, but leaves the company vulnerable since there is no backup stock if a delivery is late. As a result, the company leverages its size and scale to exert pressure on the shipping industry, setting high standards for performance and charging huge penalties for any delays on deliveries.

Home Depot success has relied on selling large volumes on high turnover by intentionally lowering gross profit margins to twenty six percent from an industry average of twenty eight to thirty two percent.[2] It has also benefited from larger cultural trends that have impacted home improvement chains. Historians are just beginning to uncover how Americans have taken to the do-it-yourself trend by looking at the early post-WWII years when, for example, power tool manufacturers started advertising to homeowners, and retailers began offering evening classes.[3] Home improvement remains popular, mostly because it is not vulnerable

---

[1] East Bay Alliance for a Sustainable Economy, "Taking the Low Road: How Independent Contracting at the Port of Oakland Endangers Public Health, Truck Drivers, and Economic Growth" (September 2007). Last accessed July 2008: http://ebase.live.radicaldesigns.org/index.php.

[2] "Building Business Builds in '82," *Chain Store Age* 59.8 (August 1983): 56–57.

[3] Carolyn Goldstein, *Do It Yourself: Home Improvement in 20th-Century America* (Washington, DC: National Building Museum, 1998); Barbara Kelly, *Expanding the American Dream: Building and Rebuilding Levittown* (Albany, NY: SUNY Press, 1993).

to fluctuations in the economy. If interest rates are high, people are more likely to stay in their homes and remodel than buy a new house. They are also more willing to do household repairs and projects themselves to save money rather than hire skilled labor. If interest rates are low, people move into new houses and do significant work themselves, especially in the first year.[4] North American consumers seem to buy into the industry line, given company revenues, but as the company expands overseas into different cultural contexts, the company will have to absorb new difficulties in logistics, and respond to changing consumer patterns.

Distribution System

To maximize the advantages of warehouse retailing, Home Depot founders Bernie Marcus and Arthur Blank devised a system that eliminated both distribution centers and distributors. In a traditional distribution system, the retailer orders goods from distributors, who place those orders with suppliers. Goods are then shipped to the retailer's distribution centers, where they are sorted and sent on trucks to individual stores. Home Depot skips those steps by acting as its own distributor. It contacts suppliers directly, contracts with trucking companies, and has orders shipped directly to stores, where pallets of goods are stored directly on shelves in the selling space. Wal-Mart, before Home Depot, eliminated distributors by contacting suppliers directly, pioneering this strategy in the discount industry. What Home Depot did that was innovative for large-scale retailers was to eliminate the distribution center step, as well as the back-room storage at each store. This allowed savings and higher profits, which made it possible to drop prices and gross margins against the industry average.

Home Depot's retailing model has frequently been copied. Many chains switched to the warehouse format in their store designs. Yet no major competitor adopted the specific distribution system espoused by Home Depot. Hechinger's, Lowe's, and Kmart's Builders Square each implemented store-level warehousing at different times, but not Home Depot's distribution system.[5] By 1991, sales by warehouse-style stores

---

[4] "Do-It-Yourself Chain Surges in Slump," *New York Times*, January 13, 1983, Section D, Page 4, Column 1.

[5] Kara Swisher, "Hardware Wars: Hechinger Strikes Back," *The Washington Post*, March 29, 1993, F1; Barbara Rudolph, "Blueprint for Trouble? K Mart Has Extraordinary Hopes for the Do-It Yourself Market," *Forbes*, January 28, 1985, 51. One exception to this is Home Quarters, which did attempt to eliminate the

represented one-fourth of the total market for the US home improvement retail market. In this still-fragmented industry, Home Depot accounted for only a small portion of stores, about five percent in 1990. Despite its modest slice of the pie, Home Depot attained and held the lead, generating per-store sales that were more than seven times the industry average. Home Depot began a trend that resulted in an estimated fifty percent decrease in the number of home improvement industry distributors during the 1980s.[6]

Home Depot's distribution system is not without attendant risks and difficulties. To succeed at such a large scale, trade-offs are required which often result in a very fragile system, the need for third-party logistics companies, and outsourced, temporary storage. Thus security and flexibility are sacrificed for efficiency. It necessitates careful balancing—one that is susceptible to collapse by the simplest outside factors, such as weather, market changes, and labor disputes. Developing new techniques such as cross-docking and transit facilities has allowed Home Depot's distribution model to continue in modified form, despite an increase in overseas goods. This model remains an integral part of the chain's business plan, contributing to its past, present, and presumably future global success.

Logistical Challenges

Without a middle party to facilitate the company's complicated orders, Home Depot was required to absorb the additional work. Home Depot arranged to receive shipments to stores during off hours. This meant that store employees would not be taken off the selling floor during busy times, and would be better utilized during late-night and early-morning hours. This arrangement required the carrier's employees to work off-hours, however it enabled a more efficient utilization of equipment. Home Depot scheduled standing daily appointments at every store to eliminate dispatching and routing negotiations between stores and carriers. Ship notices and invoicing were automated to allow store employees to prepare for each shipment prior to arrival. The chain also instituted the option of drop-trailer deliveries, where the trucker would leave the trailer at the store, passing receiving responsibilities to the employees, who would

---

distribution center. Laurel Campbell, "Home Quarters Joins Do-It-Yourself Market," *The Commercial Appeal (Memphis)*, March 13, 1992, B4.

[6] Kimberly D. Hendrix, "The 1990s: It's a Rough Time for Home Improvement Retailing," *Chain Store Age* 67.8 (August 1991): 34A–37A.

unload at their convenience. This kept the driver from losing time waiting for a trailer to be unloaded, and gave the stores more flexibility. The technology of the pallets (on which goods are stacked and transported) was adjusted to facilitate the transfer of goods. Switching from wood pallets, which had to be returned to the truck after unloading, to slipsheets, which are plastic trays that transfer from truck to store shelf and take up less space, eased logistical problems.[7]

Seasonal shifts in the home improvement industry create challenges for Home Depot. The quick turnover of large items every spring—gas grills, lawn equipment, outdoor furniture, lumber—means that operations must move equally fast. In 2002 Home Depot decided to lease short-term warehouse space near certain stores to position oversized, "high velocity" merchandise within quick reach of its emptying shelves. These multi-customer, rentable distribution centers provided much-needed extra space during critical periods for Home Depot.[8] Still, it represented only a small piece of their network. In 2004, Home Depot projected they would use only between seven and ten such rented warehouses that year, which they hoped would add resiliency to their system. This particular innovation has trickled down into related retail sectors. The third-party logistics company that consulted on the seasonal storage for Home Depot later used a similar model for Wal-Mart, arranging a seasonal direct-to-store shipping procedure that mimics Home Depot's system.[9]

Another difficulty created by this system is the increased need for less-than-truckload (LTL) shipments due to the high number of small deliveries to individual stores by suppliers. Since orders often skip the middle step of consolidation through a distributor, shipments that do not fill up an entire truck still require a trip from supplier to store, which can result in huge inefficiency. As of 2001, in addition to its annual four hundred thousand full truckload movements, the company also coordinated four million LTL movements. To deal with this, Home Depot hired a consultant to create logistics management software to automate price

---

[7] "Home Depot's Prescription for Carrier Productivity," *Transportation & Distribution* 35.9 (September 1994): 32; Robert J. Bowman, "Home Depot: How Big Hardware Retailer Makes Direct Delivery Work," *Supply Chain Brain,* July, 2002. Last accessed April 2008: www.supplychainbrain.com

[8] "USCO to Manage Home Depot Overflow Program," *The Journal of Commerce Online*, March 13 2003. Last accessed April 4, 2008: www.joc.com; Connie Robbins Gentry, "Room to Grow," *Chain Store Age* 80.4 (2004): 58.

[9] Gentry, "Room to Grow," 58.

negotiations, optimization, and ultimately, the carrier-selection process.[10] Without a location, like a distribution center, to consolidate these shipments, inefficiency was an unavoidable consequence of this system, but one that the company was quick to address.

Cross-Docking

To further minimize the problem of LTL shipments, Home Depot began researching cross-docking techniques in 1996, opening their first facility in Philadelphia that year. Long, slender buildings with loading docks on two long sides, cross-docking facilities are distribution centers without long-term storage. Shipments arrive, are unloaded on one side of the facility, consolidated with other arrivals, and repacked for delivery in the assigned bay and trailer that corresponds to each individual store. From there, stores receive one delivery per day during off hours, usually between 4:00 pm and 5:00 am. Smaller than distribution centers, cross-docking facilities, also called transit facilities, are almost always run and managed by third party logistics companies. In 2001, Home Depot announced plans to build sixteen such facilities across the country, and planned for greater expansion if they succeeded. Each facility was designed to handle cross-docking for one hundred thirty, to one hundred forty stores.[11]

The transit facilities provided greater flexibility for the supply network, and further strengthened the system without interfering with the founders' "middleman-free" vision. By 2004, Home Depot owned three types of distribution facilities in their diversified and developed network, each with its own specific tasks: cross-docking facilities, lumber warehouses, and carton distribution warehouses. In addition, they rented short-term extra space for seasonal items. Their lumber facilities are located along rail lines, and receive shipments almost exclusively by rail, usually twenty-five to thirty railcars per week. The transit facilities receive five to six hundred truckloads per week, and make the same number of outbound journeys. Carton facilities operate at about four hundred shipments per

---

[10] Robert J. Bowman, "Home Depot: An Experiment in LTL Carrier Management," *Supply Chain Brain,* July 2001. Last accessed April 2008: www.supplychainbrain.com; "Saddle Creek Open Transit Facilities," *Transportation & Distribution* 43.6 (June 2002): 20.

[11] Brae Canlen, "Fine-Tuning Distribution: Home Depot," *Home Channel News* 27.22 (December 17 2001): 28–31. For background, see Donald Waters, *Global Logistics and Distribution Planning: Strategies for Management,* fourth edition (London: Kogan Page, 2003).

week. Thus each store receives about two to five shipments per week from each type of facility.[12]

This distribution model creates certain pressures on the system with which the company must deal creatively in order to maintain its low overhead. For most of its existence, Home Depot has not sold large household appliances because they are expensive items with low turnover. Moreover, their weight and bulk makes shipping costs a large percentage of retail price. In 1999, after two years of testing, Home Depot decided to enter the appliances market. To deal with this, it signed a deal with GE in which Home Depot would stock sixty percent of items in stores, and GE would keep the remaining forty percent, shipping them directly to customers' homes after they purchased them from a Home Depot store. Home Depot's distribution system also made its webstore both late in coming and limited in success. With a lack of distribution centers from which to fill orders, Home Depot was trapped, resorting to bullying its competitors to stay out of the market. Before launching their webstore in 2000, Home Depot sent veiled threats to their suppliers, discouraging them from selling directly to consumers on the web by suggesting that the suppliers might lose Home Depot's business.[13]

Global Sourcing

The complexity of Home Depot's distribution system did not generate attention until recently, when the chain's size and geographical reach made its system seem a true accomplishment. Ascension to the spot of the US's second-largest retailer drew added interest, as did its quick-response innovations in distribution. Though Wal-Mart and Home Depot both sidestep middleman consolidators, only Home Depot has implemented innovations to eliminate the long-term warehousing of goods. While it has been successful in improving efficiency, Home Depot's increased reliance on global sourcing has added additional stress to its logistics system. In order to accommodate expansion in global sourcing, in 1992 the company opened new distribution centers to handle increased imports.[14] By 1997, three percent of Home Depot's stock derived from international sources (totaling thirty different countries). That equaled twenty thousand

[12] Gentry, "Room to Grow," 58.

[13] Bruce Upbin, "Profit in a Big Orange Box," *Forbes* 165.2 (2000): 122.

[14] "Business in Brief," *Atlanta Constitution*, November 8, 1991, G3; "Business Briefs," *The Atlanta Constitution*, May 21, 1992, J2; Sonia Murray, "Openings," *Atlanta Constitution*, May 16, 1992, C2.

containers' worth of products annually.[15] By 2001, six percent of stock, or about ninety four thousand containers, was imported from forty countries.

Home Depot soon realized that imported goods came with their own set of logistical challenges. Domestic products only have to be consolidated regionally, but overseas goods require national order consolidation to eliminate confusion, and attain an acceptable level of efficiency. Home Depot hoped to lower the cost of imported products by eliminating the "non-value-added middleman."[16] This meant rethinking sourcing and distribution. Home Depot had a few distribution centers (DCs) scattered across the country, mostly on the East and West Coasts near major shipping ports. They decided to reconsolidate these DCs: on the West Coast, the Los Angeles DC supported the Los Angeles and Long Beach ports, while on the East Coast, the Savannah, Georgia DC, which opened in 1997, replaced distribution centers near Atlanta, Miami, and New Jersey.

These new distribution centers quickly became vendors to Home Depot stores, slipping into the established distribution channel with minimal disruption. The new DCs included technological upgrades, including the shift from bar codes and early RFIDs (Radio Frequency Identification) to warehouse management software and wire-guided equipment. This allowed Home Depot to centralize its foreign procurement protocols, standardize specifications, and apply quality testing and random audit checks. Forecasting software, which used two years' worth of sales data and estimated lead and shipping times, also helped the company to predict what to order and how much.[17] Nevertheless, by 2001, more storage space was required to accommodate the increase in global sourcing. Home Depot tapped Trammell Crow, an Atlanta-based developer and real estate company, to develop $150 million worth of distribution centers. Even with these added distribution centers, the company still relied heavily on direct supplier-to-store shipments for the vast majority of their goods.[18]

Despite the temptation of a widely-expanded market base, going global with Home Depot stores proved difficult. Merely expanding to Canada

---

[15] Jean V. Murphy, "Global Sourcing Helps Home Depot Keep Prices Low, Quality High," *Supply Chain Brain*, April 1998. Last accessed March 2008: www.glscs.com/archives/4.98.HomeDepot.htm?adcode=10

[16] Connie Robbins Gentry, "Where Retailers Shop," *Chain Store Age* 78.3 (March 2002): 92–93.

[17] Murphy, "Global Sourcing Helps Home Depot Keep Prices Low, Quality High."

[18] Tony Wilbert, "Trammell Crow to Help Out at Depot," *The Atlanta Journal-Constitution*, July 30, 2001, 2E.

upset Home Depot's low-DC system. After buying a Canadian home improvement chain, Home Depot attempted to convert the former chain's traditional logistics system to the direct-from-suppliers shipping model. Home Depot decided to partner with a Canadian subsidiary of the US shipper which handled the chain's less-than-truckload shipping problem. Because the shipper has extensive North American operations, it maintains an office at every major border crossing between the United States and Canada to ease the import/export process. By electronically sending paperwork prior to a truck's arrival, brokers are able to ease past customs and move a trailer across the border in ninety seconds. The shipper also has its own network of transit facilities on both sides of the border. This facilitates the consolidation of orders, allowing each Canadian Home Depot to receive one truck-load of deliveries per day.[19]

Increasing global sourcing was especially difficult for a company with such high logistical standards. Home Depot demanded a great deal from its domestic carriers, and worked to develop reciprocally beneficial relationships with them. However, this was neither an easy nor a quick task. Home Depot designed a system that allowed overseas suppliers to achieve the same high level of service offered by domestic suppliers. The chain provided extra security for itself by keeping more than one supplier for any given product should more be needed quickly. Moreover, Home Depot retained control of all international freight forwarding, and developed a software system to track international orders. It also developed a web-based invoicing system that targeted smaller overseas suppliers.[20] Thus, establishing global sourcing and international store locations required new developments in Home Depot's corporate management that did not exist on the national level.

The Panama Canal and Savannah

In 2003, longshoremen, port operators, and carriers at the Los Angeles and Long Beach ports were at odds over labor issues, and a long port lockout ensued. Carriers were frustrated by the delays and delivery uncertainties, and began to seek alternative ports and routes. In 2004, overcrowding and understaffing created a major backup at the ports: at one time, as many as forty ocean liners were anchored off the coast of southern

---

[19] Bowman, "Home Depot: How Big Hardware Retailer Makes Direct Delivery Work."

[20] Eric Chabrow, "Supply Chains Go Global," *Information Week* 780 (April 3, 2000): 50–55; "Home Depot's Prescription for Carrier Productivity."

California, waiting to dock. This further catalyzed the search for alternatives to the congested and conflict-ridden West Coast. Previously, Home Depot used a "mini-landbridge" route, meaning, water transportation to the West Coast, then transfer to truck or rail for the remainder of the journey to the Central and/or East Coast locations. Frequent slow downs on cross-country roads and rails also contributed to the difficulty of shipping, which compelled company executives to begin considering all-water routes between Asia and the East Coast. They decided that the Panama Canal would be a more reliable, and less expensive, alternative, and began to use this new water route for shipments bound for the East Coast.[21]

Home Depot, along with Wal-Mart and others, decided that Savannah, Georgia would be a good alternative location to ship goods headed for the East Coast via the Panama Canal.[22] Savannah had a bustling port for two hundred fifty years, exporting flax, silk, and cotton; by 1988, half its docks sat empty. An explosion of Asian goods streamed into the West Coast, while most East Coast Asian shipments bypassed Savannah for Charleston and the Port of New York/New Jersey. As imports to the US increased rapidly, West Coast ports quickly became full to capacity, and shippers looked to the East Coast for back-up. Savannah stood ready to accept more cargo, and between 1994 and 2004, more than tripled the number of cargo containers it accepted. After the Port of New York/New Jersey, it became second largest importer of Asian cargo.[23]

Home Depot had a pivotal role in the ascendancy of Savannah's port. In 1995, Savannah was competing with Charleston, then the largest port in the region, for a new Home Depot distribution center. By offering tax incentives, below-market-value land, and easy access from the interstate, Savannah was able to attract Home Depot, which developed a major East Coast import distribution center near the port. The Georgia Port Authority was also able to offer expedited handling of all Home Depot containers because the state owns the terminals. Thus, labor disputes have never been a problem in Savannah. Soon, Dollar Tree, Wal-Mart, Target, and others followed Home Depot to Savannah. With proximally-located distribution centers, low traffic, and advanced preparation, drivers were

---

[21] Michael A. Levans, "Transportation Trends Tight Squeeze," *Logistics Management*, January 1, 2005. Last accessed April 2008: www.logisticsmgmt.com/article/CA495771.html?text=%22home+depot%22

[22] Neil King Jr., "Panama Canal at Crossroads," *Wall Street Journal*, January 7, 2004, B1.

[23] Daniel Machalaba, "Ship Shape: How Savannah Brought New Life to Its Aging Port," *Wall Street Journal*, August 22, 2005, A1.

able to move shipments out of the port quickly, setting records for performance, increasing profitability, and stabilizing Home Depot's import operations by realizing an all-water transit route.[24]

Home Depot took the warehousing model of retailing to a new extreme. By calibrating its operations against a network of stores rather than a single location, Home Depot built an efficient system with low overhead costs. Like Wal-Mart and other high-volume discounters, Home Depot aimed for expansion and then used size to leverage greater cost efficiency. Although warehouse retailing greatly contributed to its success, this distribution system also required sacrifices in stability and flexibility. However, by adjusting and refining its system through cross-docking, overseas shipping, and revised carrier relationships, Home Depot was able to by-pass deficiencies and profit from this unique business model. The aesthetics of their store interiors—the stenciled lettering, rough finish, concrete floors, poor lighting, tall shelving, and safety-orange color scheme—represent only one dimension of a complex and thorough system of management protocols that aim to produce high profits and market dominance. Because all pieces of the system are interconnected, any attempt to change the model would require an examination of the *entire* system, from trucker technology, to global sourcing, to the orange aprons worn by store employees. Store size and layout, employee-labor relations, supplier timetables—all these factors contribute to the complex equation that is Home Depot.

Home Depot's association with day laborers has prompted a reexamination of the place of large corporations in the exploitation of workers and their local environments. As a chain frequented by small contractors, Home Depot has become a natural setting for the informal congregation of day laborers hoping to find work from shopping contractors. While security guards threaten the laborers (who are mostly men, usually minorities, and sometimes even illegal immigrants) with fines and trespassing charges, workers' advocates believe that it should be *legal* for day laborers to congregate at Home Depot stores, even arguing that Home Depot should pay to build shelters and provide basic amenities for the workers, since the store is responsible for attracting the activity. In 2006, the City of Burbank, California adopted this approach, requiring the Home Depot to build a sheltered hiring site before opening its doors. After opening, anti-immigration protesters mobbed the hiring site, attracting national attention. Following Burbank's lead, the Los Angeles City Council considered a proposal that would require stores like Home

[24] Ibid.

Depot to pay for the construction of a small shelter with water fountains, toilets, trash cans, and shade. Despite various attempts, the city has, to date, been unsuccessful in passing such an ordinance.[25]

The debate about day laborers at Home Depot stores continues today without decisive resolution. Despite its private status, the company is a flash-point in public debates simply because it is so visible. With this status comes increased vulnerability, which, as one would imagine, could lead to the adoption of a defensive attitude. However, as Home Depot has discovered, it makes much more business sense to adapt than lock down its defenses. Opening a store in Manhattan amidst astronomical real estate costs, highly-trafficked streets, and no loading docks, meant reducing the list of required essentials, and radically altering its proven retail model. Rather than creating a high-profile debate with environmental groups, Home Depot decided to sell wood exclusively from certified sources, even though it meant a price increase for its customers.[26] As Home Depot grows, the company is evolving to meet changing conditions, and in the process, is revealing where there might be room for improvement in corporate practices.

Home Depot is just one example of a retailer who accumulates goods across vast distances, manipulating space (and people along the way) to bring together into one retail landscape an array of products that have been shorn of their geographic origins. Warehouse retailing is more than just an aesthetic designed for a particular shopping experience. It involves the daily choreography of the stores, and warehouses, that supply them. The familiar orange-themed big boxes seen along the freeway are only the tip of a larger iceberg that includes overseas shipping routes, trucking technologies, storage facilities, labor relations, and customs deals. Only by examining Home Depot's practices can one see the links between corporate history, economics, and architectural analysis. Together, these elements provide us with a window into global retailing through the back door, or rather, through the loading dock.

---

[25] Steven Greenhouse, "Front Line in Day Laborer Battle Runs Right Outside Home Depot," *New York Times*, October 10, 2005, A1; Richard Simon, "Who Should Foot the Bill for Day Laborer Centers?" *Los Angeles Times*, April 23, 2006, Washington Section.

[26] Christopher J. Chipello, "Six Timber Firms Near Pact to Avoid Some Canada Turf," *Wall Street Journal*, March 17, 2000, C6.

BIBLIOGRAPHY

Adam, Alison. "Big Girls' Blouses: Learning to Live with Polyester." In *Through the Wardrobe: Women's Relationships with Their Clothes*, eds. Ali Guy, Eileen Green and Maura Banim, 39–52. Oxford, UK: Berg, 2001.

Adorno, Theodor and Max Horkheimer, *Dialectic of Enlightenment*, trans. Edmund Jephcott. Palo Alto: Stanford University Press, 2002.

Agnew, John A. and James S. Duncan. *The Power of Place: Bringing Together Geographical and Sociological Imaginations.* Boston: Unwin Hyman. 1989.

Ahmed, Sarah. "Home and Away: Narratives of Migration and Estrangement." *International Journal of Cultural Studies* 2.3 (1998): 329–347.

Alden, Dana L, Steenkamp, Jan-Benedict E. M and Rajeev Batra. "Brand Positioning Through Advertising in Asia, North America, and Europe: The Role of Global Consumer Culture." *Journal of Marketing* 63 (1999): 75–87.

Alexander, Marina, Lenda Jo Connell, and Ann Beth Presley. "Clothing Fit Preferences of Young Female Adult Consumers." *International Journal of Clothing Science and Technology* 17.1 (2005): 52–64.

Allinson, Anne. "Japanese Mothers and Obentos: The Lunch Box as Ideological State Apparatus." *Anthropological Quarterly* 64.4 (1991): 195–208.

Appadurai, Arjun. *Modernity at Large: Cultural Dimensions of Globalization*. Minneapolis, MN: University of Minnesota Press, 1996.

Ash, Juliet and Elizabeth Wilson. *Chic Thrills: A Fashion Reader.* Berkeley: University of California Press, 1992.

Azarya, Victor. "Globalization and International Tourism in Developing Countries: Marginality as a Commercial Commodity." *Current Sociology* 52 (2004): 949–967.

Bailey, Rebecca. "Clothes Encounters of the Gynecological Kind: Medical Mandates and Maternity Modes in the USA, 1850–1990." In *Dress and Gender: Making and Meaning*, eds. Ruth Barnes and Joanne B. Eicher, 248–265, New York: Berg, 1992.

—. "Fashions in Pregnancy: An Analysis of Selected Cultural Influences, 1850–1980." PhD Dissertation, Michigan State University, 1981.

Barbosa, David. "New Land of Shoppers: China Builds Malls on Gigantic Scale." *New York Times*, May 25, 2005.

Bart, Peter."Price of Parakeet? A Rolling Pin," *The New York Times*, July 15, 1971.

Baudrillard, Jean. *The Ecstasy of Communication.* New York: Semiotext(e), 1988.

—. *Simulations*. New York: Semiotext(e), 1983.

—. "The Implosion of Meaning in the Media." In *In the Shadow of the Silent Majorities or, The End of the Social and Other Essays.* New York: Semiotext(e), 1983, 95–110.

Baumgartner, H. "Towards a Personology of the Consumer." *The Journal of Consumer Research* 29.2 (2002): 286–292.

Beale, Vicki. "Fashioning the Pregnant Body: Wearing Pregnant Bodies." PhD Dissertation, University of Sheffield, 2003.

Befu, Harumi. "Foreword: Towards Zones of Hybridity in Japan." In *Transcultural Japan: At the Borderlands of Race, Gender, and Identity,* eds. David Blake Willis and Stephen Murphy-Shigematsu, xxii–xxv. London and New York: Routledge, 2008.

Belk, Russell W. et al. "A Naturalistic Inquiry into Buyer and Seller Behavior at a Swap Meet." *The Journal of Consumer Research* 14.4 (1988).

—. "Possession and the Extended Self." *The Journal of Consumer Research* 15.2 (1988): 139–168.

Benjamin, Walter. *Illuminations,* trans. Harry Zohn. New York: Harcourt Brace Jovanovich, 1968.

—. *The Arcades Project,* trans. Howard Eiland and Kevin McLaughlin, ed. Rolf Tiedemann. Cambridge, MA: Harvard University/Belknap Press, 2002.

Benstock, Shari, and Suzanne Ferriss. *On Fashion.* New Brunswick, NJ: Rutgers University Press, 1994.

Berger, Arthur Asa. *Ads, Fads and Consumer Culture*. Lanham, MD: Rowman and Littlefield, 2007.

Berkoff, Rick. "Can You Separate the Sizzle from the Steak?" In *Mass Media and Society,* ed. Alan Wells, 298–299. Lexington, MA: Lexington Books, 1987.

Bewley, Marius. "Scott Fitzgerald's Criticism of America." *Twentieth Century Interpretations of F. Scott Fitzgerald's The Great Gatsby*, ed. Ernest H. Lockridge, 37–53. Englewood Cliffs, New Jersey: Prentice Hall, 1968.

Blumin, Stuart. *The Emergence of the Middle Class: Social Experience in the American City, 1760–1900.* Cambridge, UK: Cambridge University Press, 1989.

Bob, Clifford. *The Marketing of Rebellion: Insurgents, Media, and International Activism.* New York: Cambridge University Press, 2005.

Bolen, M. Christopher and Richard J. Caira, Jr. and Jason S. Wood, "When Scandal Becomes Vogue: The Registrability of Sexual References in Trademarks and Protection of Trademarks from Garnishment in Sexual Contexts." *Idea* 39.3 (1999): 435–471.

Bordo, Susan. *Unbearable Weight: Feminism, Western Culture, and the Body.* Berkeley: University of California Press, 1993.

Bourdieu, Pierre. *Distinction: A Social Critique of the Judgment of Taste.* London: Routledge, 1984.

Branchik, Blaine J. "Out in the Market: A History of the Gay Market Segment in the United States." *Journal of Macromarketing* 22.1 (2002): 86–97.

Brekke, Kjell Arne and Richard B. Howarth. "The Social Contingency of Wants." *Land Economics* 76 (2000): 493–503.

Bruccoli, Matthew J. *Some Sort of Epic Grandeur: The Life of F. Scott Fitzgerald.* New York: Harcourt, Brace, Jovanovich, 1981.

Bruner, Edward. *Culture on Tour: Ethnographies of Travel.* Chicago: University of Chicago Press, 2005.

Bruner, Edward and Barbara Kirshenblatt-Gimblett. "Maasai on the Lawn: Tourism Realism in East Africa." *Cultural Anthropology* 9 (1994): 435–470.

Buck-Morss, Susan. *The Dialectics of Seeing: Walter Benjamin and The Arcades Project.* Cambridge, MA: MIT Press, 1991.

Butler, R. W. "West Edmonton Mall as a Tourist Attraction." *The Canadian Geographer* 35.3 (1991): 287–295.

Byrd, Ayana and Lori L. Tharps. *Hair Story: Untangling the Roots of Black Hair in America.* New York: St. Martin's Press, 2001.

Carlisle, James. "Canada's Biggest Mall Versus the World's Toughest Mouse." *Financial Post*, June 25, 1996, 14.

Carnoy, Martin. *Sustaining the New Economy: Work, Family, and Community in the Information Age.* Cambridge, MA: Harvard University Press, 2000.

Cancian, Frank. *Economics and Prestige in a Maya Community: The Religious Cargo System in Zinacantán.* Stanford, CA: Stanford University Press, 1965.

—. *The Decline of Community in Zinacantán: Economy, Public Life, and Social Stratification, 1960–1987.* Stanford, CA: Stanford University Press, 1992.

Canlen, Brae. "Fine-Tuning Distribution: Home Depot," *Home Channel News* 27.22 (December, 17 2001): 28–31.

Cano, Lucero Morales and Avis Mysyk. "Cultural Tourism, the State, and Day of the Dead." *Annals of Tourism Research,* 31 (2004): 879–898.

Clifford, James. "Of Other Peoples: Beyond the 'Salvage' Paradigm." In *Discussions in Contemporary Culture,* ed. Hal Foster, 121–130. Seattle: Bay Press, 1987.

Cook, Tim. "West Edmonton Mall Mega-expansion Draws Ire of Residents." *The Canadian Press*, Nov. 17, 2002.

Cassidy, Marsha F. "The Cinderella Makeover: *Glamour Girl*, Television, Misery Shows, and 1950s Femininity." In *The Great American Makeover: Television, History, Nation*, ed. Dana Heller. New York: Palgrave MacMillan, 2006.

Castells, Manuel. *The Castells Reader on Cities and Social Theory,* ed. Ida Susser. Malden, MA: Blackwell, 2002.

—. *The City and the Grassroots: A Cross-Cultural Theory of Urban Social Movements.* Berkeley: University of California Press, 1983.

Castenada, Quetzil. *In the Museum of Maya Culture: Touring Chichen Itza.* Minneapolis: University of Minnesota Press, 1996.

Chabrow, Eric. "Supply Chains Go Global." *Information Week* 780 (April 3, 2000): 50–55.

Chase, John. "The Role of Consumerism in American Architecture." *Journal of Architectural Education* 44 (1991): 211–224.

Chasin, Alexandra. *Selling Out: The Gay and Lesbian Movement Goes to Market*. New York: Palgrave, 2000.

Chatterjee, Ipsita. "Packaging of Identity and Identifiable Packages: A Study of Women Commodity Negotiation through Product Packaging." *Gender, Place & Culture* 14.3 (2007): 293–316.

Ciarlo, David. "Consuming Race, Envisioning Empire: Colonialism and German Mass Culture, 1887–1914." PhD Dissertation, University of Wisconsin-Madison, 2003.

Clarke, Adele. *Situational Analysis: Grounded Theory after the Postmodern Turn*. Thousand Oaks, CA: Sage, 2005.

Cohen, Lizabeth. *Making A New Deal: Industrial Workers in Chicago, 1919–1939.* Cambridge, UK and New York: Cambridge University Press, 1990.

—. *A Consumers' Republic: The Politics of Mass Consumption in Postwar America.* New York: Knopf, 2003.

Collier, George, with Elizabeth Lowery Quaratiello. *¡Basta! Land and the Zapatista Rebellion in Chiapas.* Oakland, CA: Institute for Food and Development Policy, 1994.

Colls, Rachel. "'Looking Alright, Feeling Alright': Emotions, Sizing and the Geographies of Women's Experiences of Clothing Consumption." *Social & Cultural Geography* 5.4 (2004): 583–596.

—. "Outsize/Outside: Bodily Bigness and the Emotional Experiences of British Women Shopping for Clothes." *Gender, Place and Culture* 13.5 (2006): 529–545.

Conroy, Marianne. "Discount Dreams: Factory Outlet Malls, Consumption, and the Performance of Middle-Class Identity." *Social Text* 54 (1998): 63–83.

Cowen, Tyler. *In Praise of Commercial Culture.* Cambridge, MA: Harvard University Press, 1998.

Craig, Maxine Leed. *Ain't I a Beauty Queen: Black Women, Beauty, and the Politics of Race.* Oxford, UK: Oxford University Press, 2002.

Craik, Jennifer. *The Face of Fashion: Culture Studies in Fashion.* London: Routledge, 1994.

Crain, Mary. "Negotiating Identities in Quito's Cultural Borderlands: Native Women's Performances for the Ecuadorean Tourist Market." In *Cross-Cultural Consumption: Global Markets Local Realities,* ed. David Howes, 125–137. New York: Routledge, 1996.

Crawford, Margaret. "Suburban Life and Public Space." In *Sprawl and Public Space: Redressing the Mall*, ed. David J. Smiley, 21–30. Washington, DC: National Endowment for the Arts, 2002.

—. "The World in a Shopping Mall." In *Variations on a Theme Park: The New American City and the End of Public Space*, ed. Michael Sorkin, 3–30. New York: Hill and Wang, 1992.

Creighton, Millie. "Edutaining Children: Consumer and Gender Socialization in Japanese Marketing." *Ethnology* 33.1 (1994): 35–52.

—. "Imaging the Other in Japanese Advertising Campaigns". In *Occidentalism: Images of the West*, ed. James Carrier, 135–160. Oxford, UK: Oxford University Press, 1995.

—. "Maintaining Cultural Boundaries in Retailing: How Japanese Department Stores Domesticate 'Things Foreign'." *Modern Asian Studies* 25.4 (1991): 675–709.

—. "Marriage, Motherhood, and Career Management in a Japanese 'Counter Culture'." In *Re-Imaging Japanese Women*, ed. Anne Imamura, 192– 220. Berkeley: University of California Press, 1996.

—. "Pre-Industrial Dreaming in Post-Industrial Japan: Department Stores and the Commoditization of Community Traditions." *Japan Forum* 10.2 (1998): 1–23.

—. "Soto Others and Uchi Others: Imaging Racial Diversity, Imagining Homogeneous Japan." In *Japan's Minorities: The Illusion of Homogeneity*, ed. Michael Weiner, 211–238. London: Routledge, 1997.

—. "The Shifting Imagery of Childhood Amidst Japan's Consumer Affluence: The Birth of the '5 Pocket Child'." In *Images of the Child*, ed. H. Eiss, 75–99. Bowling Green Ohio: The Popular Press, 1994.

Crewe, Louise and Nicky Gregson. *Second-Hand Cultures.* Oxford, UK: Oxford International Publishers, Ltd., 2003.

Cronin, Anne M. *Advertising and Consumer Citizenship: Gender, Images, and Rights*. London and New York: Routledge, 2000.

Cross, John C. *Informal Politics: Street Vendors and the State in Mexico City*. Stanford, CA: Stanford University Press, 1998.

Crothers, Lane. *Globalization and American Popular Culture*. Lanham, MD: Rowman and Littlefield, 2007

Csikszentmihalyi, M. "The Cost and Benefits of Consuming." *The Journal of Consumer Research* 27.2 (2000): 267–272.

Dávila, Arlene. *Latinos Inc.: The Marketing and Making of a People.* Berkley, Los Angeles and London: University of California Press, 2001.

Davis, Fred. *Fashion, Culture and Identity.* Chicago: University of Chicago Press, 1992.

Davis, Susan. "The Theme Park: Global Industry and Cultural Form." *Media, Culture & Society* 18.3 (1996): 399–422.

Davis, Tracy C. "Theatrical Antecedents of the Mall that Ate Downtown." *Journal of Popular Culture* 24.4 (1991): 1–15.

Dear, Michael and Jennifer Wolch, eds. *The Power of Geography How Territory Shapes Social Life*. Boston: Unwin Hyman, 1989.

Debord, Guy. *Society of the Spectacle.* Cambridge, MA: Zone Books, 1995.

Decker, Jeffrey Louis. "Gatsby's Pristine Dream: The Diminishment of the Self-Made Man in the Tribal Twenties." *Novel: A Forum on Fiction* 28.1 (Autumn 1994): 5 –71.

Delhaye, Christine. "The Development of Consumption Culture and the Individualization of Female Identity." *Journal of Consumer Culture* 6.1 (2006): 87–115.

D'Emilio, John and Estelle B. Freedman. *Intimate Matters: A History of Sexuality in America.* New York: Harper and Row Publishers, 1988.

De Quincey, Thomas. *Confessions of an English Opium Eater.* New York: Penguin, 2003.

Douglas, Mary and Baron Isherwood. *The World of Goods: Towards an Anthropology of Consumption.* New York: Routledge, 1996.

Eber, Christine E. "'That They Be In the Middle, Lord:' Women, Weaving And Cultural Survival in Highland Chiapas, Mexico." In *Artisans and Cooperatives: Developing Alternative Trade for the Global Economy*, eds. Kimberly M. Grimes and B. Lynne Milgram. Tucson: University of Arizona Press, 2000.

Eber, Christine, and Brenda Rosenbaum. "'That We May Serve Beneath your Hands and Feet': Women Weavers in Highland Chiapas, Mexico." In *Crafts in the World Market: The Impact of Global Exchange on Middle American Artisans*, ed. June Nash. Albany, NY: SUNY Press, 1993.

Eberly, J. "Adjustment of Consumers' Durables Stocks: Evidence from Automobile Purchases." *The Journal of Political Economy* 102.3 (1994): 403–436.

Egley Waggoner, Catherine, and D. Lynne O'Brien Hallstein. "Feminist Ideologies Meet Fashionable Bodies: Managing the Agency/Constraint Conundrum." *Text and Performance Quarterly* 21.1 (2001): 26–46.

Enstad, Nan. *Ladies of Labor, Girls of Adventure: Working Women, Popular Culture, and Labor Politics at the Turn of the Twentieth Century.* New York: Columbia University Press, 1999.

Entwistle, Joanne, and Elizabeth Wilson. *Body Dressing.* Oxford, UK: Berg, 2001.

Ewen, Stuart. *Captains of Consciousness: Advertising and the Social Roots of Consumer Culture.* New York: McGraw-Hill, 1976.

Fabian, Johannes. *Time and the Other: How Anthropology Makes its Object.* New York: Columbia University Press, 1983.

Fairbairn, Kenneth J. "West Edmonton Mall: Entrepreneurial Innovation and Consumer Response." *The Canadian Geographer* 35.3 (1991): 261–268.

Featherstone, Mike. *Consumer Culture and Postmodernism*, second edition. Thousand Oaks, CA: Sage Publications, Inc., 2007.

Filion, Michel. "Broadcasting and Cultural Identity: The Canadian Experience." *Media, Culture & Society* 18.3 (1996): 447–467.

Fitzgerald, F. Scott. *The Great Gastby,* ed. Ruth Prigozy. New York: Oxford University Press, 1998.

—. *This Side of Paradise,* ed. James L. W. West. New York: Cambridge University Press, 1995.

Flood, Marielle K. "Changing Patterns of Interdependence: The Effects of Increasing Monetization on Gender Relations in Zinacantán, Mexico." *Research in Economic Anthropology* 15 (1994): 145–173.

Fortier, Anne-Marie. "Re-Membering Places and the Performance of Belonging(s)." *Theory, Culture & Society*. 16.3 (1999): 41–64.

Foucault, Michel. "Of Other Spaces." In *The Visual Culture Reader*, ed. Nicholas Mirzoeff, 229–236. London: Routledge, 1999.

Frank, Dana. *Purchasing Power: Consumer Organizing, Gender, and the Seattle Labor Movement, 1919–1929*. Cambridge, UK: Cambridge University Press, 1994.

Friedberg, Anne. "*Les Flâneurs du Mal(l)*: Cinema and the Postmodern Condition." *Publications of the Modern Language Association of America* 106.3 (May 1991): 419–431.

—. *Window Shopping: Cinema and the Postmodern*. Berkeley: University of California Press, 1993.

Fujita Mariko. "'It's All Mother's Fault': Childcare and the Socialization of Working Mothers in Japan." *The Journal of Japanese Studies* 15.1 (1989): 67–91.

Fuss, Diana. "Fashion and the Homospectatorial Look." In *On Fashion*, eds. Shari Benstock and Suzanne Ferriss, 211–232. New Brunswick, NJ: Rutgers University Press, 1994.

Gaines, Jane. "Fabricating the Female Body." In *Fabrications: Costume and the Female Body*, eds. Jane Gaines and Charlotte Herzog, 1–27. New York: Routledge, 1990.

Gallaher, Carolyn. "The Role of Protestant Missionaries in Mexico's Indigenous Awakening." *Bulletin of Latin American Research* 26 (2007): 88–111.

Garrett, Wilbur E. "La Ruta Maya." *National Geographic* 176 (1989): 424–479.

Gentry, Connie Robbins. "Where Retailers Shop." *Chain Store Age* 78.3 (March 2002): 92–93.

Gill, Rosalind. "Postfeminist Media Culture: Elements of a Sensibility." *European Journal of Cultural Studies* 10.2 (May 2007): 147–166.

Glaser, Barney, and Anselm Strauss. *The Discovery of Grounded Theory: Strategies for Qualitative Research*. Chicago: Aldine, 1967.

Glickman, Lawrence. *Consumer Society in American History: A Reader*. Ithaca, NY and London: Cornell University Press, 1999.

Goldstein, Carolyn. *Do It Yourself: Home Improvement in 20th-Century America*. Washington, DC: National Building Museum, 1998.

Gordon, Gary Isaac. "Peddler, Pesos, and Power: The Political Economy of Street Vending in Mexico City." PhD Dissertation, University of Chicago, 1997.

Goss, Jon. "The 'Magic of the Mall': An Analysis of Form, Function, and Meaning in the Contemporary Retail Built Environment." *Annals of the Association of American Geographers* 83 (1993): 18–47.

Gossen, Gary. "Life, Death, and Apotheosis of a Chamula Protestant Leader: Biography as Social History." In *Ethnographic Encounters in Southern Mesoamerica: Essays in Honor of Evon Zartman Vogt*, eds. Victoria R. Bricker and Gary H. Gossen. Albany, NY: SUNY Press, 1989.

Gottdiener, Mark. *New Forms of Consumption: Consumers, Culture, and Commodification.* Lanham, MD: Rowman and Littlefield, 2000.

—. *Postmodern Semiotics: Material Culture and the Forms of Postmodern Life.* London: Blackwell, 1995.

Grayson, Deborah R. "Is it Fake? Black Women's Hair as a Spectacle and Spectacular." *Camera Obscura—A Journal of Feminism and Film Theory* 36.9 (1995): 13–31.

Greenfield, Patricia. *Weaving Generations Together: Evolving Creativity in the Maya of Chiapas.* Santa Fe, NM: SAR Press, 2004.

Greenspan, A. and D. Cohen. "Motor Vehicle Stocks, Scrappage, and Sales." *The Review of Economics and Statistics* 81.3 (1999): 369–383.

Gregson, Nicky, and Vikki Beale. "Wardrobe Matter: The Sorting, Displacement and Circulation of Women's Clothing." *Geoforum* 35.6 (2004): 689–700.

Gross, Harriet, and Helen Pattison. *Sanctioning Pregnancy: A Psychological Perspective on the Paradoxes and Culture of Research.* London: Routledge, 2007.

Guha-Khasnobis, Basudeb, et al. *Linking the Formal and Informal Economy.* Oxford, UK: Oxford University Press, 2006.

Guy, Alison, and Maura Banim. "Personal Collections: Women's Clothing Use and Identity." *Journal of Gender Studies* 9.3 (2000): 313–327.

Hannerz, Ulf. "Culture between the Centre and the Periphery: Toward a Macro-Anthropology." *Ethnos* 3.4: 200–216.

—. *Transnational Connections, Culture, People, Places.* London: Routledge, 1996.

Harvey, David. *A Brief History of Neoliberalism.* Oxford, UK and New York: Oxford University Press, 2005.

Hayden, Dolores. *The Power of Place: Urban Landscapes as Public History.* Cambridge, MA: MIT Press, 1995.

Hebdige, Dick. *Subculture: The Meaning of Style*. London: Routledge, 1988.

Heidegger, Martin. *Being and Time,* trans. Joan Stambaugh. Albany, NY: SUNY Press, 1996.

Heller, Laura. "Think Pink. Shop RED. What's in a Cause?" *Retailing Today* 45.21 (2006).

Henderson, William. "Wal-Mart Puts on a Gay-Friendly Face." *Advocate*, September 26, 2006, 14.

Hendrickson, Carol. *Weaving Identities: Construction of Dress and Self in a Highland Guatemala Town*. Austin: University of Texas Press, 1995.

Hendrix, Kimberly D. "The 1990s: It's a Rough Time for Home Improvement Retailing." *Chain Store Age* 67.8 (August 1991): 34A–37A.

Hendry, Joy. "Foreign Country Theme Parks: A New Theme or an Old Japanese Pattern?" *Social Science Japan Journal* 3.2: 207–220.

Herr, Cheryl. "Terrorist Chic: Style and Domination in Contemporary Ireland." In *On Fashion*, eds. Shari Benstock and Suzanne Ferriss, 236–266. New Brunswick, NJ: Rutgers University Press, 1994.

Hesse, Monica. "Greed in the Name of Green to Worshipers of Consumption: Spending Won't Save the Earth," *Washington Post*, March 5, 2008, C01.

Hiltebeitel, Alf and Barbara D. Miller, eds. *Hair: Its Power and Meaning in Asian Cultures*. Albany, NY: SUNY Press, 1998.

Hine, Thomas. *I Want That!: How We All Became Shoppers (A Cultural History)*. New York: Harper Collins Publishers, 2002.

Hirschhorn, Clive, *The Columbia Story*. New York: Octopus Publishing Group Limited, 1999.

Hocker, Cliff and Sakina P. Spruell. "Bad Hair Day." *Black Enterprise* 31.4 (2000): 144.

Hoffman, Marilyn. "Flea Market: Big Business in US," *Christian Science Monitor*, Sept. 10, 1976.

Horgan, Dianne. "The Pregnant Woman's Place and Where to Find It." *Sex Roles* 9.3 (1983): 333–339.

hooks, bell. *Feminism is for Everybody: Passionate Politics*. Boston: South End Press, 2000.

—. *Sisters of the Yam: Black Women and Self-Recovery*. Boston: South End Press, 1993.

Horowitz, Roger and Arwen Mohun, *His and Hers: Gender, Consumption, and Technology*. Charlottesville, VA and London: University of Virginia Press, 1998.

Hough, Pamela and Stuart Hough. *Bit by the Fleas: An Insider's Guide to the Paris Flea Market.* Paris: Vilo, 2002.

Hunter, Marilyn. *Shopping for Identity: The Marketing of Ethnicity.* New York: Schocken Books, 2000.

Hurley, Andrew. *Diners, Bowling Alleys, and Trailer Parks: Chasing the American Dream in Postwar Consumer Culture.* New York: Basic Books, 2001.

Hutchinson, Brian. "Trouble in Big Mall Country." *Canadian Business* 67.9 (1994): 68–73.

Isenberg, Barbara. "Garage Sale Gone Big; Monthly 'Swap Meets' Take over Rose Bowl." *The Wall Street Journal,* October 8, 1970, 16.

Ivy, Marilyn. "Formations of Mass Culture." In *Postwar Japan as History*, ed. Andrew Gordon, 239–258. Berkeley: University of California Press, 1993.

Jackson, Kenneth T. "All the World's a Mall: Reflections on the Social and Economic Consequences of the American Shopping Center." *The American Historical Review* 101 (1996): 1111–1121.

James, Pearl. "History and Masculinity in F. Scott Fitzgerald's *This Side of Paradise.*" *Modern Fiction Studies* 51.1 (2005).

Jedrej, Charles and Mark Nuttall. *White Settlers: The Impact of Rural Repopulation in Scotland.* London: Routledge, 1996.

Jordan, Glenn and Chris Weedon. *Cultural Politics: Class, Gender, Race, and the Postmodern World.* Cambridge, MA: Basil Blackwell Inc., 1995.

Jurek, Nancy C. *Bootstrap Dreams: U. S. Microenterprise Development in an Era of Welfare Reform.* New York: Cornell University Press, 2005.

Kates, Steven. *Twenty Million New Customers! Understanding Gay Men's Consumer Behavior.* New York: The Harrington Park Press, 1998.

—. "Out of the Closet and Out on the Street!: Gay Men and Their Brand Relationships." *Psychology & Marketing* 17.6 (2000): 493–513.

Kawano Satsuki. *Ritual Practice in Modern Japan: Ordering Place, People and Action.* Honolulu: University of Hawaii Press, 2005.

Kehl, D. G. "Sangria in the Sangreal: 'The Great Gatsby' as Grail Quest." *Rocky Mountain Review of Language and Literature* 47.4 (1993): 203–217.

Kelly, Barbara. *Expanding the American Dream: Building and Rebuilding Levittown.* Albany, NY: SUNY Press, 1993.

Kilbourne, Jean. *How Advertising Changes the Way We Think and Feel.* New York, London, et al.: Touchstone, 1999.

Kinsella, Sharon. "Minstrelized Girls: Male Performers of Japan's Lolita Complex." *Japan Forum* 18.1 (2006): 65–87.

Klenck, Margaret. "The Psychological and Spiritual Efficacy of Confession," *Journal of Religion and Health* 43.2 (June 2004): 139–150.

Koestenbaum, Wayne. *Cleavage: Essays on Sex, Stars, and Aesthetics.* New York: Ballantine Books, 2000.

Kreitler, Peter Gwillim. *United We Stand: Flying the American Flag.* San Francisco: Chronicle Books, 2001.

Kuehl, John, ed. *Dear Scott/Dear Max: The Fitzgerald-Perkins Correspondence.* New York: Charles Scribner's Sons, 1971.

Kuttner, Robert. *Everything For Sale: The Virtues and Limits of Markets.* New York: Alfred A. Knopf, 1998.

Lancaster, Bill. *The Department Store: A Social History.* London and New York: Leicester University Press, 1995.

Langrehr, Frederick W. "Retail Shopping Mall Semiotics and Hedonic Consumption." *Advances in Consumer Research* 18 (1991): 428–433.

Lears, Jackson. *Fables of Abundance: A Cultural History of Advertising in America.* New York: Basic Books, 1994.

LeBesco, Kathleen., *Revolting Bodies? The Struggle to Redefine Fat Identity.* Boston: University of Massachusetts Press, 2004.

LeFebvre, Henri. *The Social Production of Space.* London: Blackwell, 1991.

Lehmann, J. "France, Japan, Europe, and Industrial Competition: The Automotive Case." *International Affairs* 68.1 (1992): 37–53.

Leinwand, Gerald. *Patriotism in America: Democracy in Action.* New York and London: Franklin Watts, 1997.

Leonard, John. "Handcraft Swapping at Drive-Ins: A Bit of California Dreaming." *The New York Times,* January 17, 1976, 44.

Leong, Sze Tsung. "…And Then There Was Shopping." In *Cultural Studies: An Anthology*, ed. Michael Ryan, 698–702. Malden, MA: Blackwell, 2008.

Lewis, Tania. "'He Needs to Face his Fears with these Five Queers!': *Queer Eye for the Straight Guy*, Makeover TV, and the Lifestyle Expert." *Television and New Media* 8.4 (2007): 285–311.

Little, Walter E. *Mayas in the Marketplace: Tourism, Globalization, and Cultural Identity.* Austin: University of Texas Press, 2004.

Longhurst, Robyn. "(Ad)dressing Pregnant Bodies in New Zealand: Clothing, Fashion, Subjectivities and Spatialities." *Gender Place and Culture* 12.4 (2005): 433–446.

—. "Corporeographies' of Pregnancy: 'Bikini Babes." *Environment and Planning D: Society and Space* 18 (2000): 453–472.

—. "(Re)presenting Shopping Centres and Bodies: Questions of Pregnancy." In *New Frontiers of Space, Bodies and Gender*, ed. Rosa Ainley, 20–34. London: Routledge, 1998.

MacCannell, Dean. *Empty Meeting Grounds: The Tourist Papers*. New York: Routledge, 1992.

MacDonald, Veronica. "Ethnic Hair Care: Acquisitions are Changing the Market, But When it Comes to Product Development, Moisturization Remains the Mantra." *Household & Personal Products Industry* 39.4 (2002): 60–69.

MacKendrick, Paul L. "The Great Gatsby and Trimalchio." *The Classical Journal* 45.7 (1950).

Magnoni, Aline, Traci Ardren and Scott Huston. "Tourism in the Mundo Maya: Inventions and (Mis)Representations of Maya Identities and Heritage." *Archaeologies* 3 (2007): 353–383.

Maitland, Barry. *The New Architecture of the Retail Mall.* London: Architecture Design and Technology Press, 1990.

Mandella, Adémola, Preston Phillips, and Anasuya Isaacs. *Authentic Hair: Photos, Poems and Prose Celebrating the Beauty and Versatility of Natural Hair.* New York: Cosmic Nubian Enterprises, 2002.

Manning, Robert D, Price, Derek V and Henry J. Rich. "Concierge or Information Desk: Teaching Social Stratification through the Malling of America." *Teaching Sociology* 25 (1997): 15–28.

Marchand, Roland. *Advertising the American Dream: Making Way for Modernity, 1920–1940.* Berkeley: University of California Press, 1985.

Marcus, George. "Ethnography in/of the World System: The Emergence of Multi-Sited Ethnography." *Annual Review of Anthropology* 24 (1995): 95–117.

Martin, Desiree A. "'Excuse the Inconvenience, but this is a Revolution': Zapatista Paradox and the Rhetoric of Tourism." *South Central Review* 21 (2004): 107–128.

Martin, Quentin E. "The First Emotional Bankrupt: F. Scott Fitzgerald's Josephine Perry." *The F. Scott Fitzgerald Review* 1.1 (2008).

Marvin, Carolyn and David W. Ingle, *Blood, Sacrifice, and the Nation: Totem Rituals and the American Flag.* Cambridge, UK and New York: Cambridge University Press, 1999.

Mattiace, Shannan. *To See With Two Eyes: Peasant Activism and Indian Autonomy in Chiapas, Mexico.* Albuquerque: University of New Mexico Press, 2003.

Maynard, Margaret. *Out of Line: Australian Women and Style.* Sydney: UNSW Press, 2001.

McClintock, Anne. *Imperial Leather: Race, Gender, and Sexuality in the Colonial Contest*. New York and London: Routledge, 1995.

McCracken, Grant. *Culture and Consumption: New Approaches to the Symbolic Character of Consumer Goods and Activities.* Bloomington, IN: Indiana University Press, 1988.

McCree, Cree. "Flea Market." *Psychology Today* 18 (June 1986).

McCrossen, Alexis, ed. *Disrupting Boundaries: Consumer Culture in the U.S.-Mexico Borderlands*. Durham, NC: Duke University Press: forthcoming.

McKenchnie, Gary and Nancy Howell. "The Flea Market Bug in Florida; It's Peak Season for Fencing Masks, Deer Heads, and Maybe a Classic Triumph." *The Washington Post,* February 19, 1995, E5.

McRobbie, Angela. "Post-feminism and Popular Culture," *Feminist Media Studies* 4.3 (November 2004): 255–264.

Megill, Allan. *Karl Marx: The Burden of Reason (Why Marx Rejected Politics and the Market).* Boston: Rowman & Littlefield Publishers, 2002.

Mellard, James M. "Counterpoint as Technique in 'The Great Gatsby.'" *The English Journal* 55.7 (October 1966): 853–859.

Miller, Daniel. *Capitalism: An Ethnographic Approach.* Washington DC: Berg, 1997.

—. et al. *Shopping, Place and Identity*. London: Routledge, 1998.

Miller, James E. "Boats Against the Current." *Twentieth Century Interpretations of F. Scott Fitzgerald's The Great Gatsby*, ed. Ernest H. Lockridge, 19–36. Englewood Cliffs, New Jersey: Prentice Hall, 1968.

Miller, Max H. "Patterns of Exchange in the Rural Sector: Flea Markets Along the Highway." *Journal of American Culture* 2.3 (1988).

Miller, Michael B. *The Bon Marché: Bourgeois Culture and the Department Store, 1869–1920.* Princeton, NJ: Princeton University Press, 1981.

Moran, Joe. *Reading the Everyday*. London: Routledge, 2005.

Morris, Meaghan. "Things to Do with Shopping Centres." *The Cultural Studies Reader*, ed. Simon During, 295–319. London: Routledge, 1993.

Morris, Jr., Walter F. *Living Maya*. New York: Harry F. Abrams. 1987.

Moruzzi, Norma Claire. "Veiled Agents: Feminine Agency and Masquerade in *The Battle of Algiers*." In *Negotiating at the Margins: The Gendered Discourses of Power and Resistance*, eds. Sue Fischer and Kathy Davis, 255–277. New Brunswick, NJ: Rutgers University Press, 1993.

Myers, Kathy. "Understanding Advertisers." In *Media Studies: A Reader*, ed. Paul Marris and Sue Thornham, 480–488. Edinburgh: Edinburgh University Press, 1996.

Myers, N. and J. Kent, "New Consumers: The Influence of Affluence on the Environment." *Proceedings of National Academy of Sciences of the United States of America* 100.8 (2003): 4963–4968.

Nash, Meredith. "Oh Baby, Baby: (Un)veiling Britney Spears' Pregnant Body." *Michigan Feminist Studies* 19 (Fall 2006–Spring 2007): 27–50.

—. "Yummy Mummies, Baby Bumps and Body Image: Shaping 'Postmodern' Pregnancy in Melbourne." PhD Dissertation, University of Melbourne, forthcoming.

Newman, David. "Borders and Bordering: Towards an Interdisciplinary Dialogue." *European Journal of Social Theory* 9 (2006): 171–186.

O'Brian, Robin. *The Peso and the Loom: The Political Economy of Maya Women's Work in Highland Chiapas, Mexico.* PhD Dissertation, University of California, Los Angeles. 1994.

O'Guinn Thomas C and Russell W. Belk. "Heaven on Earth: Consumption at Heritage Village, USA." *The Journal of Consumer Research* 16 (1989): 227–238.

Palmer, Gareth. "*Big Brother*: An Experiment in Governance." *Television and New Media* 3.3 (August 2002): 295–310.

Palmer, Kimberly. "Ethnic Hair-care Ads Show New Faces." *The Miami Herald*, Sept. 1, 2003, section G.

Parker, David. "Two Versions of the Hero." *Modern Critical Interpretations of F. Scott Fitzgerald's The Great Gatsby*, ed. Harold Bloom, 29–44. New York: Chelsea House Publishers, 1986.

Pasolini, Piers Paolo. *Roman Poems,* trans. Lawrence Ferlinghetti and Francesca Valente. San Francisco: City Lights Books, 1986.

Patterson, Martha H. *Beyond the Gibson Girl: Reimagining the American New Woman, 1895–1915*. Champaign, IL: University of Illinois Press, 2008.

Peiss, Kathy. *Cheap Amusements: Working Women and Leisure in the Turn-of-the-Century New York.* Philadelphia: Temple University Press, 1986.

—. Hope in a Jar: The Making of America's Beauty Culture. New York: Henry Holt and Company, 1998.

—. "On Beauty and the History of Business." In *Beauty and Business: Commerce, Gender, and Culture in Modern America*, ed. Philip Scranton, 7–21. New York: Routledge, 2001.

Pitts, Brenda G. "Sports Tourism and Niche Markets: Identification and Analysis of the Growing Lesbian and Gay Sports Tourism Industry." *Journal of Vacation Marketing* 5.1 (1999): 31–50.

Polhemus, Ted. *Street Style: From Sidewalk to Catwalk.* London: Thames & Hudson, 1994.

—. *Style Surfing: What to Wear in the 3rd Millennium.* London: Thames & Hudson, 1996.

Poria, Yaniv. "Assessing Gay Men and Lesbian Women's Hotel Experiences: An Exploratory Study of Sexual Orientation in the Travel Industry." *Journal of Travel Research* 44 (2006): 327–334.

Portes, Alejandro, Manuel Castells, and Lauren A. Benton, ed. *The Informal Economy: Studies in Advanced and Less Developed Countries*. Baltimore: The Johns Hopkins University Press, 1989.

Portes, Alejandro and Saskia Sassen-Koob, "Making it Underground: Comparative Material on the Informal Sector in Western Market Economies." *American Journal of Sociology* 93.1 (1987).

Prins, Harold. "Visual Media and Primitivist Perplex: Colonial Fantasies, Indigenous Imagination, and Advocacy in North America." In *Media Worlds: Anthropology on New Terrain*, eds. Faye Ginsburg, Lila Abu-Lughod and Brian Larkin, 58–74. Berkeley: University of California Press, 2002.

Prior, Molly. "Ethnic Makers Expand Lines, Taking Cue from Professional Brands." *Drug Store News* 24.14 (2002): 45–46.

Pritchard, Annette, Nigel J. Morgan, Diane Sedgely, and Andrew Jenkins. "Reaching Out to the Gay Tourist: Opportunities and Threats in an Emerging Market Segment." *Tourism Management* 19.3 (1998): 273–282.

Proust, Marcel. *Remembrance of Things Past.* New York: Vintage Books, 1982.

Rabine, Leslie W. "A Woman's Two Bodies: Fashion Magazines, Consumerism and Feminism." In *On Fashion*, eds. Shari Benstock and Suzanne Ferriss, 59–75. New Brunswick, NJ: Rutgers University Press, 1994.

Razzouk, Nabil and David Gourley. "Swap Meets: A Profile of Shoppers," *Arizona Business* 29.2 (1982).

Reid-Merrit, Patricia. *Sister Power: How Phenomenal Black Women are Rising at the Top.* New York: John Wiley & Sons, Inc., 1996.

Robertson, Jennifer. "It Takes a Village: Internationalization and Nostalgia in Postwar Japan." In *Mirror of Modernity: Invented Traditions of Modern Japan*, ed. Stephen Vlastos, 110–129. Berkeley: University of California Press, 1998.

Ronell, Avital. *Crack Wars: Literature, Addiction, Mania.* Urbana: University of Illinois Press, 2004.

Rooks, Noliwe. *Hair Raising: Beauty, Culture, and African American Women.* New Brunswick, NJ: Rutgers University Press, 1996.

Sack, Robert David. *Place, Modernity, and the Consumer's World: A Relational Framework for Geographical Analysis.* Baltimore: Johns Hopkins University Press, 1992.

Sartre, Jean-Paul. *Being and Nothingness: A Phenomenal Essay on Ontology,* trans. Hazel E. Barnes. New York: Washington Square Press, 1984.

Scanlon, Jennifer. *Inarticulate Longings: The Ladies Home Journal, Gender, and the Promises of Consumer Culture.* New York: Routledge, 1995.

—. ed. *The Gender and Consumer Society Reader.* New York: New York University Press, 2000.

Scarry, Elaine. *Resisting Representation.* New York: Oxford University Press, 1994.

Schlereth, Thomas J. "Columbia, Columbus, and Columbianism." *Journal of American History* 79.3 (December 1992): 937–968.

Schor, Juliet B. and Douglas B. Holt, eds., *The Consumer Society Reader.* New York: The New Press, 2000.

Segrave, Kerry. *Drive-in Theaters: A History from their Inception in 1933.* Jefferson, North Carolina: McFarland & Company, Inc. Publishers, 1992.

Seidman, Steven. *Beyond the Closet: The Transformation of Gay and Lesbian Life.* New York: Routledge, 2002.

Shepard, Robert J. *When Culture Goes to Market: Space, Place, and Identity in an Urban Marketplace.* New York: Peter Lang, 2008.

Sherry, Jr., John F. "A Sociological Analysis of a Midwestern American Flea Market." *The Journal of Consumer Research* 17.1 (June 1990).

Shields, Rob. "Social Spatialization and the Built Environment: the West Edmonton Mall." *Environment and Planning D: Society and Space* 7 (1989).

Skov, Lise and Brian Moeran, eds. *Women, Media and Consumption in Japan.* Surrey, UK: Curzon Press, 1996.

Slater, Don. *Consumer Culture and Modernity.* New York: Polity Press, 1997.

Smiley, David J., ed. *Sprawl and Public Space: Redressing the Mall.* Washington, DC: National Endowment for the Arts, 2002.

Smith, P. J. "Coping with Mega-Mall Development: an Urban Planning Perspective on West Edmonton Mall." *The Canadian Geographer* 35.3 (1991): 295–305.

Soderman, B. and R. Carter. "The Auto Salvage: A Space of Second Chances." *Space and Culture* 11.1 (2008): 20–38.

St. James, James. D*isco Bloodbath: A Fabulous But True Story of Murder in Clubland.* New York: Simon & Schuster, 1999.

Staudt, Kathleen. *Free Trade? Informal Economies at the U.S.-Mexico Border.* Philadelphia: Temple University Press, 1998.

—. "Informality Knows No Borders? Perspectives from El Paso-Juarez." *SAIS Review* XXI, no. 1 (2001).

Sterne, Jonathan. "Sounds like the Mall of America: Programmed Music and the Architectonics of Commercial Space." *Ethnomusicology* 41 (1997): 22–50.

Stoll, David. *Fishers of Men or Founders of Empire? The Wycliffe Bible Translators in Latin America.* London: Zed Press, 1983.

Strasser, Susan. "Making Consumption Conspicuous: Transgressive Topics Go Mainstream." *Technology and Culture* 43 (2002): 671–672.

—. "Woolworth to Wal-Mart: Mass Merchandising and the Changing Culture of Consumption." *Wal-Mart: The Face of Twenty-First Century Capitalism*, ed. Nelson Lichtenstein, 31–56. New York: The New Press: 2006.

—. Charles McGovern, and Matthias Judt. *Getting and Spending: European and American Consumer Societies in the Twentieth Century.* Cambridge, UK: Cambridge University Press 1998.

Tanaka, Keiko. "Intelligent Elegance: Women in Japanese Advertising." In *Unwrapping Japan: Society and Culture in Anthropological Perspective*, eds. Eyal Ben-Ari, Brian Moeran, and James Valentine, 78–96. Honolulu: University of Hawaii Press, 1990.

Tata, Michael Angelo. "Confessions of a D&G Label Whore," *to the quick 3* (Winter 2000): 29–39.

Taylor, Verta and Leila J. Rupp, "Chicks with Dicks, Men in Dresses: What It Means to Be a Drag Queen." *Journal of Homosexuality* 46, no. 3/4 (2004): 114–115.

Teel, Gina. "Category-killers vs. All-day Dawdlers." *Alberta Report* 20.37 (1993): 18–19.

Tehranian, Katherine. *Modernity, Space, and Power: The American City in Discourse and Practice.* Cresskill, NJ: Hampton Press, 1995.

Tenerelli, Mary J. "Ethnic Hair Fare." *Global Cosmetic Industry* 168.6 (2001): 32–33.

Tonkiss, Fran. "The Ethics of Indifference: Community and Solitude in the City." *International Journal of Cultural Studies* 6.3 (2003): 297–311.

Trilling, Lionel. *The Liberal Imagination.* Garden City, NY: Doubleday, 1953.

Tuten, Tracy L. "The Effect of Gay-Friendly and Non-Gay-Friendly Cues on Brand Attitudes: A Comparison of Heterosexual and Gay/Lesbian Reactions." *Journal of Marketing Management* 21 (2005): 441–461.

Twitchell, James B. *ADCULT USA: The Triumph of Advertising in American Culture.* New York: Columbia University Press, 1996.

—. *Branded Nation: The Marketing of Megachurch, College Inc., and Museumworld.* New York: Simon & Schuster, 2004.

Tyler, Imogen. "Skin Tight: Celebrity, Pregnancy and Subjectivity." In *Thinking Through the Skin*, eds. Sarah Ahmed and Jackie Stacey, 69–84. London: Routledge, 2001.

Underhill, Paco. *Call of the Mall.* New York: Simon & Schuster, 2004.

Van den Berghe, Pierre. *The Quest for the "Other": Ethnic Tourism in San Cristóbal, Mexico.* Seattle: University of Washington Press, 1994.

Van, Karyl and John Hahn. *Guidelines in Selling Magazines Advertising.* New York: Appleton Century Crofts, 1971.

Verburg, Peter. "The West Edmonton Mall…uh, Rocks." *Canadian Business* 70.13 (1997): 92–95.

Vogel, S. "Professional Housewife: The Career of Urban Middle Class Japanese Women." *Japan Interpreter* 12 (1978): 16–43.

Vogt, Evon Z. *Zinacantán: A Maya Community in the Highlands of Chiapas.* Cambridge, MA: Belknap Press/Harvard University Press, 1969.

Volkman, Toby Alice. "Visions and Revisions: Toraja Culture and the Tourist Gaze." *American Ethnologist* 17 (1990): 91–110.

Walker, Susannah. "Black is Profitable: The Commodification of the Afro, 1960–1975." In *Beauty and Business: Commerce, Gender, and Culture in Modern America*, ed. Philip Scranton, 254–277. New York: Routledge, 2001.

Ward, Jane. "Producing 'Pride' in West Hollywood: A Queer Cultural Capital for Queers with Cultural Capital." *Sexualities* 6 (2003): 88.

Warwick, Alexandra, and Dani Cavallaro. *Fashioning the Frame: Boundaries, Dress and the Body.* Oxford, UK: Berg, 1998.

Washbrook, Sarah. "The Chiapas Uprising of 1994: Historical Antecedents and Political Consequences." *Journal of Peasant Studies* 32 (2005): 417–449.

Waters, Donald. *Global Logistics and Distribution Planning: Strategies for Management*, fourth edition. London: Kogan Page, 2003.

Way, Brian. "The Great Gatsby." *Modern Critical Interpretations of F. Scott Fitzgerald's The Great Gatsby*, ed. Harold Bloom, 87–108. New York: Chelsea House Publishers, 1986.

Weems Jr, Robert E. *Desegregating the Dollar: African American Consumerism in the Twentieth Century.* New York: New York University Press, 1998.

Weiner, Edith and Arnold Brown. "The New Marketplace," *The Futurist* 29 (May/June) 1995: 12–14.

Welter, Barbara. "The Cult of True Womanhood, 1820–1860." *American Quarterly 18* (Summer 1966): 151–174.

White, Mimi. *Tele-Advising: Therapeutic Discourse in American Television.* Chapel Hill: University of North Carolina Press, 1992.

Whitley, John S. *F. Scott Fitzgerald: The Great Gatsby.* Southampton, England: The Camelot Press, Ltd., 1976.

Wiles, Rose. "'I'm Not Fat, I'm Pregnant': The Impact of Pregnancy on Fat Women's Body Image." In *Women and Health: Feminist Perspectives*, eds. Sue Wilkinson and Celia Kitzinger, 33–48. London: Taylor & Francis, 1994.

Williams, Peter, Phil Hubbard, David Clark, and Nigel Berkeley. "Consumption, Exclusion and Emotion: The Social Geographies of Shopping." *Social & Cultural Geography* 2.2 (2001): 203–220.

Williamson, Janice. "I-less and Gaga in the West Edmonton Mall: Towards a Pedestrian Feminist Reading." In *The Anatomy of Gender: Women's Struggle for the Body,* eds. Dawn H. Currie and Valerie Raoul, 97–115. Ottawa: Carleton University Press, 1992.

Williamson, Judith. "Decoding Advertisements." In *Media Studies: A Reader*, eds. Paul Marris and Sue Thornham, 489–491. Edinburgh: Edinburgh University Press, 1996.

Willis, David Blake, and Stephen Murphy-Shegematsu. "Transcultural Japan: Metamorphoses in the Cultural Borderlands and Beyond." In *Transcultural Japan: At the Borderlands of Race, Gender, and Identity,* eds. David Blake Willis and Stephen Murphy-Shigematsu, 3–44. London and New York: Routledge, 2008.

Wilson, Elizabeth. *Adorned in Dreams: Fashion and Modernity.* Berkeley: University of California Press, 1987.

Wilson, Robert R. "Playing and Being Played: Experiencing West Edmonton Mall." In *Pop Can: Popular Culture in Canada*, eds. Lynne Van Luven and Priscilla L. Walton, 82–90. Scarborough, Canada: Prentice Hall, 1999.

Wilson, Tamar Diana. "Introduction, the Urban Informal Sector." *Latin American Perspectives* 25.2 (1998).

Wolf, Naomi. *The Beauty Myth: How Images of Beauty are used against Women.* New York: Harper Collins, 1991.

Woloch, Nancy. *Women and the American Experience.* New York: McGraw-Hill Publishers, 2005.

Wright, Robert A. "See What They Did to the Garage Sale," *The New York Times,* July 15, 1971.

Wunderlich, Roger. "The Great Gatsby as Long Island History." *The Long Island Historical Journal* 7.1 (Fall 1994): 118–124.

Wurdinger, Victoria. *The Multicultural Client: Cuts, Styles, and Chemical Services.* Albany, NY: Milady Publishing Co., 1996.

Yeoh, Brenda S.A., and Louisa-May Khoo. "Home, Work, and Community: Skilled International Migration and Expatriate Women in Singapore." *International Migration* 36.2 (1998): 159–186.

Young, Iris Marion. "Women Recovering Our Clothes." In *On Fashion*, eds. Shari Benstock and Suzanne Ferriss, 197–210. Brunswick, NJ: Rutgers University Press, 1990.

Zlolniski, Christian. *Janitors, Street Vendors, and Activists: The Lives of Mexican Immigrants in Silicon Valley.* Berkeley: University of California Press, 2006.

—. "The Informal Economy in an Advanced Industrialized Society: Mexican Immigrant Labor in Silicon Valley," *The Yale Law Journal* 103.8 (1994).

Zukin, Sharon. *Landscapes of Power: From Detroit to Disney World.* Berkeley: University of California Press, 1991.

CONTRIBUTORS

Annessa Ann Babic received her PhD in History from Stony Brook University (2008), and is currently revising her dissertation, "Undoing Glory: Gendered Constructions of Patriotism in Twentieth Century US Society, 1917–1972," for publication. She is a social and cultural historian, with specialties in consumption, nationalism, and image theory. Currently she is working on research projects examining the relationship between American and Turkish women's magazines and their role in international relations. She is also working on a project examining the imagery and rhetoric used by the American Legion to create the veteran vs. the soldier. She is the recipient of numerous grants and fellowships, and a two-time teaching fellow. She received a Peter Rollins-Michael Schoenecke Travel Grant from the Popular Culture and American Culture Associations (PCA/ACA) for her paper "Wonder Women Fetishes and Fantasies: The Image of the Patriotic Female during World War II." Dr. Babic has published on topics as varied as terrorism in the post 9-11 age to American patriotism, and has presented at conferences outside her field and around the globe. She has also contributed to *Lupus Now* (a magazine for Lupus patients and those seeking material on the disease). Her most recent essay/memoir is "Just Cut My Wings and Let Me Fly." She is currently a Visiting Assistant Professor of History at Old Dominion University (Virginia).

Peter Clandfield worked for Fantasyland Parks and Attractions, West Edmonton Mall, 1986–1989, and is currently teaching in the Department of English Studies, Nipissing University, North Bay, Ontario. He has published articles and book chapters on literary and cinematic representations of urban and suburban development and redevelopment, and is working on a book-length study of the same subject. His research interests also include contemporary Scottish literature; theories and practices of censorship; representations of cultural and racial hybridity; and crime fiction.

Millie Creighton is a Japan specialist and Associate Professor in the Department of Anthropology at the University of British Columbia, where she serves on the Executive Management Boards of the Center for

Japanese Research and the Center for Korean Research. She has conducted extensive research on Japanese department stores, consumerism, tourism, popular culture, gender, minorities, work and leisure, place, nostalgia, identity, and performance forms such as *taiko* and *kyogen*. She was awarded the Canon Prize for her analysis of contemporary Japanese identity and nostalgia as reflected through department store retailing and other forms of consumerism. She has conducted and published research on contemporary tourism campaigns invoking the modern Japanese desire to reinvigorate icons of Japanese identity and past lifeways, modern uses of historical eras, and tourism to, or invoking associations of, foreign countries. She has also conducted research on *Nikkei* (people of Japanese descent) and their international networking.

Veronica Davidov is a cultural and visual anthropologist, who specializes in cultural commodification, production of value, tourism, and postcolonial fantasies of alterity. She has conducted fieldwork in Ecuador and Peru focusing on tourism in the Napo Quichua and Uros Islands communities, respectively. She received her PhD from New York University in 2008, and is currently a lecturer in the Globalization and Diversity program at Maastricht University in the Netherlands.

Amparo Pamela Fabe is an economist and sociologist who studies consumer behavior among teenagers and adults in the Philippines. She has a MA in Sociology and one in Economics, and is currently a PhD Candidate in Economic Sociology at the University of the Philippines. She has done consulting work for Filipino retailers like Ayala Center Cebu and Gaisano, Incorporated. She has completed studies on the typology of consumption and cultural capital. Her most recent study is a national survey on the consumption patterns of college students in five areas: fashion, fragrance, entertainment, cellular phones, and digital cameras.

Daniel Farr is a doctoral candidate in sociology at the State University of New York at Albany. His dissertation seeks to address parental aspiration among young gay men. He works at the intersections of masculinity/ gender, sexualities, media, and the family. His research is informed by an educational background in women's studies and anthropology. He is currently working on several forthcoming articles and chapters addressing various aspects of media and culture. Several of his pieces address queer-based visual media including the film "Latter Days," and the television series "The L-Word," "Queer as Folks," and "Queer Eye for the Straight

Guy." He is a visiting assistant professor of sociology at Randolph College.

Gretchen Guenther, MS, CPA, has recently accepted an Assistant Professorship at the School of Business, College of Saint Rose, New York. Her primary teaching areas are not-for-profit, financial, and managerial accounting. Additionally, she is interested in understanding the experience of GLBT individuals in the areas of finance, accounting, and sports. Her BS and MS are both in accounting from the College of Saint Rose.

Elizabeth Johnson, a cultural historian and black feminist, joined the College of Arts and Sciences at Governors State University in 2008 as an Assistant Professor of History. Her research interests include hair and body aesthetics and African American history. Professor Johnson earned her PhD in American Culture Studies at Bowling Green State University in 2004, and her BS at Jackson State University in 1988. Before her appointment at Governors State, she was Assistant Professor of History at SUNY Dutchess Community College (2004–2008).

Jennifer Le Zotte is a doctoral student in the Department of History at the University of Virginia. Currently, she is exploring the relationship between primary consumer culture and flea markets, thrift stores, and garage sales in twentieth-century America. Her BS is in journalism and MA in American history, both from the University of Florida.

Meredith Nash is a PhD Candidate in Gender Studies at the University of Melbourne and creator of "The Baby Bump Project," a web initiative that provides a space for women to evaluate critically celebrity pregnancy and mainstream media representations of pregnant bodies. Her current research interests include: practices of the pregnant "self," celebrity pregnancy, "baby bump" culture, and pregnant embodiment. She has published widely on pregnancy and motherhood in both academic and mainstream publications.

Robin O'Brian is an Assistant Professor of Anthropology at Elmira College, in Elmira, New York. She holds degrees in Anthropology from UCLA and the California State University. Dr. O'Brian has conducted research in Chiapas, Mexico on Maya women's household and economic work. She has also published on women's labor, traditional weaving, and Maya women's encounter with tourism. In 2006, Dr. O'Brian was one of twenty four faculty members selected nationally to participate in "Maya Worlds," a traveling institute about ancient and contemporary Maya society. She is currently developing a new research project examining economic and social change in one Maya community since the development of the Ruta Maya.

Ayokunle Olumuyiwa Omobowale holds a Doctorate degree in Sociology from the University of Ibadan. His PhD thesis was entitled "Political Clientelism and Rural Development in Selected Communities in Ibadan, Nigeria." He is interested in the Sociology of Development, Rural Sociology, Political Sociology and Medical Sociology. In 2007, he won the University of Ibadan Postgraduate School Award for scholarly publication. He was a lecturer at the University of Lagos, Lagos, Nigeria, from April 2007 to May 2008. Currently, he is a lecturer of Sociology at Nigeria's premier university, the University of Ibadan, Ibadan.

Sara Stevens is a PhD candidate at Princeton University's School of Architecture. She holds a Master of Environmental Design from Yale University, where her research focused on familiar architectural formats of the suburban landscape and the underlying networks of business and finance that produce them. Currently, she is studying the legal framework of deed restrictions in the early twentieth century, and the relation between scientific rationalization and urban planning in the Progressive Era.

Michael Angelo Tata received his MA in Creative Writing/Poetry from Temple University, his MA in Liberal Studies from the New School for Social Research, and his PhD in English Literature through the CUNY Graduate Center. His poetry has been exhibited as sculpture in "The Weather," a multimedia exhibit at the Parlor Gallery (Lancaster, PA), and as fashion through the Long Beach Foundation for the Arts. His poetry and criticism have appeared in the journals *Blood Lotus, Origami Condom, LinQ, FRIGG, Nebula, M/C, Ugly Couch*, *Lit, Lungfull, eye: rhyme, kenning, Bad Subjects, Found Object, Rhizomes* and *to the quick,* as well as the Critical Studies compilation *From Virgin Land to Disney World: Nature and Its Discontents in the USA of Yesterday and Today* (Editions Rodopi, 2001) and the Madonna Studies anthology *Madonna's Drowned Worlds: New Approaches to Her Cultural Transformations* (Ashgate UK, 2004). His first book of poems, *The Multiplication of Joy into Integers*, won Blue Light Press' 2003 poetry prize. His poetry has also appeared in the collections *This New Breed: Bad Boys, Gents and Barbarians 2* (Windstorm, 2004) and *Bordered Sexualities* (San Diego

State, forthcoming 2008). He is currently American editor for Australia's interdisciplinary journal *Nebula*, and editor-in-chief of iPublishing.

Brigette Thompson is a socio-cultural anthropologist. She received her MA in Sociology and Social Anthropology from Central European University, and her BA in Anthropology from the University of Texas at San Antonio. Her interests include home, belonging, and identity; the body, pregnancy, and childbirth; and social theory, global health, and masculinity. She currently works in Academic Affairs at Trinity University, where she advises international students and scholars. Additionally, she is an instructor in Trinity's International Studies department.

Tanfer Emin Tunc received her PhD in History from the State University of New York at Stony Brook (2005). She is a social and cultural historian of the modern United States, specializing in women's history/literature; gender, sexuality, and reproduction; and feminist theory. The recipient of her field's most prestigious grants and fellowships (including awards from the National Science Foundation, the Woodrow Wilson Foundation of Princeton University, Rockefeller University, Duke University, the University of Michigan, Smith College, the American Historical Association, the National Women's Studies Association, the Society for the History of Technology, and the Francis C. Wood Institute for the History of Medicine at the College of Physicians of Philadelphia), Dr. Tunc has presented at conferences all over the world. She has also published on topics as diverse as consumer culture, reproductive technologies, and women in the American novel. She is currently an Assistant Professor of American Culture and Literature at Hacettepe University (Ankara, Turkey).

Brett Westbrook was born and raised in Austin, TX. She earned a BA in German at the University of Oklahoma, an MA in English at the University of California at Berkeley, and a PhD from the University of California at Davis. For the past ten years, she has worked in Academic Affairs at the University of Texas at Austin and as an adjunct faculty member at St. Edward's University, where she teaches American literature, film and literature of the American West, and a senior Capstone course. Recent publications include "Feminism and the Limits of Genre in 'The Outlaw Josey Wales' and 'Fistful of Dollars,'" in *New Perspectives on Clint Eastwood*, University of Utah Press (2007) and, with Dr. Kathleen Brown, "The Politics of Reconciliation in John Ford's Cavalry

Trilogy: Adapting James Warner Bellah's Short Stories," in *Westerns: Paperback Novels and Movies from Hollywood*, Paul Varner (editor), Cambridge Scholars Publishing, 2007.

INDEX